'There Ain't
No Black in the
Union Jack'

'There Ain't No Black in the Union Jack'

The cultural politics of race and nation

Paul Gilroy

Hutchinson
London Melbourne Sydney Auckland Johannesburg

Hutchinson Education

An imprint of Century Hutchinson Ltd

62–65 Chandos Place, London WC2N 4NW

Century Hutchinson Australia Pty Ltd
PO Box 496, 16–22 Church Street, Hawthorn,
Victoria 3122, Australia

Century Hutchinson New Zealand Ltd
PO Box 40–086, Glenfield, Auckland 10
New Zealand

Century Hutchinson South Africa (Pty) Ltd
PO Box 337, Berglvei 2012, South Africa

First published 1987

Phototypeset in Linotron Palatino
by Input Typesetting Ltd, London

Printed and bound in Great Britain

British Library Cataloguing in Publication Data
Gilroy, Paul
   'There ain't no black in the Union Jack':
   the cultural politics of 'race' and nation.
   1. Great Britain—Race relations
   2. Great Britain—Politics and
   government—1979–
   I. Title
   323.1'41   DA125.A1

ISBN 0 09 167951 6

To Pat's memory,
and to Marcus's future

The Courtesies of order, of ruly forms pursued from a heart of rage and terror or grief defame the truth of every human crisis. And that, indeed, is the plan: To defuse and to deform the motivating truth of critical human response to pain. . . . If you make and keep my life horrible, then when I can tell the truth, it will be a horrible truth; it will not sound good or look good, or God willing, feel good to you, either. There is nothing good about the evils of a life forced into useless and impotent drift and privation. There is very little that is attractive or soothing about being strangled to death, whether it is the literal death of the body or the actual death of the soul that lying, that the humiliation and the evil of self-denial guarantees. Extremity demands, and justifies an extreme response. Violation invites, teaches violence. Less than that, less than a scream or a fist, less than the absolute cessation of normal events in the lock of abnormal duress is a lie and, worse than that, it is a blasphemous ridicule of the self. (June Jordan, *Civil Wars*)

There is no escaping what the future holds. We are going back, *back* to something earlier, maybe better, maybe worse, maybe something more terrifyingly human! These few hundred years of freedom, empire building, voting, liberty, democracy – these will be regarded as the *romantic* centuries in human history. There will be in that future no trial by jury, no writs of habeas corpus, no freedom of speech, of religion – all that is being buried and not by communists and fascists alone, but by their opponents as well. All hands are shovelling clay onto the body of freedom before it even dies, while it lies breathing its last. . . . (Richard Wright, *The Outsider*)

. . . the only agent on which we can premise future radical change emerges from the melding of traditional groups into a public sphere, a body politic, a community imbued with a sense of cultural and spiritual continuity and renewal. This community, however, is constituted only in the ever-present act of an ever-dynamic effort of public self-assertion that yields a sharp sense of selfhood. Collectivity thus melds with individuality to produce rounded human beings in a rounded society. Direct action assumes the form of direct democracy: the participatory forms of freedom rest on face-to-face assemblies, rotation of public functions, and, where possible, consensus. (Murray Bookchin, *Were We Wrong?*)

Contents

Acknowledgements

Many people have contributed to this book in different ways and I would like to thank them all publicly. Convention dictates that I bear the ultimate responsibility for it but all my friends, teachers and associates named below have played a part in its development and I am deeply grateful to all of them. If I was truthful, I'd admit that all I have done is cobble their ideas together.

Richard Johnson and Stuart Hall supplied detailed critical comments on early drafts and I am grateful for their precious time and their pedagogic patience.

Mandy Rose, Trisha Bohn, Courtney Griffiths, Jan McKenley, Joe Sim, Derrick McLintock, Dick Hebdige, Terry Daniels, Errol Lawrence, Pratibha Parmar, Chetan Bhatt, John Solomos, Patrick Wright and Beryl Gilroy gave comments on various parts of it. All of them encouraged and challenged me in the most productive way possible by their disagreements. You're all broader than broadway.

Lloyd Brown couldn't have been more generous and his encyclopaedic knowledge of black musics is second to none. I really am in his debt, especially for 'Go Away Little Boy' and 'Red, Black and Green'.

Valuable and useful material were selflessly passed to me by Hazel Carby, Max Farrar, Val Wilmer, Mark Ainley, Pete Ayrton, Darla-Jane Gilroy, Rick Fawcett and Lawrence Marlow who were also encouraging.

Enrico Stennett and Daddy Peckings told me a dread history that I would never have found out otherwise. Chapter 5 is part of a campaign to have Peckings' Askew Road shop made into a national monument.

I was greatly strengthened by the encouragement of Val Amos, Isaac Julien, Kobena Mercer, Cora Kaplan, Simon Jones, Claire DeMuth, Helen Walker and Jo Mayne. They all made helpful suggestions and, more importantly, made me believe I could and had to do it.

Amana Smith and her family and Angela Napoleon and hers looked after my son so that I could get the time to write. An extra thank you to them. Glen Bor, David Bor, Francis Ware, Kate Pullinger, Nick Robin, Nicola Stephenson, Sarah Martin and many of

9

ACKNOWLEDGEMENTS

the others listed above baby-sat so that I could go out 'in the field'.

Gill Lawrence arrested the deterioration in my eyesight by typing the last sixty pages of the manuscript; I am especially grateful to her.

The difficulties of actually writing were constantly mediated by the pleasures of listening to the NYC guitar mafia: David Spinoza, Steve Khan, Bill Connors, John Tropea, Hiram Bullock, John Scofield, Howard 'Buzz' Feiten, Cornell Dupree, Eric Gale, Marcus Miller and of course, Anthony Jackson. If this book is half as interesting as his bass playing I shall be delighted.

Most importantly, this project has rested on the love and help provided to me by Vron Ware. Her intellectual insights, political intuition and technical skills as an editor have improved the final product beyond measure and I am particularly grateful for her patience, forbearance and wise counsel.

Introduction

I dreamed I was in Yorkshire, going from Gomersal Hill-Top to Cleckheaton;
and about the middle of the lane I thought I saw Satan coming to meet me
in the shape of a tall, black man, and the hair of his head like snakes . . .
(John Nelson, stone-mason of Birstall, quoted by E. P. Thompson in *The
Making of the English Working Class*).

Long ago, writing to illuminate patterns of racial sentiment and
conflict very different from those which characterize Britain in the
1980s, the great black scholar and activist, W. E. B. DuBois, identified
an 'unasked question' that constituted a barrier between the world
and those who live within the veil of colour. The question was,
according to DuBois, 'How does it feel to be a problem?'
  Racism does not, of course, move tidily and unchanged through
time and history. It assumes new forms and articulates new antagonisms in different situations. Yet something of the process which
DuBois identified still endures, or has been recreated in crisis-bound
Britain. The idea that blacks comprise a problem, or more accurately
a series of problems, is today expressed at the core of racist reasoning.
It is closely related to a second idea which is equally pernicious, just
as popular and again integral to racial meanings. This defines blacks
as forever victims, objects rather than subjects, beings that feel yet
lack the ability to think, and remain incapable of considered behaviour in an active mode. The oscillation between black as problem and
black as victim has become, today, the principal mechanism through
which 'race' is pushed outside of history and into the realm of
natural, inevitable events. This capacity to evacuate any historical
dimension to black life remains a fundamental achievement of racist
ideologies in this country. It generates some complex problems in
racial politics which will not be easily solved. Racism is not akin to
a coat of paint on the external structures of social relations which
can be scraped off if the right ideological tools and political elbow
grease are conscientiously applied to the task. Seeing racism in this
way, as something peripheral, marginal to the essential patterns of
social and political life can, in its worst manifestations, simply
endorse the view of blacks as an external problem, an alien presence
visited on Britain from the outside.
  If nothing else, this book sets out to vindicate the proposition

11

that the substantive challenge awaiting those who would break the alternating current of racism between problem and victim status lies in the possibility of representing a black presence outside these categories. This reintroduction of history is not a minimal aim. Racism rests on the ability to contain blacks in the present, to repress and to deny the past.

The book has a second more parochial aim related to its origins in the field of cultural studies. It seeks to provide, more implicitly than explicitly, a corrective to the more ethnocentric dimensions of that discipline. I have grown gradually more and more weary of having to deal with the effects of striving to analyse culture within neat, homogeneous national units reflecting the 'lived relations' involved; with the invisibility of 'race' within the field and, most importantly, with the forms of nationalism endorsed by a discipline which, in spite of itself, tends towards a morbid celebration of England and Englishness from which blacks are systematically excluded. Discussing the works of Thomas Carlyle or John Ruskin without mentioning their positions on the Nigger Question and the Morant Bay Rebellion of 1865 was an early symptom of this difficulty. The exclusion of the work of black radicals and cultural critics, particularly C. L. R. James, from the field of cultural studies was a second source of bewilderment to me (Hamilton, 1984).* It was only towards the end of writing this book that I began to appreciate how symptomatic these strategic silences were. They mask the hidden history not merely of blacks in this country, but of the complex historical relationship between working-class radicalism and the struggle against slavery which is just beginning to be investigated (Fryer, 1984; Linebaugh, 1982, 1984; Bolt and Drescher, 1980; and Walvin, 1985).

The promise of future investigations does not provide much comfort in the present. Today even where the issue of 'race' stares cultural studies in the face in the quote from Thompson above or in Barthes's famous image (1972) of a 'negro soldier saluting the French flag' the epistemology and ontology of 'race' are being studiously conjured out of consideration:

The Negro who salutes is not the symbol of the French Empire: he has too much presence, he appears as a rich, fully experienced, spontaneous, innocent, indisputable image . . . at the same time this presence is tamed . . . as form, its meaning is shallow, isolated, impoverished.

The marginalization of 'race' and racism has persisted even where cultural studies have identified themselves with socialist and feminist political aspirations. This is perhaps a consequence of the imperatives of what are identified as 'national popular' struggles as well as a

---

* Full references quoted in the text are contained in the Bibliography beginning on p. 251.

desire to construct national interests and roads to socialism using a political language which, as we shall see in Chapter 2, is saturated with racial connotations. Recovering the representation of blacks from the condition of isolated impoverishment, which has been allocated them on the basis of perceived spontaneity and innocence, is a long-term task far beyond the scope of this book. What follows is a cultural analysis which does not pretend to address many of the important historical and structural issues arising, for example, in the political economy of black settlement. The full complexity of contemporary 'race' politics has not been dealt with. I have focused instead on how 'race' and racism articulate various forms of action, some of which are not usually dignified by the labels of formal politics.

Chapter 1 looks at the question of 'race' and class. Some of the most influential formulations in this area are accorded critical scrutiny and it is tentatively suggested that class analysis should be substantially reworked in the light of its encounter with 'race'. Chapter 2 addresses the relationship between contemporary notions of 'race' on both sides of the colour line, and the ideas of nation and national belonging. It is argued that these give the new racism a substantial part of its newness. By defining 'race' and ethnicity as cultural absolutes, blacks themselves and parts of the anti-racist movement risk endorsing the explanatory frameworks and political definitions of the new right. Chapter 3 covers representations of the law as a national institution. In this context, black law-breaking comes gradually to be seen as proof of the incompatibility of blacks with Britishness. Ideologies of legality and of blacks as a high-crime group are also identified as constitutive of the new racism. Chapter 4 turns to the issue of anti-racism and uses a comparative study of two different phases of anti-racist mobilization to further clarify the relationship between 'race' and nation as well as to highlight some of the difficulties in developing a popular anti-racist cultural politics. Chapter 5 covers the expressive culture of black Britain. It shows that culture does not develop along ethnically absolute lines but in complex, dynamic patterns of syncretism in which new definitions of what it means to be black emerge from raw materials provided by black populations elsewhere in the diaspora. The final chapter returns to the problem of agency outlined at the start of the book and argues that much of what is commonly identified as 'racial' politics can also be interpreted as fall-out from the struggles of urban social movements for community and autonomy. The first two chapters effectively state the political and theoretical problems which are explored in the empirical studies which make up Chapters 3, 4 and 5. The final chapter returns to the issue of 'race' and class in the light of these 'case studies' of the intersection between culture and politics

13

and suggests a general framework for re-conceptualizing class in terms which derive from recent theories of social movements.

My overall approach necessarily involves political and theoretical opposition of the study of 'race' as an issue which is marginal to the normal processes by which British society has developed. 'Race' will be presented as an effect of a number of discourses and practices which have become more crucial to the inner workings of this society as the national crisis has deepened. In Britain, 'race' cannot be adequately understood if it is falsely divorced or abstracted from other social relations. The chapters which follow will also argue that 'race' cannot be reduced to the effects of these other relations.

1 'Race', class and agency

The race question is subsidiary to the class question in politics, and to think of imperialism in terms of race is disastrous. But to neglect the racial factor as merely incidental is an error only less grave than to make it fundamental (C. L. R. James).

Hearing . . . that you are a zealous friend for the Abolition of that Accursed traffick denominated the Slave Trade I inferred from that you was a friend to freedom on the broad basis of the Rights of Man for I am pretty persuaded that no Man who is an advocate from principle for liberty for a Black Man but will strenuously promote and support the rights of a white man & vice versa (Thomas Hardy, 1792).

This chapter is not intended to provide an account of 'race' which is designed to function as an alternative to the sociology of 'race relations' as it is presently defined.[1] However, as an introduction to what follows, a brief critique of that sub-discipline of sociology can serve to clarify some basic theoretical and political issues. It has been pointed out (Gabriel and Ben-Tovim, 1979) that sociological writing on 'race relations' falls into three categories reflecting the analysis of structures, meanings and culture. The sociology of 'race' can therefore be seen to fracture along the 'fault lines' (Craib, 1984) which traverse its parent discipline. These are the effects of the epistemological and ontological problems which arise in trying to reconcile the study of structures with the study of meaning and action.

These tensions are not confined to academic theories. They also appear in explicitly political writing on 'race' and racism. Here the most sophisticated and ambitious writers have tried to operate across these divisions. But the problems are particularly acute where writers have resisted the idea that 'race' and class belong to separate spheres of experience with different epistemological and ontological valencies and used Marxian and neo-Marxian approaches to confront the question of historical agency posed by the relationship between 'race' and class.

A non-reductive understanding of how these different collectivities interrelate has been sought by various black writers within the approach broadly suggested by C. L. R. James's words above. Hall's

---

* Superior figures refer to the Notes and references sections following each chapter.

use of the concept of 'articulation' (UNESCO, 1980) is, for example, an attempt to address the political and intellectual problems which arise in combining analysis of 'race' and racism as structuring relations in society with an understanding of them as ideologies shaping political action and giving it powerful common-sense meanings. The distinction between racism and racialism which emerges in the work of Sivanandan (1982) serves a similar function.

Roy Bhaskar (1979; 1980) has argued that societies and agents have different properties even if there are complex relationships of dependency between them. His position suggests that it may be useful to be more explicit about the different ways in which racism is both a property of structures and a source of meanings. He proposes a 'transformative' model of human action in which societies provide raw material for human agents to act on and thereby produce societies over time. This insight emphasizes a view of society as a process rather than a finished edifice. It can provide a framework for separating out the different analytical issues surrounding 'race'. The discourse of 'race', its ontology and the articulation between them are three interrelated aspects of a single political and theoretical problem. Their analytical separation takes place in the context of a theoretical position which can be enhanced and extended by a theory of culture. Indeed, this perspective on 'race' and racism depends on a theory which presents the cultural not as an intrinsic property of ethnic particularity but as a mediating space between agents and structures in which their reciprocal dependency is created and secured. It is, in Craib's phrase, a 'hinge linking the teleological "door" of agency to the structural frame of society' (1984).

In the sociology of 'race relations', idealists of various political persuasions have studied racial meanings as an autonomous tradition of scientific inquiry (Banton and Harwood, 1977) or in an ideological instance which, entire of itself, 'intervenes only subsequently' if at all in the economic relations of British society (Gabriel and Ben-Tovim, 1978). On the other side, there are writers who have sought to reduce 'race' to the inherent effects of various structures – relations of production, and markets (Sivanandan, 1982; Rex, 1979). Between these poles, sometimes literally papering over the stress-induced cracks, is a third tendency which has defined 'race' as a cultural phenomenon. This group has made 'race' into a synonym for ethnicity and a sign for the sense of separateness which endows groups with an exclusive, collective identity (Lawrence, 1982). For these writers, blacks live not in the castle of their skin but behind the sturdy walls of discrete ethnic identities.

This book aims to highlight some of the limitations in each of these approaches. It criticizes their conceptualizations of culture and provides an extended argument, both implicit and explicit, that a materialist theory of culture has much to contribute to 'race relations'

16

analysis. The initiative must be recaptured from those whose view of culture is less supple, more absolute and reluctant to address the complex syncretisms which have been a feature of the junction between 'race' and class in contemporary Britain.

Culture can be presented as a field articulating the life-world of subjects (albeit de-centred) and the structures created by human activity. However the contemporary tendency towards ethnic absolutism, explored in Chapter 2, comes to view it as an impermeable shell, eternally dividing one 'race' or ethnic group from another. Apart from the theoretical difficulties with this position, it has crucial political deficiencies. I shall argue that it replicates among black and anti-racists, positions which are characteristic of the new right.

The argument below seeks to introduce a more sophisticated theory of culture into the political analysis of 'race' and racism in Britain by claiming the term back from ethnicity. The active, dynamic aspects of cultural life have been emphasized. This is a calculated challenge to the absolutist definitions of 'race' and ethnicity which are shared by contemporary racism, a substantial current in the sociology of 'race', and much liberal anti-racism.

Racial meanings are examined not as an autonomous branch of ideology, but as a salient feature in a general process whereby culture mediates the world of agents and the structures which are created by their social praxis. These meanings are sources of the individual and collective actions which give culture its materiality. The terrain of meaning and action is also a field of historical development through struggle. The view of 'race' as an eternal, essential factor of division in society will also be challenged by showing some of the ways in which 'race' and racism have featured in contemporary Britain's complex political antagonisms, marking distinct patterns of social and political subordination and de-subordination, resistance and negotiation.

These aims take this book inevitably into areas in which various forms of class theory have made important contributions. Class analysis has helped to illuminate the contours of historical development which have seen racism change from one determinate period to the next. It is necessary then to clarify how the concepts 'race' and class will be used below and how they will be thought to combine and contradict. The final chapter argues in detail that the vocabulary of class analysis may itself be insufficient to address the political struggles charted in Chapters 3, 4 and 5. It is useful, therefore, to begin with a critical evaluation of the work of some of the writers who have tried to bring the terms 'race' and class into some sort of mutual relation.

Though its presence makes life difficult for the theorist, the concept of class cannot be entirely banished from inquiries into racial politics, not least because it has an obvious value in locating the practice of racial groups in relation to the contradiction between capital and labour. However, where forms of political action develop which demand more than the reappropriation of material production, and where that production and the accumulation of capital depend not on exploitation alone but on control of information and communication systems, its use must be carefully specified. It is important to recognize the difficulties which attend the concept and to appreciate that its use in the politics and history of Britain's black settlers has often been economistic and reductive, seeking to subordinate the self-organization of blacks to the mythical discipline of a unified working class and its representative political institutions.

Theoretical and political debates over the status of 'race' relative to class exemplify a more general crisis in the field of Marxist analytical writing. This has its roots not only in the strategic political crises of the workers' movements in the overdeveloped countries (Mouffe and Laclau, 1985; Gorz, 1982) but also in the theoretical challenges posed for class-based analysis by writers and thinkers from radical traditions struggling against forms of subordination which are not obviously or directly related to class. These may be based on gender, 'race', ethnicity or age and are often found in political locations removed from the workplace. Mass unemployment and consumer-oriented people's capitalism have combined in novel ways to further undermine both the theory and practice of the left. Marx's own method ought to have taught his disciples that there are necessarily historical and political limits to the validity of his insights. Unfortunately some of the most anachronistic strands in Marxian thought have lived on like residual dinosaurs in the lost valley of 'race relations' analysis.

At the structural level, it has become imperative to question the analytic priority accorded by the Marxian tradition to forms of production which directly generate surplus value. This priority is no longer justified either by the diminishing size or the political character of this group of workers. Less than 30 per cent of Britain's working population now performs work of this type.

The failure of these workers to match the predictive logic of reductive Marxism and constitute a socialist vanguard, advancing towards the transformation of society, has been recently underlined. The masculinism and craft traditions which distinguish them as a group have been successfully appealed to by the family-centred populist ideology of Thatcherite conservatism. Bea Campbell (1983) puts it bluntly: 'The Tories have claimed [the] tradition of male craft and sex chauvinism, so important in the organization of the working class men's movement, for the right.'

Millions of women (who now form 40 per cent of the total working population) and low-paid workers have now been unionized in the public sector. Here the junction between 'race', gender and organized

18

class politics is being encountered as an urgent problem. The immediate issues raised by the presence of women, blacks and other subordinate groups in the political institutions of the working class carry with them profound theoretical questions which reach into the heart of Marxian explanation. What is the working class today? What gender is it? What colour is it? How, in the light of its obvious segmentation, is it to be unified? Is this unification still possible or even desirable?

The relationship between manufacturing and service work, the role of the state as an employer and as a provider of income, and the growth of structural unemployment, all indicate the need to rework contemporary class analysis and the conceptions of class struggle which support it. Class analysis must be opened up so that it can be supplemented by additional categories which reflect different histories of subordination as well as the 'historical and moral' elements Marx identified as determining different values for different types of labour power (*Capital* I quoted by G. Rubin, 1975).

A third of Britain's workforce is now employed by the state in central or local government as well as in publicly owned corporations. The complex experiential chemistry of class, 'race' and gender revealed, for example, by examination of public sector employment, yields an important reminder of the limitations of analysis based exclusively on a narrow conception of class. Where the conditions of subordination constructed by these forms of oppression are lived out, they cannot be empirically disentangled.

Feminist critiques of Marxism have emphasized the political privileges attached by it to work outside the home and the way it has devalued labour performed in the private sphere. They point towards the same critical conclusion even when, as in some socialist feminist writing, a reconstruction of class theory is proposed.[2] If class analysis is to retain a place in explaining contemporary politics in general and the relationships between black and white workers, citizens, neighbours and friends in particular, it must be ruthlessly modernized.

Though it is a necessary part of the analytic framework proposed here, the contradiction between capital and labour is not sufficient; it simply cannot by itself generate a complete account of the struggles through which the social movement of blacks dissolves and then transcends the formal divisions of class. In some struggles, workers and shopkeepers have created political solidarity in the name of 'race' and community. In others, the action of black workers may be linked in complex ways to those of the black unemployed. It has been suggested, for example, that the industrial action in which health service workers confronted the government during the autumn and winter of 1982–3 cannot be understood unless the issue of its relationship to the urban protests of summer 1981 is explained. The Race

19

Today Collective have argued that these two apparently distinct conflicts can be shown to have common roots not simply in the black populations that spearheaded them, but in a self-conscious community's struggles against various, different manifestations of pauperization. The political activities of black workers in the health service are necessarily tied to those of their children in the streets.[3]

This example illustrates the need for a political and theoretical vocabulary capable of linking the organization of service workers to that of unemployed young people. It underlines the fact that there is nothing to be gained from attempts to use the concept class as if its meaning had been unaffected by the changes in capital accumulation and the division of labour which have resulted from the revolution in new technology.

The place of black labour in the processes which transform workers into a class and distribute surplus labour power in society raises a series of fundamental doubts about the degree of homogeneity which can be ascribed to today's 'English working class'. It is severely divided not only between those in and out of work, but between workers in the various sectors of waged employment, between men and women, and between older and younger people. Conflicts around 'race', nation and ethnicity must be examined in the light of these other divisions where the unity of a single 'working class' cannot be assumed but remains to be created. It must be emphasized, then, that class is used below in a tentative and even provisional manner. The concept is useful to the extent that it ties political struggles to the goal of reappropriating the material structures of production but the antagonisms which form around 'race' and racism are not limited by this aim. Accordingly, class has been shorn of the positivistic certainties which came to be associated with it in the period when industrial production was ascendant. These are now an outmoded, residual presence in both sociological writing on 'race' and socialist political analysis of racism.

Race for itself and class in itself

Writers who have tried to theorize the relationship between 'race' and class in contemporary Britain can be divided into three basic tendencies. These form around the same 'fault lines' which divide the sociologies of systems from the sociologies of action. Each features a distinct paradigm or problematic for the 'race'/class relationship and each is marked by an equally clear political orientation.

The first tendency operates on the boundaries of Weberian and Marxist analysis and argues that economic relations have a primacy in determining the character of 'race' politics. In its Weberian inflection, it views blacks as members of an 'underclass' (Rex and

Tomlinson, 1979) while in the parallel Marxist version, this idea is conveyed by the term 'sub-proleteriat'. The point of departure for both variations is recognition of the ways in which Britain's black polulations are subject to particularly intense forms of disadvantage and exploitation. For the Weberians, an underclass status results from the accumulated effect of losing struggles in the distributive sphere. In other words, faring consistently badly in the markets for jobs, housing and education. This structural position constitutes the objective basis for an 'underclass in itself'. This appears where 'instead of identifying with working-class *culture* [my emphasis] community or politics they [the blacks] formed their own organisations and became in effect a separate under-privileged class' (Rex and Tomlinson, 1979, p. 275).

The version of this argument, which is cast in Marxist language, lays greater emphasis on the effect of *production* relations in generating and reproducing the underclass/sub-proleteriat with its distinct political identity. Racial structuration is thus imposed by capital. But it is compounded and deepened by the state institutions and agencies which seek to regulate the ebb and flow of black labour power in capital's interests. Thus, the role and position of migrant labour in late capitalism as well as the political and legal contradictions around citizenship and settlement in Britain have been important objects of concern to this tendency.

The value of these arguments lies in their insistence on the real effects of racial division inside the working class and in the suggestion that sectional class interests expressed along the lines of 'race' and colour are not epiphenomena of capitalist development and cannot therefore be banished by incantation of the voluntaristic slogans like 'black and white unite and fight'.

In the Marxist version of this approach, the term sub-proleteriat is noteworthy because it allows black leftists a means to retain a significant but vague link with class theory. This link has a rhetorical dimension as well as an analytical one. It encourages activists to open a dialogue with the political forces of 'the left' while directing their energies towards the development of relatively autonomous black political activity, focused by the ways in which racism reaches into the lives of the black working class. Whereas, for the Weberian writers, market relations secure and reproduce the divisions between the racially distinct underclass and the class structure as a whole, Marxists address the effects of racist ideology and racialist practice which fracture the political superstructure and the economic base in turn. The most sophisticated version of the Marxian variation on these themes is found in the work of Sivanandan. He describes the relationship between racism and capitalism as an essentially instrumental and even functionalist one in which 'Capital requires racism not for racism's sake but for the sake of capital' (1980). Where

21

capitalism depends on racism in this way, and this is Sivanandan's analysis of post-war Britain, struggles against racism become a priori struggles against capitalism.

Both versions of this argument see the transposition of struggle between economic and political levels of the social formation as a straightforward question. 'Race' conceived in class terms acts as a conductor between the two.

The second analytical tendency which can be identified claims its warrant from the rigours of political economy and in the name of Marxian science, sets out to outflank the first position from the left. This approach has been typified in the recent work of Robert Miles. His position begins by emphasizing the familiar observation that 'races' as they appear in society have no basis in the raw materials of human biology.[4] There is, of course, only one human race, but for Miles this observation is entangled with a demolition of the sociology of 'race relations' and becomes the trigger for an intense critique of all attempts to use the concept 'race' in either description or analysis. It is as if the recognition of the limited value of 'race' as an analytic tool provided, in itself, a coherent theory of contemporary racisms. Miles writes on occasions as if he believes that banishing the concept 'race' is a means to abolish racism:

I recognize that people do conceive of themselves and others as belonging to 'races' and do describe certain sorts of situation and relations as being 'race relations', but I am also arguing that these categories of everyday life cannot automatically be taken up and employed analytically by an inquiry which aspires to objective or scientific status (1982, p. 42).

In a later work (Miles, 1984), the complex and contradictory ways in which actual social forces recognize themselves as 'races' and organize themselves in political life on the basis of constructed racial sensibility are brushed aside in what amounts to an attempt to reduce the complexities of social life to a set of theoretical concepts.

The supposed dichotomy between 'race' and class becomes a mere 'false construction' (Miles, 1984) and ' . . . the totality of "black people in Britain" cannot be adequately analysed as a "race" outside or in opposition to class relations'. 'Race' is nothing more than an ideological effect, a phenomenal form masking real, economic relationships in a manner analogous to a mirage. To use 'race' in analysis and thus to respect the diverse ways in which it endows action with meaning is to capitulate to mere ideology. Miles therefore attacks black writers who have initiated a dialogue with Marxism over racism in Britain because they use 'race', in spite of its illusory status, to 'encourage the formation of a particular political force'. He clearly disagrees with the political strategy these authors propose and makes his disagreement explicit through a negative evaluation of the politics of black autonomy. The idea is to be dismissed not only because it is based on idealist theoretical foundations but because it represents a political threat to a deeper class unity:

> . . . the political and ideological reaction of those who remain the object of racism will be increasingly a movement towards a complete break with the struggles and institutions that arise of out production relations. Once this happens, the politics of 'race' are likely to predominate amongst those excluded by racism, leading to a strategy of absolute autonomy (Miles, 1984, pp. 231–2).

Miles describes racism and racialization as having 'autonomous but limited effects' but does not specify how much autonomy his own political strategy will cede to blacks in Britain.

Racism, it is argued, originates and is reproduced in particular forms of the struggle between capital and labour – specifically in the modern period, the employment of migrant labour. Thus although racism is rigorously defined in terms of the Marxian theory of ideology, it becomes a problem which can be solved satisfactorily at the economic level. Here, shared class positions in the processes of production provide 'a material and political basis for the development of anti-racist practice within the working class'. This position effectively articulates a theoretical statement of the 'black and white unite and fight' variety. The consciousness of groups which define themselves in, or organize around, what become racial discourses is rendered illegitimate because of its roots in ideology. It is consistently counterposed to the apparently unlimited potential of an ideal category of workers. This group, the repository of legitimate and authentic class feeling, is able to transcend racial particularity in political practice uncontaminated by non-class subjectivity. Class is confined to the workplace and the pure solidarity of workers apparently flows from their position in the immediate processes of production. The form of class consciousness, which Miles identifies as non-ideological, emerges only in this narrow conception of production relations. The possibility that either the political and cultural life of 'races' or their experiences of racial subordination can become unifying factors enabling groups to act across the formal lines of class is vigorously criticized.

This perspective presents Marxism as a privileged science allowing unique access to fundamental historical issues which are denied to analysts writing from other perspectives. Dogmatism is particularly evident in Miles's discussion of class relations inside the black communities. The effects of popular and institutional racisms in drawing together various black groups with different histories is unexplored. The idea that these relationships might create a new definition of black out of various different experiences of racial subordination is not entertained. Blacks are presented, not as a potentially cohesive group but as 'a population of significantly distinct historical

23

origins, occupying different class positions' (Miles, 1984). A complete discontinuity is introduced between the interests of the black *petit bourgeois* and working-class black settlers on the basis of their objectively contradictory class positions. Yet the construction of the Black Community as a complex and inclusive collectivity with a distinctive political language undermines Miles's position. The formal lines of class have been blurred recently not just by the explicitly anti-racist actions of the black *petit bourgeois* which will be examined in Chapter 4, but by the struggles of black teachers, business people and even media workers.

Examining the way that these groups are formed and sometimes reproduce can point to a view of 'race' as a political category. As such, its meanings are unfixed and subject to the outcomes of struggle. There can be no guarantee that conflicts over the meaning of 'race' will always be resolved in a politically radical or progressive direction, but it would be foolish to deny the black *petit bourgeois* the capacity to 'change sides' which Marx and Engels describe so cryptically in *The Communist Manifesto* (Marx and Engels, 1973).

If journalists, teachers, sociologists and other members of the professional and managerial classes can be theorized into contradictory class locations and from there, take up the needs of the working class by joining its political institutions, perhaps even becoming its organic intellectuals, there seems no reason why the black *petit bourgeois* in both its 'old' and 'new' guises should not be able to do something similar. Indeed, common history, culture and language, as well as the effects of racism, may all enhance this possibility. For example, where neighbourhood shops acquire the role of community institutions, it is possible for their proprietors to develop a sense of the connections between their lives and those of their working-class clients. As a result, they may go on to provide them with goods on credit when they strike. This type of connection has been a notable feature of some industrial disputes, particularly where a black workforce lives in close proximity and is able to make its politics simultaneously in both work and non-workspace (Mala Dhondy, 1974).

Miles notes that common involvement of black and white workers in the trades union and labour movements can lead to common struggle. However he and Annie Phizaclea have argued for a complete separation between this 'class unity' and various forms of ethnic organization (1980). I shall try and demonstrate that the language and culture of black radicalism is more complex in its relation to class than this simple polarized schema suggests.

Phizaclea and Miles also find it hard to grasp that what they call 'ethnic organization' is not reducible to anti-racism. I shall show in Chapters 4 and 5 that anti-racism is not and probably has never been an adequate heading under which the content, scope and direction of black protest and self-organization can be assessed. Black political action has often been articulated through what appears to be a utopian political language. The distance from economism which has characterized it has baffled critics who would measure it by Eurocentric yardsticks and are consequently unable to perceive the sophisticated critique of capitalism which informs the social movement of blacks in the overdeveloped countries. This critique has, in Richard Wright's words, 'become a tradition, in fact a kind of culture' (Padmore, 1956). This social movement has a variety of goals other than the elimination of racist ideology.

In any case, looking at the contradictions in political consciousness formed at work tells less than half the story. Work is not the only place where complex and important political relationships between black and white Britons have been created. 'Race' can be shown to be relevant to the politics of consumption as well as to the politics of production, and Chapters 4 and 5 below look at some of the connections between black and white youth in detail as part of an argument that the issue of 'race' has become a central theme and referent in virtually all youth cultures in this country.

Miles and his collaborators regard the dissolving of 'race' into class as a necessary and desirable step. The third tendency which can be identified shares the idea of a fundamental split between 'race' and class but argues for the opposite strategic conclusions. For writers in this group, the distance between 'race' and class is the result not of their different epistemological values in Marxist science but of the fact that racism inhabits a general ideological instance in the social formation. It does not appear to have any contact with class politics. The task of the radical theorist of 'race' and racism is revealed as the production of critiques of official 'race' policy and the formulation of alternative 'rational policy recommendations' which can facilitate the 'rational political interventions' of central and local governments (Gabriel and Ben Tovim, 1979). There are several problems, both political and theoretical, with this position. Its plausibility relies on a positive evaluation of the capacity of state institutions to act as an agent for the elimination of racism. This cannot be taken for granted at either level of government. We shall see, in Chapter 4 for example, that even where a progressive, radical local authority acts in the name of anti-racism its practices may reinforce the very ideologies it is seeking to challenge.

At a theoretical level, this tendency identifies 'race' in a variety of political struggles which are distinguished from class antagonisms on the basis that they are primarily 'popular democratic' and not therefore inscribed by class.

The struggle for racial equality and racial justice . . . needs to be seen primarily as a popular democratic struggle which . . . entails, in current conditions of British parliamentary democracy, a complex, detailed and

25

realistic war of position to be waged by the ethnic minorities and anti-racist organisations, involving the application of a consistent disposition of forces to those key areas of the local state in which constructive developments can successfully be fought for (Ben Tovim *et al.*, 1981)

The formulations 'national popular' and 'popular democratic' derive from a reading of Gramsci articulated most notably by Ernesto Laclau (1977) which I have criticized elsewhere (CCCS, 1982). They accord with the strategic thinking of the European communist parties (Balibar *et al.*, 1980). The political danger in this approach is twofold. Its enthusiasm for the language of nation and a national focus leads to the contemporary association between British racism and British nationalism being overlooked. When coupled with political pragmatism which demands from the left a populist appeal to match the authoritarian populist (Hall, 1985) appeal of the right, there is a further risk that forms of nationalism which are themselves coloured with racial connotations will be endorsed. This problem is explored in detail in the next chapter. Second, the logic of this approach reduces the construction of anti-racist politics to the development of those forms of democracy which are congruent with a pluralist national identity. Rabstein locates anti-racism in precisely this way, seeing it as the construction of a

national democratic alliance whose strategy for the democratisation of life in Britain is linked to a national liberation struggle aimed at asserting a new pluralist national identity through struggling around race issues in the first instance (1981, p. 99).

Like Miles, these authors insist on locating racism in a discrete ideological instance. They would, however, tend to disagree with his mechanistic suggestion that political conflicts can be addressed by appealing to a fundamental unity of workers based on their common class position. For this tendency, racism is bad ideology and it must be combated not, as he would have it, in the realm of economic contradictions but by good (popular democratic) ideology. This can be pumped into people's heads by a variety of means and is orchestrated by rational state intervention expressed in clearly focused policies. Race relations legislation, multi-cultural education policies and racism awareness training are some of the favoured vehicles for accomplishing this transformation. Ben Tovim *et al.* identify the means of its elaboration in the 'hegemonic' activities of 'black para-professionals'.

The difficulties I have identified in these positions involve more than simply a critique of the way that each deploys the concept 'race'. If it is accepted that one of the definitive characteristics of contemporary racism is its capacity first to define blacks in the problem/victim couplet and then expel them from historical being altogether, then anti-racism must be able to respond by revealing and restoring the historical dimensions of black life in this country. However, none of the models of the 'race'/class relationship discussed above are adequate to this task. Despite their differences, the first two positions centre on the idea that the historical process emerges (either directly or complexly) from the 'economic' antagonisms arising out of production or market relations. The third breaks with this idea but the price of its divergence is that 'race', defined in the ideological instance, loses contact with both history and class politics. It becomes a policy issue.

Racism is not a unitary event based on psychological aberration nor some ahistorical antipathy to blacks which is the cultural legacy of empire and which continues to saturate the consciousness of all white Britons regardless of age, gender, income or circumstances. It must be understood as a process. Bringing blacks into history outside the categories of problem and victim, and establishing the historical character of racism in opposition to the idea that it is an eternal or natural phenomenon, depends on a capacity to comprehend political, ideological and economic change. It is here that a revised and reworked concept of class may be of value provided that, as I have suggested earlier, the dialectic between forces and relations of production is stripped of its nineteenth-century content and the concept is not confined to the immediate relations of production.

The three approaches I have criticized all seek to negotiate a position for 'race' and ethnicity in relation to an overarching class structure. By contrast, the path I have chosen pays less attention to the issue of the epistemological relation of 'race' to class and to the status of 'race' as a distinct order of social phenomena *sui generis*. The pursuit of a platonist answer to the question of where 'races' slide between the world of real relations and the world of phenomenal forms must, I believe, be given secondary status. The primary problem for analysis of racial antagonism which occurs within the broad framework of historical materialism must be the manner in which racial meanings, solidarity and identities provide the basis for action. Different patterns of 'racial' activity and political struggle will appear in determinate historical conditions. They are not conceived as a straightforward alternative to class struggle at the level of economic analysis, but must be recognized to be potentially both an alternative to class consciousness at the political level and as a factor in the contingent processes in which classes are themselves formed. It may be felt, for example, that in Britain during the late 1980s 'race', whatever we think of its ideological origins, provides a more potent means to organize and to focus the grievances of certain inner-city populations than the languages of class politics with which it must, in a limited sense, compete. We shall see in Chapter 2 how the voice of this class politics has acquired racial referents and connotations through its relationship to the language of nationalism. Recognizing

27

these developments need not lead, as it does in the work of Glazer and Moynihan (1975), to a situation in which racial or ethnic politics is crudely counterposed to class as a basis for collective action but rather to a finer discrimination which appreciates the complex interplay between struggles based around different forms of social subordination.

Class formation

Wallerstein (1979) has argued forcefully that 'class analysis loses its power of explanation whenever it moves towards formal models and away from dialectical dynamics'. To reconstruct class so that it is adequate to the task I have outlined involves turning it away from being a polarized concept and towards becoming a multi-modal one. The emphasis found in traditional Marxist writing about 'race' must therefore be inverted: 'race' can no longer be reduced to an effect of the economic antagonisms arising from production, and class must be understood in terms qualified by the vitality of struggles articulated through 'race'. However, clarification of what class consciousness and struggles consist of in contemporary Britain is, in itself, difficult. The growth of populist political forms which appeal to national sentiment, seemingly above and beyond the narrow concerns of class, has been matched by a detachment or distancing between the poor and their traditional means of political representation – the trades union and labour movements. The effect of these developments can be seen in the proliferation of political subjectivities apparently unrelated to class and often based on ascriptive criteria (age, 'race', gender). We shall see in Chapter 6 that political action premised on 'race' and openly against racism can contribute to new social movements of this type.

These shifts are part of a crisis of representation in the organizations and institutions of the working-class movement and this must be acknowledged in any revised notion of class. They render the assessment of class feeling very complex. This crisis has structural and conjunctural, national and international dimensions. Its structural aspects include not only the ways in which new technology and recession now circumscribe the range of economic options available to Britain but also the demographic factors which are associated with the uneven development of national decline. The latter has precipitated important changes in the regional bases of the working-class movement (G. Williams, 1982; Massey, 1984; Massey and Miles, 1984). These are significant because, like the politics of anti-racism, they point to the limits of a political strategy based on appeals to a homogeneous and cohesive nation.

Where the crisis of representation has been acknowledged by the left, discussion has centred on the electoral implications of the dislocation between the represented and their representatives. In particular, the question of whether the Labour Party will be able to survive this upheaval has been explored, as has the related discussion of the peculiar qualities of Thatcherite conservatism which have enabled it to maintain a limited but none the less effective 'historic bloc'[5] amidst the debris of deindustrialization (Hobsbawm, 1984; 1985). These issues, however important, constitute only a fraction of the problems in which the crisis of representation is manifest. It can also be apprehended through the populist politics of 'race' and nation which has emerged at the centre of Britain's attempts to make sense of national decline.

The resultant racialization of British political life has passed through various phases since the end of the Second World War. Chapter 3 examines some of the ways in which racist ideologies have changed during this period. It is important at this stage of the argument to recognize that the populist impulse in recent patterns of racialization is a response to the crisis of representation. The right has created a language of nation which gains populist power from calculated ambiguities that allow it to transmit itself as a language of 'race'. At the same time, the political resources of the white working class are unable to offer a vision, language or practice capable of providing an alternative. They are currently unable to represent the class as a class, that is outside of the categories in which capital structures and reproduces it by means of 'race'. Where this means of representation has been articulated, as we shall see in Chapters 4 and 5, its relationship to class organization and to the languages of class politics had been tenuous.

There must be caution in any attempt to adapt Gramsci's commentary on the genesis of Italian Fascism to contemporary British conditions. However, his remarks capture something of the relationship between this crisis and the emergence of authoritarian and nationalist political forces:

At a certain point in their historical lives, social classes become detached from their traditional parties. In other words, the traditional parties in that particular organizational form, with the particular men who constitute, represent and lead them, as its expression. When such crises occur, the immediate situation becomes delicate and dangerous, because the field is open for violent situations, for the activities of unknown forces, represented by charismatic 'men of destiny' (1971, p. 210).

In contemporary Britain, the politics of 'race' has provided the site for just such a detachment. Locating 'race' and racism in a Gramscian analysis based on hegemony poses the question of class in an acute form. It points to a view of the causality of class as a complex, multi-determined process in which racialization currently plays a key part.

29

The positions of dominant and subordinate groups are ascribed by 'race'. It assigns and fixes their positions relative to each other and with respect to the basic structures of society, simultaneously legitimating these ascribed positions. Racism plays an active role, articulating political, cultural and economic elements into a complex and contradictory unity. It ensures, though this need not always be the case, that for contemporary Britain 'race is the modality in which class is lived', the medium in which it is appropriated and 'fought through' (Hall, 1980).

Looking at 'race' in this way underlines the contingent and discontinuous nature of class formation. Analysing it requires careful attention to the necessary displacement of 'relative autonomy' between the economic, ideological and political instances in any social formation. This problem is glossed over by the Marxian writers criticized above. The range of possible outcomes within the formation of any particular class may be determined primarily by economic considerations but 'in the last instance' it will be rooted in the results of ongoing processes of conflict. Class in concrete historical conditions is therefore the effect of struggles.

Adam Prezworski (1977) has used this insight to develop the idea that class struggle should be broadly defined. It should encompass struggles which bring classes into being as well as struggles between organized class forces which are relatively rare. His break with the economistic definitions of class characteristic of much avowedly Marxist writing on 'race' is readily apparent. He draws an important distinction between 'the determination of objective ideological and political relations by objective economic relations' and the multiplex, reciprocal relationship of determination of struggles by the structured totality of social relations. In specific historical circumstances, particular patterns of class formation involve both types of determination. Objective conditions structure the range of possibilities, but precise outcomes emerge directly from struggles. Prezworski concludes that 'all conflicts . . . can be understood in historical terms if and only if they are viewed as effects of and in turn having effects upon class formation'. This statement is offered as a methodological postulate for a complex, non-reductionist radicalism based on Marxism. It has been clarified further by Katznelson who concludes his own discussion of class thus:

Class society exists even where it is not signified; but how and why it is signified in particular ways in particular places and times is the study of class formation (1981, p. 207).

Whether this position merits the name Marxism and its precise lineage within the tradition of Marxist–humanist writing are interesting questions beyond the scope of this chapter (Thompson, 1978; Soper, 1986). However, the expanded conception of class formation to which it refers can contribute significantly to an alternative view of the 'race'/class relationship in several ways. First, it suggests that an analysis based on class formation can render the connections between history and concrete struggles, structure and process, intelligible even in situations where collective actors define themselves and organize as 'races', people, maroons, ghost-dancers or slaves rather than as a class. Second, when struggles about class formation are being discussed, that is struggles which have the effect of organizing or dis-organizing classes, the possibility of reciprocal determination between 'race' and class politics can be identified.

The emphasis on class formation leads to the conclusion that when struggling to form and to reproduce, classes are only *potentially* constituted. It allows for the historical analysis of periods when the language and politics of class may be entirely absent, as well as periods like our own when the reappropriation of material production is only one goal among many in the heterogeneous practice of social movements. From this perspective, even the most resolutely autonomous organization of black workers, claimants or schoolchildren does not necessarily represent a simple threat to the organic unity and interests of a fixed and predetermined working class. Class politics in this model do not precede the encounter between black and white, they are created or destroyed in it. This must be the beginning of an answer to those who would relegate black struggles to the realm of 'non-class' contradictions (Maclennan, 1984) and in the process deprive them of the capacity to shape or define class antagonism (Boddy and Fudge, 1984) A class formation problematic also provides a third political and theoretical opportunity. It permits the effects of racism to be located structurally and historically in relation to the conflict between capital and labour.

One of the effects of reciprocal determination between 'race' and class struggles has been the creation of what Cedric Robinson has called a 'racial capitalism'. Without wishing to enter debates over the extent to which racial differentiation has been integral to capitalist development (Wolf, 1982), it seems important to recognize that the tendency to 'exaggerate regional, subcultural and dialectical differences into racial ones' (Robinson, 1982) has been a remarkable feature of continuity across the various economic expressions of the capitalist world system and their ideological conditions of existence. This subject has not always received due consideration in the historiography of nation states and national capitals (Linebaugh, 1982; 1984; and Sweeny, 1984).

If it is to continue to be useful, class analysis like class struggle cannot be confined to the individuals who occupy positions in the immediate processes of production, nor even to the actions of the 'collective labourer in hand and brain'. The mis-match between the quantity of labour available and the actual labour necessary for

31

capitalist production has created structural unemployment. This surplus labour power appears in particular social forms. Its distribution demands an acknowledgement of the political potential of groups banished from the world of work and wages. The organization (if any) of surplus populations is at the very core of class formation in contemporary Britain and involves a unique accommodation between black and white. How are groups based in the surplus population to combine if at all with the residues of the trades union and labour movements? How does political consciousness change when people move forever away from the possibility of waged work and accept the state as the provider of their income? How do the politics of 'race' and nation organize and disorganize these groups in struggle?

The effects of racialization are certainly visible in the distance between the economic marginality of surplus population and their political centrality. The riots of 1981 and 1985 are remembered as somehow racial events. Given that a minority – between 29 per cent and 33 per cent – of those arrested in 1981 were 'non-white' it is essential to ask how this memory has been constructed?

Those uprisings and the 'mini-riots' which have continued sporadically in the period between them point to the importance of the surplus population. It is prominent not only in representations of national decline but in the processes which turn workers and non-workers alike into a class, or at least into an urban social movement, conscious of its discrete collective interests at local level.

The notion of an articulated ensemble of social relations structured in dominance has been proposed by Hall (1980) as a basic concept in the analysis of racially segmented societies. It is readily compatible with the emphasis on class formation proposed here. Both express a shift away from seeing exploitation as the sole route to political consciousness and encourage consideration of the effects of subordination based in forms of power which have at best a partial and ambiguous connection with the extraction of surplus value. These include subjectivities and struggles constituted around gender, sexuality, generation, the consumption and distribution of state services and ecological and regional conflicts as well as those defined by 'race'. It is easy to see how some of these forms of struggle move beyond the particularity in which they originate. For example, whether or not it can be called feminist (Loach, 1985), the organization of women in the coal strike of 1984–5 qualified and transformed the meaning of class in that dispute and affected the ability of all social forces in support of the struggle to act politically as a group. New kinds of solidarity and new patterns of communication between different areas of the country were brought into being. Similarly the struggle of miners' dependants to claim the state benefits to which they were entitled, articulated a political connection between those whose claims were based on the strike and other claimants whose relationship to work was more distant. These examples illustrate a process which is being repeated in smaller and less visible patterns on an every-day basis. The class element in these struggles can be defined in their commitment to the reappropriation of the material structures of production. Yet they will not be limited by this aim which is a necessary but not a sufficient means of realizing their plural desires.

Struggles over the quality and direction of urban policing which emerged in the aftermath of the 1981 riots are the most obvious recent case in which a 'sectoral' struggle often articulated around ideas about 'race' has been carried into the institutional mainstream of working-class politics.[6] These conflicts have highlighted the contra-diction between local and national governments and revealed novel links between local state bureaucracies and street-level politics, some of which will be discussed in Chapter 4. Their outcome has clear implications for the ability of all radical forces to organize and engage in political activity.

The most apparently disparate struggles can be related analytically to the processes of class formation by looking directly at their effects rather than solely at the intentions of the people who conduct them. Political antagonism is manifest in a variety of organizational forms. The class formation problematic requires that organization is viewed as a theoretical problem in its own right. If, at one level, the unity of the working class must remain a symbolic unity (Laclau and Mouffe, 1985), at another, radical and critical political organizations and movements negotiate with each other (regardless of their sectarian origins) and may even be forced in the course of a particular struggle to try and co-ordinate their actions. The institutional struc-ture of the state plays a role here particularly in potentially unifying the various components of the surplus population. The state's insti-tutions map out the strategic configuration of political conflicts. This is defined against them and may be unified by their operations. They provide a material context for the development of movements and organizations as well as an important basis for any relationship between them:

. . . institutional patterns shape mass movements by shaping the collectivity out of which protest can arise. Institutional life aggregates people or disperses them, moulds group identities and draws people into settings in which collective action can erupt . . . institutional roles determine the stra-tegic opportunities for defiance, for it is typically by rebelling against the rules and authorities that people protest. . . . The unemployed do not and cannot strike even when they perceive that those who own the factories and businesses are to blame for their troubles. Instead they riot in the streets where they are forced to linger, or storm the relief centres and it is difficult to imagine them doing otherwise (Piven and Cloward, 1977, p. 22).

The form of the state structures the form of political struggles. Where

33

state institutions impose racial categories, the struggle against racism will be a struggle against the state. People encounter these agencies in a variety of different roles: client, critic and beneficiary as well as employee. The institutional structure of schools, housing authorities and social security offices allows the individuals involved in operating them to articulate political relationships which may require state servants to side with their 'clients' against their managers. Opposition to ethnic monitoring by DHSS staff or their strikes against the introduction of specialist claims control units illustrates this. Thus new kinds of political struggle can be solidified by the very institutions which are deployed to answer their demands and to channel them into fragmented individualized solutions: into separate cases and claims. This synchronization and unification can also be fostered by a political language which defines all those who challenge the dominant order as a common, natural enemy. Miners and blacks discover that they share being labelled 'the enemy within'.

All this is not merely a more complex way of saying that the discourses of powerless and dispossessed groups will tend to resonate for one another. That is certainly true and the depth of support for the miners' struggle in the black communities bears it out.[7] I am suggesting that these heterogenous struggles somehow encompass class and are in the process of moving beyond the challenge to the mode of production which defines class politics. What this means for the social movement of blacks in this country will be explored through an examination of expressive culture in Chapter 5. The general argument can be summed up like this. New types of class relations are being shaped and reproduced in the novel economic conditions we inhabit. The scale of these changes, which can be glimpsed through the pertinence of a populist politics of 'race' and nation, is such that it calls the vocabulary and analytic frameworks of class analysis into question. It emphasizes the fact that class is not something given in economic antagonisms which can be expressed straightforwardly in political formations. It no longer has a monopoly of the political stage, if indeed it ever had one.[8]

At present, narrowly class-based political action has to compete against a variety of popular politics of which the populist development that can be identified by the shorthand term the 'new racism' is only one important example. The rise of this new racism can be located in a crisis of political representation in the organizations of the working-class movement. Unless class analysis is to be restricted to those rare occasions on which self-conscious social groups articulate their political struggles through languages of class (Stedman Jones, 1983), the notion of class struggle must be redefined. Prezworski suggests that it can include struggles to form classes: struggles about what class is to be at any particular moment. Rather than being guaranteed in the inevitable progress from class in itself to class for itself, class today is a contingent and necessarily indeterminate affair. It would, however, be mistaken to simply label any political struggle which has the potential for universalizing the issue of emancipation as class struggle. The obvious alternative, pending the replacement of class as a category in the long term, seems to be to reserve the concept for those elements within the politics of social movements which relate to the contradiction between capital and labour and to the mode of production which makes that contradiction intelligible. Social movements centred on the experience of subordination as well as exploitation include class but are not reducible to it. Where it enables political action and organization, 'race' falls into this category.

The most visible of recent changes in class relations involve the genesis of a professional and managerial class (Carter, 1985) and the expansion of surplus labour which appears in society in a number of contradictory forms: 'housewives', 'black youth', 'trainees', 'the middle class' and 'claimants'. This surplus population must be examined in its own right as a potential class and in its relationship to other classes and class fractions. However, the novelty of the conditions we inhabit means that the concept of alliances is not always appropriate to the relationships these groups make with other new social forces or with the labour movement. Its connotations of formality and permanence are at odds with the unevenness and spontaneity which have, for example, marked the history of anti-racist association. Under certain conditions black and white women may be able to make common cause, but they may also have different needs which result in conflicting demands in relation to, say, policing. The results of their encounters may be to disorganize each group yet they may still have important effects on the meaning and scope of class politics and organization. It is more important that these conflicts and combinations commence at the point where the tactical repertoire and analytical vocabulary of class starts to break down.

In organizational terms, many of the new social movements rely on mass mobilizational rather than mass membership. This is a tactic which has entered the political strategies of the women's and peace movements in Britain from black America's civil rights movement. The language of political relationships like Jesse Jackson's 'Rainbow Coalition' (Marable, 1985) may be important not only for its challenge to the central place of work-based politics but for the way it facilitates this activist orientation in the face of the bureaucratic mass membership strategy (Piven and Cloward, 1977) associated with electoral politics in general and the labour movement in particular.

Assessment of struggles apparently unrelated to class must pose the question of agency in its most acute form. How and why did the groups involved come to be organized? What are the limits of their action? What are its effects likely to bring for the future?

It is not just the content and effects of struggles around 'race' which reveal connections with class organization and politics. To the extent that they provide bases for collective action, the historical, cultural and kinship ties which give 'race' meaning must also be evaluated. How do these ties and the race consciousness which they foster compare with the forms of collective association based on work, wages and exploitation? They may overlap in the experience of black people who work, but even if they cannot be sublimated into discrete mutually exclusive categories, they need to be distinguished.

In a fascinating study, Craig Calhoun (1982) has looked at the heterogeneity and complexity of class in the context of popular radicalism during the first industrial revolution. He has identified several types of political language and mobilization which became grouped together under the term 'working class'. He distinguishes helpfully between workers who struggled 'on the basis of strong community foundations but against the preponderant forces of economic change' and those who 'fought on a weaker basis but within the emergent industrial order'. These groups are distinguished by their different places in relation to the process of industrialization, just as the groups I have been discussing can be distinguished according to their different positions within the processes of de-industrialization which have attended the second industrial revolution. Calhoun argues that 'both the social organisational basis and the consciousness which preceded the emergence of the modern working class were more likely foundations for radical collective action' than the class consciousness of the period. He views the politics of class as having created forms of action and consciousness which were less radical than traditional 'populist' movements centred on notions of community. Traditional communities are themselves viewed as 'the crucial social foundation for radical collective action'.

Calhoun identifies the roots of this diminishing radicalism in the 'development of formal organisations which could mobilize workers for national action. On an ideological level, the key to [it] was the development of an argument of exploitation based on the labour theory of value'. His differentiation of the complexity of class and its accompanying forms of radicalism can help to illuminate some of the ways that racial politics comes to fragment and disorganize the working class today.

I have pointed out elsewhere the use which black settlers have made of notions of community in their self-organization (Gilroy, 1981). Looking at the forms of collective action in which the idea of community has been prominent is also a means to connect the spatial and territorial dimensions of class formation with the political struggles discussed above (Katznelson, 1981). It raises the specificity of urban politics and of cities as locations in which the social division of labour achieves geographical expression. This is important because the national economic crisis and the crisis of representation in the working-class movement display patterns of uneven territorial development. It may, therefore, become hard to distinguish the subjectivity based around 'race' from feelings of neighbourhood, region and locality. Black settlers who are concentrated in small areas within Britain's urban centres experience these connections in one form. The white racist for whom the presence of black neighbours becomes a symbol of urban degeneration experiences them differently.

It must also be repeated that radical ties and traditions which were formed in the nexus of imperial development and anti-colonial struggle are an enduring resource in the political practice of black Britain. These legacies are, of course, reshaped around the particular relations of exploitation and oppression which have arisen in post-war Britain. They have appeared not only in struggles around work (Beetham, 1970) but in the reproduction of classes and 'races' which becomes youth culture. The institutions they create: temples, churches, clubs, cafés and blues dances confound any Eurocentric idea of where the line dividing politics and culture should fall. The distinction between public and private spheres cuts through the life of their households and communities in a similar manner. Traditional solidarity mediates and adapts the institutions of the British political system against which it is defined. The varieties of radicalism constituted in this disorganic relationship, offer a profound challenge to anyone seeking to contain them within a concept of ethnicity.

The political consciousness of black settlers and their children draws on histories and memories of struggle beyond Britain's borders. They are combined, not only with the effects of insertion into an ailing industrial order at distinctive points but with the experience of banishment from production which has occurred with disproportionate frequency along lines marked by 'race'.

The history of this fusion is, for example, expressed in the continuity of protest which links the 1981 riots with the Health Service strike which followed them. Its economic dimensions are beyond the scope of this book but some of its cultural manifestations will be explored below. The social movement it has created out of poverty, exploitation and racial subordination is ideologically and organizationally distinct from the forms of political practice which emanate from the shrinking industrial core of the trades union and labour movements. Like Calhoun's early industrial labourers, the low-paid, black or female workers in today's public sector are not always well-served by the forms of organization which connect their grassroots activity through union membership to a bureaucracy premised on the need for co-ordinated national action. The traditional politics which defines the black communities and aids them in their radicalism inside and outside work, against the state as well as against capital, must be claimed back from the superstructure and the ideological instance.

Race formation

A further word about the conception of 'race' which informs this chapter is now required. The forms of economic coercion involved in, for example, plantation slavery, migrant labour and apartheid, are all important reminders of the fact that 'race' can become a distinctive feature at the level of economic development. Having accepted this possibility, I have tried to demonstrate the advantages of emphasizing that 'race' is a political category that can accommodate various meanings which are in turn determined by struggle. In arguing this, I am not suggesting that the differences between individuals which come to be seen as 'racial' have an objective basis. These differences do not bear with them a unique or constant order of determinate effects which applies regardless of the conditions in which they have to exist. 'Race' has to be socially and politically constructed and elaborate ideological work is done to secure and maintain the different forms of 'racialization' which have characterized capitalist development. Recognizing this makes it all the more important to compare and evaluate the different historical situations in which 'race' has become politically pertinent.

This project does not lead inexorably to an idealist theory of 'race relations situations'. It can be used to introduce the idea of race formation.[9] This refers both to the transformation of phenotypical variation into concrete systems of differentiation based on 'race' and colour and to the appeals to spurious biological theory which have been a feature of the history of 'races'. Race formation also includes the manner in which 'races' become organized in politics, particularly where racial differentiation has become a feature of institutional structures – legal subjectivity of citizenship – as well as individual interaction. If it is conceived as a continuous and contingent process in the same sense as class formation, race formation can also relate the release of political forces which define themselves and organize around notions of 'race' to the meaning and extent of class relationships. The concept supports the idea that racial meanings can change, can be struggled over. Rather than talking about racism in the singular, analysts should therefore be talking about racisms in the plural. These are not just different over time but may vary within the same social formation or historical conjuncture.

In this approach, biology cannot be wholly dismissed as a factor in the formation and reproduction of 'race'. It is better to confine phenotypes to a relatively autonomous realm of biological determinations which can ascribe a variety of social effects. Accepting that skin 'colour', however meaningless we know it to be, has a strictly limited material basis in biology, opens up the possibility of engaging with theories of signification which can highlight the elasticity and the emptiness of 'racial' signifiers as well as the ideological work which has to be done in order to turn them into signifiers in the first place. This perspective underscores the definition of 'race' as an open political category, for it is struggle that determines which definition of 'race' will prevail and the conditions under which they will endure or wither away.

The contemporary politics of racial differentiation in this country illustrates this well. The naming of 'races' here has recently undergone a significant shift. It has moved away from political definitions of black based on the possibility of Afro-Asian unity and towards more restricted alternative formulations which have confined the concept of blackness to people of African descent. This process has occurred despite the unifying tendencies of racist activity which regards the racial characteristics of both 'Pakis' and 'niggers' as being equally worthy of hatred. This development has its origins in an understanding of 'race' which stresses the obstacles to political accommodation erected between groups by culture and ethnicity. Its conception of cultural differences as fixed, solid almost biological properties of human relations is, as we shall see in the next chapter, similar to the theory of 'racial' and national differences propounded by the radical right. It has been amplified and reflected politically in special state policy and provision for 'ethnic minorities' (invariably defined so that they coincide with the old idea of biological 'races'). These policy initiatives have played a part in the fracturing of the inclusive definition of black. They have institutionalized the desire to meet minority needs which are perceived to be distinct and separate though formally equal. Ethnic minority provision on independent television's Channel 4 provides an important case study of this fracturing process (Gilroy, 1983).

These ideas about the cultural limits of 'race' have been encouraged by the development of specifically 'anti-racist' interventions by local state apparatuses. They have become associated with a resurgent black nationalism and expressed in a layer of political activity often itself funded by local government. A variety of pseudo-pluralism has been fostered in which a culturally defined ethnic particularity has become the basis of political association. The degree to which the anti-racist strategy of local governments has relied on ideas of absolute cultural difference between ethnic and 'racial' groups to systematize its own funding policies must be explored in depth. The causality of these developments is difficult to identify. However, the movement towards this understanding of 'race' dates precisely from the aftermath of the 1981 riots and is intimately bound up with governmental responses to those protests. Chapter 4 will demonstrate

39

how the struggle among blacks over the scope and meaning of 'race' overlaps with the way in which 'race' has been defined and addressed politically by the agencies of the local state. The campaign to secure parliamentary places for black MPs and for the development of 'black sections' inside the Labour Party has been one of very few voices holding on to the idea of Afro-Asian unity although in their case, the political basis for this alliance remains vague (Proffitt, undated).

The most urgent task facing analysis of 'race' and racism in Britain involves identifying the limits to forms of political action in which the structures of racial feeling are uppermost.

The processes of 'race' and class formation are not identical. The former is not reducible to the latter even where they become mutually entangled. The very emptiness of racial signifiers, the sense in which 'race' is meaningless, contains a warning that its political vitality and volatility may increase as the practices and ideologies which comprise it become less stable and more contradictory. The evolution of racism from vulgar to cultural forms described by Fanon has introduced a new variety which stresses complex difference rather than simple hierarchy (Fanon, 1967). Thus today's British racism, anchored in national decline rather than imperial expansion overseas, does not necessarily proceed through readily apparent notions of superiority and inferiority. The order of racial power relations has become more subtle and elusive than that. Recognizing this fundamental development provides part of the key to understanding how radical and conservative, socialist and openly racist theories and explanations of 'race' have been able to converge dramatically. This coming together is a characteristic feature of contemporary 'race' politics in Britain and is explored in the next chapter.

Notes and references

1 I am taking Robert Miles's (1982) analysis of the sub-discipline as my starting point. I am in broad agreement with his criticisms of the positions outlined by Banton, Banton and Harwood and Rex.

2 See Johanna Brenner and Maria Ramas, 'Re-Thinking Women's Oppression', *New Left Review* 144, March/April 1984, and the replies by Michelle Barrett in *NLR* 146, July/August 1984, and Jane Lewis in *NLR* 149, January/February 1985, for an indication of recent debates over the relationship between women's oppression and class relations. The biological arguments in Brenner and Ramas's position offer an important opportunity to link analysis of women's subordination with investigation into 'race' and racism. They are careful to state their opposition to any form of biological determinism. The authors argue: 'We do propose . . . to take seriously Timpanaro's suggestion that the relationship between

the natural and the social must be built into the analysis' (p. 47). On the relative autonomy of biology see Timpanaro (1972) and Soper in Mepham and Hillel-Rubin (eds) (1979).

3 *Race Today* March/April 1983. For a critical discussion of this position see Hall *et al.* (1979), chapter 10.

4 For a crisp summary of the biological arguments around 'race' see Rose and Lewontin (1983). Benedict (1943) is also of interest.

5 On the 'Historic Bloc' see Buci-Glucksmann (1980), chapter 12, sections 5 and 6. For clarification of how the idea of Authoritarian Populism has been used in the context of contemporary Britain see Hall (1985) and the two articles by Jessop *et al.* *NLR* 147, September/October 1984, *NLR* 153, September/October 1985.

6 The work of the Greater London Council's Police Committee Support Unit set up by the Labour administration in 1982 illustrates this point. In the period between January 1982 and April 1986, when the GLC was abolished, the unit funded the work of numerous community and research-based projects into policing and produced a wide variety of informational and campaigning materials relating to the politics of policing and criminal justice matters. Some of the most important initiatives undertaken by this unit included the publication of the newsletter *Policing London*, the production of videos, travelling exhibitions, posters, leaflets and Ranking Ann's anti-police bill record 'Kill The Police Bill' on the unit's own 'Rough Justice' label in 1984.

7 A well attended rally: 'Black People's Solidarity with the Miners' was held at London's County Hall on 7 December 1984. It featured various cultural performances and speakers from various groups including the Asian Collective of East London, the Black Consciousness Movement, and the Pan-African Congress. The leaflet by which the event was organized included these lines:

Black People Say – Miners Must Win! No Pit Closures!! No Job Losses!!! As Black People We Know what it is to be under seize [sic] as a community As Black People we know what is state violence As Black people we know what is unemployment Our Struggle, Miners Struggle. The same Miners Complete Victory Is Our Victory. Miners Defeat is not only our defeat but defeat of all workers. The experience of Irish people, Black People and The Miners are Same.

8 Gorz (1982) is one of the writers who has clearly argued that Marx's view of the proleteriat as a universal class is evidence of residual Hegelianism even in his mature work. See also Jean-François Lyotard's 'Complexity and The Sublime' in (ed.) Appignanesi (1986). This point will be developed further in Chapter 6 below.

9 The concept of 'race formation' can be used following Bhaskar's advice to distinguish between the different ways in which 'race' and racism appear in the world agents and in the structures they create. It allows for a complex view of the articulation between the two:

41

It should be understood as a process: (1) through which an unstable and contradictory set of social practices and beliefs are articulated in an ideology based fundamentally on race; (2) through which the particular ideology thus generated is enforced by a system of racial subjection having both institutional and individual means of reproduction at its disposal; and (3) through which new instabilities and contradictions emerge at a subsequent historical point and challenge the pre-existing system once more (Omi and Winant, 1983).

2 'The whisper wakes, the shudder plays': 'race', nation and ethnic absolutism

The Queen Mother swayed in a gentle dance when one of three steel bands began playing a lilting reggae tune. Five yards away, swaying with her, were a group of Rastafarians wearing the red, yellow and green tea cosy hats which are the badge of their pot-smoking set (*Daily Mail*, 21.4.83).

The nation has been and is still being, eroded and hollowed out from within by implantation of unassimilated and unassimilable populations. . . alien wedges in the heartland of the state (Enoch Powell, 9.4.76).

Methinks I see in my mind a noble and puissant Nation rousing herself like a strong man after sleep, and shaking her invincible locks (Milton).

Racism has been described above as a discontinuous and unevenly developed process. It exists in plural form, and I have suggested that it can change, assuming different shapes and articulating different political relations. Racist ideologies and practices have distinct meanings bounded by historical circumstances and determined in struggle. This chapter moves away from general argument to focus on the distinctive characteristics of the racism which currently runs through life in Britain.

This particular form, which Martin Barker (1981) and others[1] have labelled 'the new racism', will be examined below with a view to focusing on the nature of its newness – the job it does in rendering our national crisis intelligible. It will be argued that its novelty lies in the capacity to link discourses of patriotism, nationalism, xenophobia, Englishness, Britishness, militarism and gender difference into a complex system which gives 'race' its contemporary meaning. These themes combine to provide a definition of 'race' in terms of culture and identity. What new right philosopher John Casey has called 'The whole life of the people'.[2] 'Race' differences are displayed in culture which is reproduced in educational institutions and, above all, in family life. Families are therefore not only the nation in microcosm, its key components, but act as the means to turn social processes into natural, instinctive ones.

These ideas have hosted an extraordinary convergence between left and right, between liberals and conservatives and between racists and some avowed anti-racists. These politically opposed groups have come together around an agreed definition of what 'race' adds up

43

to. Their agreement can itself be understood as marking the newness of a new racism which confounds the traditional distinctions between left and right. Conservative thinkers, whether or not they follow the *Salisbury Review* in arguing that 'the consciousness of nationhood is the highest form of political consciousness,'[3] are forced by the nature of their beliefs to be open about their philosophies of race and national belonging. The British left, caught between a formal declaration of internationalism and the lure of a pragmatic, popular patriotism (Seabrook, 1986), is less explicit and has been confounded by the shifting relationship between national sentiment, 'race' and class politics.[4] This difficulty is encountered in acute form by English socialist writers but it can be traced back into the writings of Marx and Engels (1973).

'Race', nation and the rhetoric of order

In his thoughtful study of nationalism, *Imagined Communities*, Benedict Anderson seeks to clarify the relationship between racism and nationalism by challenging Tom Nairn's (1977) argument that these two forms of ideology are fundamentally related in that the former derives from the latter. Anderson's conclusion is worth stating at length:

The fact of the matter is that nationalism thinks in terms of historical destinies, while racism dreams of eternal contaminations transmitted from the origins of time through an endless sequence of loathsome copulations. . . . The dreams of racism actually have their origins in the ideologies of class, rather than those of nation: above all in claims to divinity among rulers and to blue or white blood and breeding among aristocracies. No surprise then that . . . on the whole, racism and anti-semitism manifest themselves, not across national boundaries but within them. In other words they justify not so much foreign wars as domestic repression and domination (Anderson, 1983, p. 136).

In support of this point, Anderson cites the fact that regardless of its internal 'race' politics, South Africa continues to enjoy amicable diplomatic relations with prominent black politicians from various African states. This is a curious example because the formulation of the apartheid system, in particular the homelands policy, can be read as an attempt to externalize those 'internal' 'race' problems by representing them as the interaction of separate states which rest on distinct cultural and historical identities (Wolpe, 1980).

Anderson's theory claims that racism is essentially antithetical to nationalism because nations are made possible in and through print languages rather than notions of biological difference and kinship. Thus, he argues that anyone can in theory learn the language of the nation they seek to join and through the process of naturalization

44

become a citizen enjoying formal equality under its laws. Whatever objections can be made to Anderson's general argument, his privileging of the written word over the spoken word for example, it simply does not apply in the English/British case. The politics of 'race' in this country is fired by conceptions of national belonging and homogeneity which not only blur the distinction between 'race' and nation, but rely on that very ambiguity for their effect. Phrases like 'the Island Race' and 'the Bulldog Breed' vividly convey the manner in which this nation is represented in terms which are simultaneously biological and cultural. It is important to recognize that the legal concept of patriality, introduced by the Immigration Act of 1968, codified this cultural biology of 'race' into statute law as part of a strategy for the exclusion of black settlers (WING, 1984). This act specified that immigration controls would not apply to any would-be settler who could claim national membership on the basis that one of their grandparents had been born in the UK. The Nationality Act of 1981 rationalized the legal vocabulary involved so that patrials are now known as British citizens.

A further objection to Anderson's position emerges from consideration of how the process of black settlement has been continually described in military metaphors which offer war and conquest as the central analogies for immigration. The enemy within, the unarmed invasion, alien encampments, alien territory and new commonwealth occupation have all been used to describe the black presence in this way. Enoch Powell, whose careful choice of symbols and metaphors suggests precise calculation, typifies this ideological strand:

It is . . . truly when he looks into the eyes of Asia that the Englishman comes face to face with those who would dispute with him the possession of his native land.[5]

This language of war and invasion is the clearest illustration of the way in which the discourses which together constitute 'race' direct attention to national boundaries, focusing attention on the entry and exit of blacks. The new racism is primarily concerned with mechanisms of inclusion and exclusion. It specifies who may legitimately belong to the national community and simultaneously advances reasons for the segregation or banishment of those whose 'origin, sentiment or citizenship' assigns them elsewhere. The excluded are not always conceived as a cohesive rival nation. West Indians, for example, are seen as a bastard people occupying an indeterminate space between the Britishness which is their colonial legacy and an amorphous, ahistorical relationship with the dark continent and those parts of the new world where they have been able to reconstitute it. Asians on the other hand, as the Powell quote above suggests, are understood to be bound by cultural and biological ties which merit the status of a fully formed, alternative national identity. They

45

pose a threat to the British way of life by virtue of their strength and cohesion. For different reasons, both groups are judged to be incompatible with authentic forms of Englishness (Lawrence, 1982). The obviousness of the differences they manifest in their cultural lives underlines the need to maintain strong and effective controls on who may enter Britain. The process of national decline is presented as coinciding with the dilution of once homogeneous and continuous national stock by alien strains. Alien cultures come to embody a threat which, in turn, invites the conclusion that national decline and weakness have been precipitated by the arrival of blacks. The operation of banishing blacks, repatriating them to the places which are congruent with their ethnicity and culture, becomes doubly desirable. It assists in the process of making Britain great again and restores an ethnic symmetry to a world distorted by imperial adventure and migration.

What must be explained, then, is how the limits of 'race' have come to coincide so precisely with national frontiers. This is a central achievement of the new racism. 'Race' is bounded on all sides by the sea. The effect of this ideological operation is visible in the way that the word 'immigrant' became synonymous with the word 'black' during the 1970s. It is still felt today as black settlers and their British-born children are denied authentic national membership on the basis of their 'race' and, at the same time, prevented from aligning themselves within the 'British race' on the grounds that their national allegiance inevitably lies elsewhere. This racist logic has pinpointed obstacles to genuine belonging in the culture and identity of the alien interlopers. Both are central to the theories of 'race' and nation which have emerged from the political and philosophical work of writers associated with Britain's 'new right' (Gamble, 1974; Levitas, 1986).

As part of their lament that the national heart no longer beats as one, Peregrine Worsthorne has pointed out that 'though Britain is a multi-racial society, it is still a long way from being a multi-racial nation'.[6] This is an important distinction which was also made fourteen years earlier by Enoch Powell. He drew attention to the difference between the merely formal membership of the national community provided by its laws, and the more substantive membership which derives from the historic ties of language, custom and 'race'. Parliament, suggested Powell, can change the law, but national sentiment transcends such narrow considerations: 'the West Indian does not by being born in England, become an Englishman. In law, he becomes a United Kingdom citizen by birth; in fact he is a West Indian or an Asian still'.[7]

It has been revealed that, at the suggestion of Churchill, a Conservative cabinet discussed the possibility of using 'Keep Britain White' as an electoral slogan as early as 1955 (Macmillan, 1973). Yet it is in the period between Powell's and Worsthorne's statements above that a truly popular politics of 'race' and nation flowered in Britain. Its growth, emanating mainly though not exclusively from the right (Rex, 1968; see also *Guardian*, 30.9.65) marks the divergence of what can loosely be called the patrician and populist orientations in the modern Conservative Party.

The 'metaphysics of Britishness' (Carter, 1983) which links patriotism, xenophobia, militarism, and nationalism into a series of statements on 'race' was a key element in the challenge to the old leadership between 1964 and 1970 and in the reconstitution of the party under Thatcher. These themes have been fundamental to the popularity of the party and conservative intellectuals have not concealed their instrumental use. The langauge of one nation provides a link between the populist effect of 'race' and a more general project which has attempted to align the British People with an anti-statism and in particular with Conservative criticism of the 'guilty public schoolboys' of the liberal intelligentsia who have wrecked the country with their consensual approach to politics. They are the men who imposed mass immigration on a reluctant populace.

'Race' is also identified as a means by which the mass of the population may be directly addressed. As Maurice Cowling puts it,

Mr Powell attaches the highest value to working class opinion. It is one of his special audiences and one, moreover, that he thinks deserves a better diet than the awful pieties with which Mr Jenkins and his allies had hoped to lead it into a liberal future (Cowling, 1978; see also Foot, 1969).

The themes of national culture and identity have long histories inside the Conservative political tradition (Bennett, 1962). Yet the populist[8] form in which they emerge as Powellism breaks decisively with its predecessors even if its object, the conception of a 'unity of national sentiment transcending classes' (Cowling, 1978) remains the same. The reconstitution of Powellism as Thatcherism (Barnett, 1984; and Worsthorne, *Sunday Telegraph*, 12.6.83) points to the consolidation of a new political language which has became progressively more dominant within the representation of the present crisis and which, more specifically, has solved a profound political problem for the right. The 'one nation' message has been a means to escape from the shadows of paternalism which were the undoing of Alec Douglas Home. The national symbols of Powellism/Thatcherism are significant not only because a populist orientation is their primary characteristic. Conservative intellectuals have been candid about the role these ideas have played in the rebirth of their party which, in the period after Wilson, lacked a language adequate to its social and political vision. This problem was described vividly in an editorial which looked at the 1970s in the first issue of the new right journal *Salisbury Review*: 'never before had it seemed so hard to recreate the verbal symbols, the images and axioms, through which the concept of authority could be renewed'. The solution to it involved making 'race' and nation the framework for a rhetoric of order through which modern conservatism could voice populist protest against Britain's post-imperial plight and marshal its historic bloc. Enoch Powell's superficially simple question 'what kind of people are we?' summoned those very images and axioms and answered itself powerfully in the negative. 'We' were not muggers, 'we' were not illegal immigrants, 'we' were not criminals, Rastafarians, aliens or purveyors of arranged marriages. 'We' were the lonely old lady taunted by 'wide-grinning piccaninnies'. 'We' were the only white child in a class full of blacks. 'We' were the white man, frightened that in fifteen to twenty years, 'the black man would have the whip hand over us'. The black presence is thus constructed as a problem or threat against which a homogeneous, white, national 'we' could be unified. To put this operation into perspective, it must be emphasized that these were not the only images and definitions of nationhood which were mobilized during this period. Other voices from the left and from the black communities themselves were to be heard. Even within the right there were alternative conceptualizations of the relationship between 'race' and nation which were more in keeping with a patrician reading of imperial history. On behalf of the populist new right, Powell has had to challenge these as well as the 'madness' of the liberal integrationists. His attack on the Queen's Christmas message of 1983 and by implication on the 'multi-racialist' stance of other members of the royal household is particularly revealing. It crystalizes some of the competing definitions of the nation which are even now in play.

Powell attacked the Queen's attachment to the Commonwealth and rebuked her advisers for not encouraging her to speak more as a 'British monarch to the British Nation'. She was, said Powell, 'more concerned for the susceptibilities and prejudices of a vociferous minority of newcomers than for the great mass of her subjects'. The racial message in this last sentence characteristically derives its full power from the absence of any overt reference to the black presence. The *Sun* picked up the inferred racial message and splashed the headlines 'Enoch Raps Queen. She must speak up more for whites' across its front page.[9] Powell censured the Queen further, for mouthing speeches which 'suggest that she has the interests and affairs of other countries, in other continents, as much or more at heart than those of her own people'. The *Sun* acknowledged the use of political 'code words' in Mr Powell's outburst and provided a summary of his 'basic message' in plain English. 'The Queen has allowed herself to be used as a mouthpiece for racial minorities, and ought to spend more time speaking out for the white majority.'

Powell's speech ended with a warning to those who were responsible for misleading the Crown and thereby disrupting the consti tutional balance between monarch and people. It is a cogent if cryptic statement of his populism: 'The place of the crown in the affections of the people would be threatened if they began to sense that the crown was not in unique and exclusive sympathy with the people of the United Kingdom which their mutual dependance ought to imply.' The message in this last point is a little obscure but is similar to that which emerges from Powell's earlier comments on the relationship between formal (legal) citizenship and the substantive cultural identity which defines genuine membership of the British nation. Monarchs come and go, but the historic continuity which constructs the British people has a longer life span than any individual sovereign and, in Powell's view, a political privilege.

I have already introduced the idea that the new racism's newness can be gauged by its capacity to operate across the broad range of political opinion. This claim can be pursued further. The distinction which Powell and Worsthorne make between authentic and inauthentic types of national belonging, appears in an almost identical form in the work of Raymond Williams (Williams, 1983; Mulhern, 1984). It provides a striking example of the way in which the cultural dimensions of the new racism confound the left/right distinction.

Williams combines a discussion of 'race' with comments on patriotism and nationalism. However, his understanding of 'race' is restricted to the social and cultural tensions surrounding the arrival of 'new peoples'. For him, as with the right, 'race' problems begin with immigration. Resentment of 'unfamiliar neighbours' is seen as the beginning of a process which ends in ideological specifications of 'race' and 'superiority'. Williams, working his way towards a 'new and substantial kind of socialism', draws precisely the same picture of the relationship between 'race', national identity and citizenship as Powell:

. . . it is a serious misunderstanding . . . to suppose that the problems of social identity are resolved by formal (merely legal) definitions. For unevenly and at times precariously, but always through long experience substantially, an effective awareness of social identity depends on actual and sustained social relationships. To reduce social identity to formal legal definitions, at the level of the state, is to collude in the alienated superficialities of 'the nation' which are limited functional terms of the modern ruling class (Williams, 1983, p. 195).

These remarks are part of Williams's response to anti-racists who would answer the denial that blacks can be British by saying 'They are as British as you are.' He dismisses this reply as 'the standard liberal' variety. His alternative conception stresses that social identity is a product of 'long experience'. But this prompts the question – how long is long enough to become a genuine Brit? His insistence that the origins of racial conflicts lie in the hostility between strangers in the city makes little sense given the effects of the 1971 Immigration

Act in halting primary black settlement. More disturbingly, these arguments effectively deny that blacks can share a significant 'social identity' with their white neighbours who, in contrast to more recent arrivals, inhabit what Williams calls 'rooted settlements' articulated by 'lived and formed identities'. He describes the emergence of racial conflict where

an English working man (English in the terms of sustained modern integration) protests at the arrival or presence of 'foreigners' or 'aliens' and now goes on to specify them as 'blacks'.

Williams does not appear to recognize black as anything other than the subordinate moment in an ideology of racial supremacy. His use of the term 'social identity' is both significant and misleading. It minimizes the specificities of nationalism and ideologies of national identity and diverts attention from analysis of the political processes by which national and social identities have been aligned. Several questions which are absolutely central to contemporary 'race' politics are thus obscured. Under what conditions is national identity able to displace or dominate the equally 'lived and formed' identities which are based on age, gender, region, neighbourhood or ethnicity? How has it come to be expressed in racially exclusive forms? What happens when 'social identities' become expressed in conflicting political organizations and movements and when they appeal to the authority of nature and biology to rationalize the relations of domination and subordination which exist between them? How these social identities relate to the conspicuous differences of language and culture is unclear except where Williams points out that the forms of identity fostered by the 'artificial order' of the nation state are incomplete and empty when compared to 'full social identities in their real diversity'. This does not, of course, make them any the less vicious. Where racism demands repatriation and pivots on the exclusion of certain groups from the imagined community of the nation, the contradictions around citizenship that Williams dismisses as 'alienated superficialities' remain important constituents of the political field. They provide an important point of entry into the nation's sense of itself. Where racial oppression is practised with the connivance of legal institutions – the police and the courts – national and legal subjectivity will also become the focus of political antagonism. Williams's discussion of 'race' and nation does not address these issues and is notable for its refusal to examine the concept of racism which has its own historic relationship with ideologies of Englishness, Britishness and national belonging.

Quite apart from Williams's apparent endorsement of the presuppositions of the new racism, the strategic silences in his work contribute directly to its strength and resiliance. The image Williams has chosen to convey his grasp of 'race' and nation, that of a resentful

English working man, intimidated by the alterity of his alien neighbours is, as we shall see below, redolent of other aspects of modern Conservative racism and nationalism.

The national community in peace and war

The imagery of black settlement as an invasion and the close association between the racism and nationalism make it impossible to discuss the contemporary politics of 'race' without reference to the war with Argentina during 1982. The war analogy of black settlement laid the discursive foundations on which connections could be made between conflict abroad and the subversive activities of the fifth column within. The supreme expression of this theme was Margaret Thatcher's speech at Cheltenham on 3 July 1982. This defined the 'Falklands Factor' so as to link the struggle against the 'Argies' with the battle against British workers: the NUR and ASLEF (the rail unions) whose industrial actions were to be undone by the fact that such activities did not 'match the spirit' of the reborn Britain.

What has indeed happened is that now once again Britain is not prepared to be pushed around. We have ceased to be a nation in retreat. We have instead a new-found confidence – born in the economic battles at home and tested and found true 8,000 miles away. That confidence comes from the rediscovery of ourselves and grows with the recovery of our self respect.

This speech, like Powell's critique of the royal household, made no open references to the issue of 'race'. Other new right thinkers were less circumspect. Wars, it was argued, are key moments in the process of national self-realization – the willingness to lay down one's life being the definition of a true patriot. The great distance involved and the tenuous constitutional connection between Britain and Port Stanley led commentators to speculate about the nature of the ties which could bind our national destiny to the fate of our distant 'kith and kin' in the South Atlantic. Peregrine Worsthorne went straight to the point:

If the Falkland Islanders were British citizens with black or brown skins, spoke with strange accents or worshipped different Gods it is doubtful whether the Royal Navy and Marines would today be fighting for their liberation.[10]

The Falklands episode celebrated the cultural and spiritual continuity which could transcend 8000 miles and call the nation to arms in defence of its own distant people. Images of the nation at war were also used to draw attention to problems inherent in 'multi-racialism' at home. There was a rich irony discovered in the contrast between the intimacy of the 'natural' if long-distance relationship with the

Falklanders and the more difficult task of relating to alien intruders who persisted in disrupting life in Britain and were not seen to be laying down their lives for the greater good. Again Worsthorne was the first to point this out: 'Most Britons today identify more easily with those of the same stock 8000 miles away . . . than they do with West Indian or Asian immigrants living next door.'[11] His potent image draws directly on Powell and emphasizes the strength of the cultural ties which mark the boundaries of 'race' as well as the exclusion of blacks from the definitions of nationality which matter most. The article from which it comes was as important for its recognition of the interrelationship of black and white life in the urban context as for the invocation of a mystic nationhood which would only be revealed on the battlefield. In the heat of combat, the nation would discover, or rather remember, what truly 'turned it on'. The implicit need to recognize and devalue the quality of 'transracial' relationships between neighbours contains a tacit acknowledgement that such relationships do exist, even if the white Britons involved relinquish their membership of Worsthorne's nation at the point at which these friendships are conceived.

The popular power of patriotism revealed by the Falklands episode was not lost on commentators of the left. Their responses to it have significantly been characterized by a reluctance to challenge the model of national greatness and the metaphysical order of belonging on which it rests. In an influential piece which noted that the Falklands had 'stirred up an ugly nationalist sediment which would cloud our cultural and political life', E. P. Thompson argued that we would pay for the war 'for a long time in rapes and racism in our cities' (Thompson, 1982). Eric Hobsbawm, on the other hand, advanced a resolute polemic in favour of a 'left patriotism'. Patriotism, he wrote, would only spill over into undesirable xenophobia, racism and jingoism if the left allowed it to be 'falsely' separated from the sentiments and aspirations of the working class. It is dangerous, he continued 'to leave patriotism exclusively to the right' and, in language reminiscent of Thompson's own frequent invocations of the popular traditions of British radicalism, he made a plea for a political orientation which could demonstrate radical patriotism and class consciousness could be yoked together in front of the socialist cart:

The dangers of . . . patriotism always were and still are obvious, not least because it was and is enormously vulnerable to ruling-class jingoism, to anti-foreign nationalism and of course in our days to racism. . . . The reason why nobody pays much attention to the, let's call it, jingoism of the chartists is that it was combined with and masked by an enormous militant class consciousness. It's when the two are separated, that the dangers are particulary obvious. Conversely when the two go together in harness, they multiply not only the force of the working class but its capacity to place itself at the head of a broad coalition for social change and they even give it the possibility of wrestling hegemony from the class enemy.[12]

In a similar article, principally notable for its blank refusal to use the words 'race' or racism, Robert Gray of the Communist Party's 'Theory and Ideology Committee' attacked 'national nihilism in the name of abstract internationalism' and argued that what was required was a 'redefinition of the interests of the nation around the alternative leadership of the working class' (Gray, 1982). None of these contributions, even those which concede the unfortunate ambiguities in nationalist ideology, make any attempt to show how this valuable redefinition might be achieved. Apart from pointing out the conspicuous success of nationalist sentiment in renovating the Tory project, few arguments are made which justify the need to make the nation state a primary focus of radical political consciousness. It is as if the only problem with nationalism is that the Tories have secured a near exclusive monopoly of it.

The possibility of politically significant connections between nationalism and contemporary racism is either unseen or felt to be unworthy of detailed discussion. More importantly, the types of subjectivity which nationalisms bring into being and put to work pass unquestioned. The problem has become how socialists can (re)possess them from the right.

Two anachronistic images of Britain lurk behind these omissions. The first depicts the nation as a homogeneous and cohesive formation in which an even and consensual cultural field provides the context for hegemonic struggle. The second is attached to the idea that this country is, and must continue to be, a major world power. Patriotism, even in its combative proto-socialist form, is empty without a filling of national pride. British socialists have so far, remained silent about how this misplaced pride can be detached from the vestigial desire for imperial greatness which has so disfigured recent political life (Barnett, 1983a; The Sun, 25.5.82).

The frequency with which Labour's senior spokespeople invoke the national interest as a verbal bludgeon introduces another note of caution. What is this interest? How is it created? How can it be identified? And where does it reside? If appealing to it is nothing more than a rhetorical motif, why has it become necessary at this moment in time? What needs does it address in those who respond to it? Michael Ignatieff's discussion of the 1984–5 coal dispute illustrates some of these difficulties.[13] Throughout this article, the national interest is taken for granted as a meaningful analytic category. 'No one lives apart from the national community', writes Ignatieff. Governments which fail to uphold it lose their electoral support. The police and the courts are its own institutions.

Like many socialists in the post-Falklands period, Ignatieff argues

53

that 'The left crucially overestimates Mrs Thatcher's electoral appeal if it believes that she has succeeded in monopolising the language of "one nation".' He opts to ignore the regional conflicts which were also at the heart of the coal dispute and which, I would argue, call into question the viability and desirability of the appeal to national unity to which he aspires. There is no reason why a political language based on the invocation of national identity should be the most effective where people recognize and define themselves primarily in terms of *regional* or *local* tradition. No coherent argument is provided as to why, for example, socialists should answer the voices of Wales, Yorkshire or Tyneside – all places where regional traditions are a key axis of political organization – with a language of the British national interest. 'Geordie', 'Hinny', 'Brummie' or 'Scouse' may all be political identities which are more in harmony with the advancement of socialist politics in this country than those conjured into being by the phrase 'fellow Britons' or even by the word citizen, given the way in which citizenship is allocated and withheld on racial grounds. These regional or local subjectivities simply do not articulate with 'race' in quite the same way as their national equivalent.

Colin Mercer's discussion of nation[14] parallels Ignatieff's and arrives at a similar image of British socialism: held to ransom by its national culture. Mercer 'owns up' to a 'sneaking admiration for Enoch Powell's prose' and thus recognizes his complicity in 'certain pleasures of Englishness'. He describes himself and by extension his audience of left cultural politicians, as unable either to 'interrupt' or 'stand outside' the complex combination of discursive effects that provide pleasure at the very moment in which 'Englishness' is constituted. The possibility that this particular brand of 'Englishness' may also enjoy a class character is left unexplored.

When it comes to their patriotism, it would appear that England's left intellectuals become so many radical rabbits transfixed and immobile in the path of an onrushing populist nationalism. How does the language of public good they propose, a necessary addition to radical speech if ever there was one, become the language of a nation so cohesive that 'no one lives outside the national community'? Indeed, the suggestion that no one lives outside the national community is only plausible if the issue of racism is excluded. What is being described by these writers is a national community, not imagined in the way that Benedict Anderson has suggested, but actual. The construction of that community is overlooked. It is accepted a priori as the structure around which the struggle to gain hegemony must take place.

The work of other socialist thinkers can be used to show that the images of paralysis which emerge from the work of Mercer and Ignatieff are only mild cases of this patriotic English disease. Where these two are simply inert in the face of national identity and its pleasures, E. P. Thompson, for example, is positively enthusiastic. He begins his pamphlet analysing the 1983 election by declaring 'whatever doubts we have, we can all think of things in the British way of life which we like, and we would want to protect these from attack' (1983). Thompson laments the fact that 'a large part of our free press has been bought, over our heads by money (some of it foreign money)'. For him, the activities of the womens' peace movement are 'characteristically British', their mass action at the Greenham Common airbase on 12 December 1982 was 'a very untidy, low-key, British sort of do'. Thompson's version of Britishness locates the lingering greatness of the nation in the inheritance of popular resistance as well as in cultural achievements:

This has not only been a nation of bullies. It has been a nation of poets and inventors, of thinkers and of scientists, held in some regard in the world. It has been, for a time, no less than ancient Greece before us, a place of innovation in human culture (Thompson, 1983, p. 34).

It is tempting to dispute the special status which Thompson accords to British culture and in particular his suggestion that modern Britain and ancient Greece are the primary innovators in human culture. However, these claims are not the main issue. What is more important is the way in which the preferred elements of English/British culture and society are described as if their existence somehow invalidated the side of our national heritage from which socialists are inclined to disassociate themselves.

Nationhood is not an empty receptacle which can be simply and spontaneously filled with alternative concepts according to the dictates of political pragmatism. The ideological theme of national belonging may be malleable to some extent but its links with the discourses of classes and 'races' and the organizational realities of these groups are not arbitrary. They are confined by historical and political factors which limit the extent to which nationalism becomes socialist at the moment that its litany is repeated by socialists. The intention may be radical but the effects are unpredictable, particularly where culture is also conceived within discrete, separable, national units coterminous with the boundaries of the nation state.

Having said this, it is impossible to deny that the language of the nation offers British socialists a rare opportunity. Through it, they can, like Thompson, begin to say 'we' and 'our' rather than 'I' and 'my'. It encourages them to speak beyond the margins of sectional interest to which they are confined by party and ideology. But there is a problem in these plural forms: who do they include, or, more precisely for our purposes, do they help to reproduce blackness and Englishness as mutually exclusive categories? Why is the racial inflection in the language of nation continually overlooked? And why are contemporary appeals to 'the people' in danger of transmitting themselves as appeals to the white people?

An answer to these questions can only begin from recognition of the way that Britain's languages of 'race' and nation have been articulated together. The effect of their combination can be registered even where 'race' is not overtly referred to, or where it is discussed outside of crude notions of superiority and inferiority. The discourses of nation and people are saturated with racial connotations. Attempts to constitute the poor or the working class as a class across racial lines are thus disrupted. This problem will have to be acknowledged directly if socialists are to move beyond puzzling over why black Britons (who as a disproportionately underprivileged group, ought to be their stalwart supporters) remain suspicious and distant from the political institutions of the working-class movement (Fitzgerald, 1984; Studlar, 1983; 1984; 1985).

Labour's occasional attempts to address nationalist sentiment have, as Anthony Barnett has demonstrated (1982), been a site of further difficulties. However, the concept of 'Churchillism' with which Barnett has tried to pin down the patriotic junction of Labourism and 'Thatcherism' is not adequate to all the permutations of Labour's failure. It plays down the specific attributes and appeal of socialist nationalism and suggests that the 'fatal dementia of national pride' has been injected into British socialism from the outside. However, left nationalism is a more organic, historic property of British socialism. Michael Foot's benign view of Enoch Powell's 'rivers of blood' intervention as a 'tragic irony' and 'pathos' (Foot, 1986) and Neil Kinnock's recent claim to working-class patriotism:

> . . . a confident and generous patriotism of freedom and fairness, not one of prejudice, vanity, or the patriotism of the 'presidential puppet' . . . a patriotism that is forgotten when the chequebook is waved . . . a patriotism which holds that our values are not for sale to anyone at any price at any time.[15]

suggest a longer pedigree for 'Churchillism' than the association of 'Tory belligerents, Labour reformists, revolutionary anti-fascists, and the liberal intelligentsia' which Barnett (1982) proposes as its genealogy. If the writings of left intellectuals are anything to go by, it is born from something altogether more cultural than political; something rooted, not in the end of empire, but in the imperial experience itself (Mackenzie, 1984; 1986). A more complex illustration of these problems can be found in Tony Benn's (1982) attempt to define the British crisis in terms of a descent into colonial status. *New Socialist*, the Labour Party journal introduced his piece thus:

> . . . the British establishment has opted for survival as the colonial administrators of a subject country. Tony Benn calls for the Labour movement to lead a national liberation struggle and restore to us our democratic rights.

Benn's description of the socialist struggle against the Thatcher government as a national liberation struggle was certainly imaginative. It was a clear attempt to harness for the left the yearning for a return to national greatness which has been used effectively by the right. It addressed the British inability to accept the end of empire and the national discomfort at the loss of world pre-eminence. It substitutes a stark image of reduced national status for the metaphysical yearning for greatness amplified by both Conservatives and the Alliance parties in their 1983 election manifestos (Barnett, 1983a). Yet the bloodshed and ruthless mass violence characteristic of decolonization have not, other than in the six counties of Northern Ireland, been evident in recent British politics. The effect of Benn's words on black citizens for whom decolonization is a memory rather than a metaphor is hard to estimate. It is, however, difficult to resist the conclusion that his choice of imagery trivialized the bitter complexities of anti-colonial struggle.

I am not suggesting that the differences between Labour and Conservative languages of nation and patriotism are insignificant, but rather that these languages overlap significantly. In contemporary Britain, statements about nation are invariably also statements about 'race'. The Conservatives appear to recognize this and seek to play with the ambiguities which this situation creates. Their recent statements on the theme of Britishness betray a sophisticated grasp of the interface between 'race' and nation created in the post-'rivers of blood' era. During the coal dispute, for example, in a speech on the enduring power of the national constitution entitled 'Why Democracy Will Last', Mrs Thatcher invoked the memory of the Somerset case of 1772. Lord Mansfield's famous judgment in this case declared that British slaveholders could no longer compel their slaves to leave the country against their will (Fryer, 1984; Shyllon, 1977; 1974). It matters little that Mrs Thatcher quoted the case wrongly, suggesting that it brought slavery in this country to an end. With no trace of irony, her speech boldly articulates an apparently anti-racist position at the heart of a nationalist and authoritarian statement in which the mining communities were identified as 'enemies within'.[16]

The Conservatives' ethnic election poster of 1983 provides further insight into the right's grasp of these complexities. The poster was presumably intended to exploit ambiguities between 'race' and nation and to salve the sense of exclusion experienced by the blacks who were its target. The poster appeared in the ethnic minority press during May 1983 and was attacked by black spokespeople for suggesting that the categories black and British were mutually exclusive. It set an image of a young black man, smartly dressed in a suit with wide lapels and flared trousers, above the caption 'Labour says he's black. Tories say he's British'. The text which followed set out to reassure readers that 'with Conservatives there are no "blacks"

57

With the Conservatives, there are no 'blacks', no 'whites', just people.

Conservatives believe that treating minorities as equals encourages the majority to treat them as equals.

Yet the Labour Party aim to treat you as a 'special case', as a group all on your own.

Is setting you apart from the rest of society a sensible way to overcome racial prejudice and social inequality?

The question is, should we really divide the British people instead of uniting them?

WHOSE PROMISES ARE YOU TO BELIEVE?

When Labour were in government, they promised to repeal Immigration Acts passed in 1962 and 1971. Both promises were broken.

This time, they are promising to throw out the British Nationality Act, which gives full and equal citizenship to everyone permanently settled in Britain.

But how do the Conservatives' promises compare?

We said that we'd abolish the 'SUS' law.

We kept our promise.

We said we'd recruit more coloured policemen, get the police back into the community, and train them for a better understanding of your needs.

We kept our promise.

PUTTING THE ECONOMY BACK ON ITS FEET.

The Conservatives have always said that the only long term answer to our economic problems was to conquer inflation.

Inflation is now lower than it's been for over a decade, keeping all prices stable, with the price of food now hardly rising at all.

Meanwhile, many businesses throughout Britain are recovering, leading to thousands of new jobs.

Firstly, in our traditional industries, but just as importantly in new technology areas such as micro-electronics.

In other words, the medicine is working.

Yet Labour want to change everything, and put us back to square one.

They intend to increase taxation. They intend to increase the National Debt.

They promise import and export controls.

Cast your mind back to the last Labour government. Labour's methods didn't work then.

They won't work now.

A BETTER BRITAIN FOR ALL OF US.

The Conservatives believe that everyone wants to work hard and be rewarded for it.

Those rewards will only come about by creating a mood of equal opportunity for everyone in Britain, regardless of their race, creed or colour.

The difference you're voting for is this:

To the Labour Party, you're a black person.

To the Conservatives, you're a British Citizen.

Vote Conservative, and you vote for a more equal, more prosperous Britain.

LABOUR SAYS HE'S BLACK.
TORIES SAY HE'S BRITISH.

CONSERVATIVE ☒

Figure 1 Conservative Party election poster, 1983

or "whites", just people'. A variant on the one nation theme emerged, entwined with criticism of Labour for treating blacks 'as a "special case", as a group all on your own'. At one level, the poster states that the category of citizen and the formal belonging which it bestows on its black holders are essentially colourless, or at least colour-blind. Yet as the writings of Powell and Worsthorne above illustrate, populist racism does not recognize the legal membership of the national community conferred by its legislation as a substantive guarantee of Britishness. 'Race' is, therefore, despite the text, being defined beyond these legal definitions in the sphere of culture. There is more to Britishness than a passport. Nationhood, as Alfred Sherman pointed out in 1976,

remains . . . man's main focus of identity, his link with the wider world, with past and future, 'a partnership with those who are living, those who are dead and those who are to be born'. . . . It includes national character reflected in the way of life . . . a passport or residence permit does not automatically implant national values or patriotism.[17]

At this point the slightly too large suit worn by the young man, with its unfashionable cut and connotations of a job interview, becomes a key signifier. It conveys what is being asked of the black readers as the price of admission to the colour-blind form of citizenship promised by the text. Blacks are being invited to forsake all that marks them out as culturally distinct before real Britishness can be guaranteed. National culture is present in the young man's clothing. Isolated and shorn of the mugger's key icons – a tea-cosy hat and the dreadlocks of Rastafari – he is redeemed by his suit, the signifier of British civilization. The image of black youth as a problem is thus contained and rendered assimilable. The wolf is transformed by his sheep's clothing. The solitary maleness of the figure is also highly significant. It avoids the hidden threat of excessive fertility which is a constant presence in the representation of black women (Parmar, 1985). This lone young man is incapable of swamping 'us'. He is alone because the logics of racist discourse militate against the possibility of making British blackness visible in a family or an inter-generational group.[18] The black family is presented as incomplete, deviant and ruptured.

Culture and identity in nations and families

The conception of nationness which emerges from the writings and speeches cited above involves a distinct theory of culture and identity which can be described as ethnic absolutism. Most clearly but by no means exclusively theorized in the work of the new right, it views nations as culturally homogeneous 'communities of sentiment' in which a sense of patriotic belonging can and should grow to become an important source of moral and political ideas.

The new racism which is articulated by these premises tends to deny that 'race' is a meaningful biological category. 'Race' is seen instead as a cultural issue. Enoch Powell has, for example, referred to skin colour as a 'uniform' for political conflict (1978). He has even attacked the policy of 'ethnic monitoring' because it involves a spurious attempt to categorize people by their non-existent biological 'race'.[19]

Mrs Lurline Champagne, a black nurse and delegate to the Conservative Party conference in 1985, was given an ovation 'much longer than most ministers' by her party after she declared 'I am a Conservative, black and British and proud of all three.' This was hardly the action of an organization which understands 'racial' differences as a matter of biological hierarchy. The superficial pluralism represented by her ovation masks new, cultural definitions of 'race' which are just as intractable. Mrs Champagne was, in her moment of glory, the exception that proved the rule. For contemporary Britain, the limits of nation coincide with the lines of 'race'.

The cultural definition of 'race' is sometimes conveyed in attempts to define the English as a 'race' separable from the Scots, Welsh, and Irish whose skin colour they share. Britishness, if it is discussed rather than simply extrapolated from Englishness, is seen to emerge as the sum of these cultures. Alien (i.e. black) cultures have been introduced into this country with disastrous effect: 'the indigenous population perceives its own predicament as that of physical pressure and attack'.[20] The increased competition for limited resources and the variety of disruptive behaviours introduced by the immigrant population create problems for the national community. The most profound difficulties are uncovered by trying to dilute our nationhood and national culture so that they can accommodate alien interlopers and their formally but not substantively British children. The most important recent example of this type of cultural conflict was the controversy around attempts to dismiss the Bradford Headmaster Ray Honeyford.

Honeyford published a series of articles in *The Times Educational Supplement* and *Salisbury Review* (Seidel, 1985) arguing, among other things, for a culturalist view of 'race' and racial conflict. From this perspective, he stressed the role of schools as agencies for socializing 'Afro-Asian settler children' into the mores which racially harmonious life in contemporary Britain required of them. He argued that the presence of these alien children in British schools was an impediment to the education of white children and sought to rescue educational theory from the clutches of the multi-culturalists who would teach all our pupils to denigrate the British Empire. . . . The multi-culturalists are a curious mixture: well-meaning liberals and clergymen suffering from a rapidly dating post-imperial guilt; teachers building a career by jumping onto the latest educational bandwaggon; a small but increasing group of professional Asian and West Indian intellectuals; and a hard core of left-wing political extremists often with a background of polytechnic sociology (Honeyford, 1983, p. 13).

Honeyford's antipathy towards anti-racism was second only to his patriotic reverence for the sanctity of British culture, jeopardized by the 'alien wedge'. His stand created demands that he should be sacked for violating the 'anti-racist policy' of the education authority who employed him to head a school in which the majority of pupils were black. The anti-racists, who were quick to brand him a racist, were less able to demonstrate why and how this was the case. His plight, beleaguered while black parents organized to withdraw their children from his school, became a populist rallying point for the new right (Butt, 1985), illustrating the destructive consequences of local authority anti-racism in general. Honeyford was presented as a martyr in the popular press.[21] The detail of Honeyford's cultural racism is less important here than the fact that its very cultural qualities prevented it from being recognized as racism at all. Culture almost biologized by its proximity to 'race' becomes so potent a force that it can block and interrupt indefinitely what was once thought to be a 'natural' long-term process of assimilation in which schools played a crucial role (Carby, 1982). The manifest cultural differences visible in public – at school – originate and are reproduced in private – in black families. They become the focus of resentment because they will not allow blacks to yield to Britishness. The attachment to non-British cultures which endures in black communities and from which much of their apparent strength and cohesion derives, is cited as the final proof that the entry of aliens into the national community is not only hazardous but practically impossible. Repatriation is therefore the only logical political solution to this problem and has the additional value of being a populist proposal.

The absolutist view of black and white cultures, as fixed, mutually impermeable expressions of racial and national identity, is a ubiquitous theme in racial 'common sense' (Lawrence, 1982), but it is far from secure. It is constantly under challenge from the activities of blacks who pass through the cultural and ideological net which is supposed to screen Englishness from them, and from the complex organic process which renders black Britons partially soluble in the national culture which their presence helps transform.

The Falklands war was not, therefore, the only moment at which the discourses of 'race' and nation erupted into popular politics and culture. They are always there, being struggled over. Racial differentiation, national belonging and the contradictory identities and ethnicities they map out are, for example, a continuous presence in press coverage of the royal family, in sports reporting, where the nation assumes its everyday shape, and in coverage of deportations under British immigration law. All are important sites on which the limits of the nation as well as its character are routinely established.

The emergence of black athletes, often very successful, in British colours has generated some interesting material bearing significant ideological contradictions. When the young black boxer Frank Bruno is hailed 'the Brawn of Britain' but tells the popular papers that 'if he wasn't Britain's hottest heavyweight prospect for years . . . he would like to be Princess Di . . . because she's got so much going for her'[22] his words are a window on these contradictions. Decathlete Daley Thompson's refusal to carry the Union Jack at the Commonwealth Games in September 1982 was an earlier example. His reluctance was interpreted by some commentators as evidence of his partial commitment to Britishness and Britain.[23] Thompson told the management of the English team that he did not want to carry the flag and refused to provide any further explanation. He was tracked down to his quarters but reporters could not speak to him because 'he was said to be asleep'. Phil Hubble, a white swimmer, was asked to take Thompson's place. He told The Times 'Naturally, I'm very proud and honoured.' Thompson's coarse banter with Princess Anne at the Olympic Games in Los Angeles may provide evidence of his rehabilitation, but the questioning of black commitment to national identity remains a sub-text of the sports pages.[24]

The problem appeared in somewhat different form during 1984 when the South African runner Zola Budd obtained British Citizenship within ten days of her application.[25] Though her father claimed citizenship by descent, Ms Budd was not granted hers under the patriality rules which operate to exclude blacks. The Home Office admitted that her ancestry had been taken into account in their decision, but she was not naturalized; she did not need to be. The ties were there for all to see. Her grandfather's house in now decaying inner-city Hackney was discovered by the Daily Mail[26] and paraded as evidence of her historic British roots. Even when she spoke to reporters in Afrikaans, the possibility that her culture might erect obstacles to her being truly British was unmentioned. Unlike black settlers and their children, Zola was recognized as being of 'kith and kin' – an important category in the folk grammar of contemporary racism. The term is used to indicate the durability of national ties which do cross over into the territory of other states, and to establish the common identity of the sons and daughters of Britannia who have come to inhabit what is known as the old commonwealth: Canada, Australia, New Zealand, and now the Falklands. Zola's Englishness was felt to be so far beyond dispute that when young blacks demonstrated against her reluctance to denounce apartheid, reports of their protest branded them as alien traitors and unBritish racists. They were deprived of the right to belong to the national community and their action at South London's Crystal Palace stadium prompted the *Sun* to suggest that they 'return to their original homelands. There is no place for them in Britain'.[27] In Parliament, a Tory MP asked the Prime Minister if she agreed that the campaign against Budd was 'petty minded and despicable' and asked her further to condemn the demonstrators 'ignorant abuse of South Africa'. Mrs Thatcher replied 'I agree with my honorable friend. I thought the treatment of a 17 year old girl was utterly appalling and a disgrace to those who meted it out to her.'[28]

Perhaps because it involves the public fragmentation of family units, the coverage of deportations has become a second important space in which the contradictions around 'race', culture and national belonging are aired. The image of isolated Asian women reluctantly climbing aboard the aircraft which will repatriate them and their children has become a particularly potent signifier of the victim status of the whole Asian community. It is proof that this group has been brought to grief by cultural values which burden them with overlarge families and refine the natural cunning that leads them to persistently strive to evade immigration laws (Parmar, 1984; Sherman, 1979).

One case which throws the complex fusion of 'race' and nation into stark relief did not end in the deportation of the Asian family who had initially been told to quit Britain. The case of Rodney and Gail Pereira is interesting because it demonstrates how the absolutist conception of ethnicity and national membership can be disrupted by its own cultural definitions of who is and who isn't a true Brit. The Pereiras did not hail from an inner city. They were denizens of Bishop's Waltham in rural Hampshire. Their campaign to stay ended in success after a Home Office minister used his discretion under the act to allow them to remain in Britain legally. Their white neighbours had campaigned vociferously in their favour and publicly celebrated the victory which had been gained by bombarding the Home Office with 'blizzard of petition forms'.[29] The *Daily Mail* also lent its support, yet it was not this campaign which swung official opinion in the Pereiras' favour. In a leader article in *The Times*, new right ideologue and associate editor of the newspaper, Ronald Butt, explained that the minister concerned had been impressed by the

... approach that Mr and Mrs Pereira had to living in Britain and the attitude towards them of their English neighbours ... they played an active part in village life ... they were popular ... in short, they showed a positive commitment to Britain and to the English way of life which gave their case an aspect beyond the simple convenience to themselves of living here.[30]

The *Daily Telegraph* told its readers that the Pereiras 'who are English speaking Roman Catholics ... feared that they would be discriminated against in India'.[31] The other papers provided myriad illustrations of the way that the couple and their 3-year-old daughter Keira had become integrated into life in their pastoral idyll. The *Guardian* revealed that despite the child's foreign name, she had 'played a mouse on her Sunday school's float of Noah's Ark at this year's May carnival'.[32] Among hundreds of offers of help received by the couple was an anonymous promise of £100,000! The process of transformation from alien to Briton is conveyed vividly in an accumulation of details like these.

Butt used his discussion of their case to attack the redefinition of racism which has meant that it is understood no longer as merely 'disliking individuals because of the colour of their skin'. In his opinion, the new definition wrongly criticized as racist the 'preference for accepting people with a strong inclination to be assimilated into the British community and who are in numbers which assist this process'. He described the anti-racists who operate this expanded definition of racism as being anxious only about people who, unlike the Pereiras, have 'little commitment to English life and culture'. His opposition to anti-racism then turned to attempts to develop multi-cultural educational curricula. He concluded:

The case of the Pereiras has helped us to understand what the argument has always been really about – and that is much more identity and culture than colour.

This definition of 'race' terms of identity and culture is not the exclusive property of the new right. It has also been articulated recently by some tendencies and groupings inside the black and anti-racist movements who, though opposed to Butt's conclusions, manage to duplicate in precise detail many of his underlying assumptions about the content and scope of racial difference. Nowhere has this been more clearly stated than in discussion of the issue of 'transracial' fostering and adoption.

This debate which flared in 1983[33] has centred on the issue of whether white families can provide adequately for the needs of the black foster-child or adoptee. This question has been central to the political organization of groups of black workers in social services and local authorities.

The Association of Black Social Workers and Allied Professionals (ABSWAP) submitted evidence to the House of Commons Select Committee in March 1983 which dealt with the topic in detail (ABSWAP, 1983). Their submission provides an opportunity to gauge the understanding of 'race' which informs the demand that black children be placed exclusively with black families. If such families cannot be found, the evidence suggests that black children remain in local authority institutions where they can be nurtured to a 'positive black identity' by black staff. ABSWAP is centrally concerned with the issue of ethnic cultures and their role in establishing 'race'. The latter is understood almost exclusively in terms of the formation of an individual 'racial identity'. This process is placed in jeopardy by putting black children in white families. ABSWAP suggests that the essential ingredient in any substitute home for black children in care is its capacity to enhance the child's 'positive black identity'. This identity, which is understood to be wholly discontinuous with white identity regardless of age, gender, class or neighbourhood considerations, arises where the child's blackness is mirrored by those around it, where role models are to hand, and where the child is adequately protected from racial abuse. A more sophisticated version of the same theory is advanced elsewhere by John Small, President of the Association (1984). He argues that 'the issue of [racial] identity should be given priority above all other factors' and explains the existence of 'identity confusion' in black children adopted by whites as the result of the children's internalization of parental super-egos which contain a negative concept of black people.

ABSWAP defines 'transracial' placements as 'a microcosm of the oppression of black people in this society' because 'black children are being used to satisfy the needs of white families'. Their evidence continues:

The most valuable resource of any ethnic group are its children. . . . The black community cannot possibly maintain any dignity in this country . . . if black children are taken away from their parents and reared exclusively [sic] by another race. . . .Transracial placements poses [sic] the most dangerous threat to the harmonious society to which we aspire. . . . It is in essence 'internal colonialism' and a new form of slave trade, but this time only black children are used (ABSWAP, 1983).

The organization states that the interests of the black child are paramount, but this rapidly becomes a tautology. These interests are simultaneously identified in a primary need for 'security and belonging' which can only be met 'within a family or community which is similar in cultural and racial characteristics'.

The definition of 'race' which informs these arguments elides the realms of culture and biology in the same way as the volkish new-right preoccupation with 'kith and kin'. Its political counterpart is a variety of black cultural nationalism which relies on mystical and essentialist ideas of a transcendental blackness (Marable, 1981; 1984). Both ABSWAP and Small reject the term 'mixed race' not because they believe there is only one 'race' which therefore cannot be mixed, but because the term is said to imply 'the superior race quotient' (sic) and carry with it an implicit notion of domination and subordination. The effect of their theory is to further fragment the possibility of an expanded political definition of blackness which can encompass

65

diverse 'racial' histories from Africa, Asia and the Caribbean. It also consigns children of what they call 'mixed parentage' to racial inde- terminancy, particularly if they are brought up by a single white parent. These children could also have found space in a more politi- cally focused definition of 'race'.

The tone of ABSWAP and Small's work suggests that anyone who concedes that a black child may be better off in a white household than in a local authority home, is advocating the kidnapping of young blacks and their compulsory rearing by whites. Theirs is the voice of a black nationalism which, though it may have political pertinence in other social formations, is sadly misplaced in this country where the black population is too small, too diverse and too fragmented to be conceptualized as a single cohesive nation. There are several other fundamental objections which can be registered to these arguments and the theory of 'race' and culture which they espouse. They reduce the complexity of self-image and personality formation in the black child to the single issue of 'race'/colour. The personality which expresses an ahistorical essence of blackness and which is judged by the black professionals to be the only identity which can match the needs of the black child (gender is again indeterminate), is guaran- teed to emerge once the process of state-regulated, professionalized colour-matching is complete. This schema depends on a thoroughly idealized conception of black family life which does nothing more than simply invert the pathological assumptions which apparently characterize much of social work intervention in this area (Stubbs, 1985). The juggling of children through ethnic categories and their shunting between adoptive and foster parents on the basis of 'race' and culture has been seized on by the new right as further proof of the disastrous consequences of local authority anti-racism (Kerridge, 1985).

At this point it becomes important to ask why much needed criti- cism of the way that racism is institutionalized in social work practice gets subsumed by the rhetoric of black cultural nationalism. The beginnings of an answer to this question can be found by looking at the ideology of ethnic absolutism as part of the response of black professionals to the political contradictions they experience working inside local government bureaucracies. The attempt to view blacks as a culturally homogeneous national unit may be more significant for what it reveals about the internal politics of social services depart- ments (SSDs) than for any light it sheds on the contemporary meaning of 'races'. Emphasizing ethnic particularity has become an important means to rationalize the practice of these departments. It organizes their clients into discrete groups with separate needs and problems which have been identified as expressive of the various cultures they inhabit. It is possible to see the invocation of racial identity and culture in the mystic forms of kinship and blood characteristic of cultural nationalism as the means with which black professionals in these institutions have sought to justify the special quality of their relationships with their black clients. These ideas provide a superficially coherent ideological reply to the contradictory position black professionals occupy. Their perch in the institutions of the local state is contradictory in both class and 'race' terms. Their membership of the professional and managerial class and the power relationships which their jobs give them relative to a largely poor and dispossessed clientele, call notions of simple racial solidarity into question. Yet, while these black social workers and allied professionals are local state servants with statutory obligations to other government agencies, their job and status do not completely insulate them from the 'race' politics of the client group which calls out to them across the boundaries of class division. This ideology of black cultural nationalism is their response. Barney Rooney (1980) has pinpointed some of these problems:

What really happens is that you recruit black people as social workers to relieve alienation, but you recruit only those who have nothing to do with the alienated sections, either in racial or cultural background, or indeed in the work which they undertake, but they attract members of their own communities . . . to social services.

Paul Stubbs has suggested that an important part of SSDs responses to increased work with black clients has been the introduction of black workers who are formally and informally allocated the work of dealing with black clients (Stubbs, 1985). He argues that their ability to do this work in the manner which is expected by the SSDs hinges on the capacity to measure professional relationships and competences against the allegiance prompted by shared ethnic identity. This ability has become, he argues, the basis on which black staff are evaluated by superiors and colleagues. If this is so, the intensity with which black cultural nationalism emerges from the ABSWAP material can be interpreted. Its origins may lie in the management of potential conflicts between professionalism and 'racial' identification. The variety of ethnic absolutism which is produced, banishes, or at least salves, the pain which grows in the tension of trying to be black and professional at the same time. It has settled on the issue of 'transracial' fostering and adoption not only because of the obvious emotional charge attached to the central symbols involved – mother, child, family – but because of the need to articulate an answer, however confused, to the racist theory of black families as pathologically disorganized and deficient. The strength and durability of black families can be asserted in the face of this negative portrait only if the issue of why black children are taken into care in the first place is avoided. On a television discussion of these issues the chair of ABSWAP, David Divine, repeatedly claimed that the 'black community has been denied the right to look after its own'.[34] This position dovetails with the Thatcherite rolling back of social services and health care provision (Bull and Wilding, 1983) and provides an important example of how the political strategy of black nationalism can intersect with the programme of the radical right.

Conclusion

This chapter has sought to identify the links between the discourses of 'race' and nation and to use their proximity as an argument against the pre-eminent place which the idea of nationhood continues to enjoy in the work of English socialists and the practice of black cultural nationalists. Apart from the overlap with the concerns and premises of the right, there are other reasons why the language of nation has become an inappropriate one for the black movement and the socialist movement in Britain. The uneven development of national crisis has, for example, exacerbated regional differences to the point that we can speak routinely of two nations – north and south. These nations, which sometimes appear to co-exist with difficulty, are more than simply competing metaphors of Englishness (Weiner, 1981). The difference between them is rooted in the mode of production and is expressed not least in the different relationships each enjoys to national decline and de-industrialization. The industrial geography of the present crisis and changes in the geographies of class hierarchy and gender patterns of employment have been identified by Doreen Massey (1984) who has concluded that a new spatial division of labour is being created. This must be taken into account in discussions of the political language and concepts which radicals will require if they are to end the dominance of authoritarian populist nationalism.

Quite apart from 'racial' and gender considerations, the steady fragmentation of national unity and its recomposition along new economic and regional axes, militates against the language of patriotism and people retaining its wide popular appeal. Changes in Britain are matched by changes outside, in the character and composition of capital which has begun to organize itself into productive structures and operations which transcend the limits of the nation state and cannot therefore be combated by workers' organizations trapped and confused within national borders. The need to develop international dialogues and means of organization which can connect locality and immediacy across the international division of labour is perhaps more readily apparent to black populations who define themselves as part of a diaspora, and who have recent experience of migration as well as acute memories of slavery and international indenture.

I have not intended to suggest that the attempt to turn these insights into political practice necessitates the abandonment of any idea of Englishness or Britishness. We are all, no doubt, fond of things which appear unique to our national culture – queueing perhaps, or the sound of leather on willow. What must be sacrificed is the language of British nationalism which is stained with the memory of imperial greatness. What must be challenged is the way that these apparently unique customs and practices are understood as expressions of a pure and homogeneous nationality. British socialists often interpret the things they like or wish to encourage as repositories and emblems of national sentiment. Socialists from Orwell to Thompson have tried to find the answer to their marginalization in the creation of a popular patriotism, and described the oppression of the working class in nationalist images as diverse as 'the Norman yoke' (Hobsbawm, 1978), and Tony Benn's colonial analogy discussed above. Their output owes its nationalist dimensions to several sources. It has been forged not only in the peculiarities of the route which brought the English proleteriat into being within national limits (Linebaugh, 1982; 1984) marked by the early liquidation of the peasant class and the protracted dominance of the aristocracy, but also by the concepts and methods of historical materialism itself. These have been shown to play a role in the reproduction of a blind spot around nationalism as far as Marxists are concerned (Gellner, 1983; Kitching, 1985; Nimni, 1985; Nairn, 1977). Marx and Engels' assertion that the workers have no fatherland sits uncomfortably beside their practice as German nationalists and its accompanying theory of historic and non-historic peoples which differentiated between 'the large viable European nations' and the 'ruins of peoples' (*Volkerabfalle*) which are found here and there and which are no longer capable of national existence (Robinson, 1983). Their dismissal of the nationalist movements which might arise from among 'historyless' peoples (*Geschitlossen Volker*) whose national communities did not conform to the precise equation of state and language which could guarantee them historical being, is one of the fundamental moments in which the Eurocentrism and statism of Marxism are brought into being. It illustrates the limitations that history has placed on the value of Marxian insights which may not be appropriate to the analysis of the relationship between 'race', nation and class in the post-industrial era. This legacy must be re-examined and dealt with if the hold of nationalism on today's socialists is to be broken. Its inversion in the form of black cultural nationalism simply replicates the problem.

69

Notes

1 Barker's concept has been usefully developed by Mark Duffield (1984) and Errol Lawrence (1982).
2 'One Nation The Politics of Race' *Salisbury Review*, no. 1. See also Casey's 'Tradition and Authority', in Cowling (ed.) (1978), *Conservative Essays*.
3 Editorial *Salisbury Review*, no. 1., 1983.
4 The works of Anthony Barnett and Patrick Wright are honourable and notable exceptions here. Wright, in particular, tries to break the deadlock between these tendencies in a bold and innovative manner. The success of his attempt is, however, qualified by the fact that it is secured on the terrain of history. Barnett has consistently pointed to the profound relationship between Labourism and nationalism as well as to the contemporary dangers inherent in a populist nationalism.
5 Speech at Southall, 4.11.71.
6 *Sunday Telegraph*, 27.6.82.
7 Speech at Eastbourne, 16.11.68.
8 Jose Nun has produced a definitive discussion of this concept in his exchange with Ernesto Laclau in *Latin American Research Unit Studies*, **3**, nos. 2–3, 1980.
9 *Sun*, 21.1.84.
10 *Sunday Telegraph*, 23.5.82.
11 *Sunday Telegraph*, 27.6.82.
12 *Guardian*, 20.12.82, reprinted from *Marxism Today*, January 1983.
13 *New Statesman*, 14.12.84.
14 *Formations*, **1**, no. 1 (1983), p. 99.
15 *Guardian*, 8.3.86; see also reply by Hugo Young 'The love that dares to speak its name too often', *Guardian*, 11.3.86.
16 Speech at the Carlton Club, 26.11.1984.
17 *Sunday Telegraph*, 8.9.76.
18 The best example of this is the contrast between television situation comedies featuring blacks and whites. It is notable that none of the series featuring blacks seem able to portray inter-generational relations between black characters or show their experiences over time, in a diachronic dimension.

　　The BBC series 'Frontline' (1985) about the relationship between two black brothers, one a 'Rasta', the other a policeman, began significantly with the death of their mother. An equivalent programme centred on a fractured white family in which notions of locality and 'ethnicity' play a similar role – 'Only Fools and Horses' – builds its humour out of the tension between generations.
19 *Guardian*, 11.3.85.
20 Speech to Stretford Young Conservatives, 21.1.77.
21 A good selection of the many articles on Honeyford's case would include *Daily Mail*, 17.12.85, 18.12.85. The *Sun*, 12.4.85, 20.6.85, 30.11.85. The

Spectator, 22.6.85, and the Centre for Policy Studies pamphlet 'The Trials of Ray Honeyford: Problems in multi-cultural education' (1985).

22   *Mirror*, 24.2.86.

23   *The Times* and *Sun*, 28.9.82.

24   As far as 'race' and the Royals is concerned see Helen Chappell's 'The Wedding and The People', *New Society*, 30.7.81., and coverage of the discovery of a 'Little Black Sambo' book in Prince William's nursery, the Sun, 26.9.85. Away from the domestic scene, the Queen's 1985 tour of the Caribbean saw her confronted with a 'giant roasted rat' at a State Banquet in Belize. This meal, and the monarch's polite 'picking at it' neatly symbolized the cultural difference between us and them. The story featured on the front page of the *Mirror*, 12.10.85.

    A good range of coverage from various sports about the contradictions between 'race' and nation can be gained from the following. Geoff Capes, an ex-police officer and currently Britain's strongest man, is something of a John Bull figure in the popular press. His relationship with an Asian woman for whom he abandoned his wife and children was the subject of a detailed article 'Why Do They Sneer At My Black Beauty?' in the *Sun*, 27.11.84.

    There is plenty of cricket coverage which deals directly with 'race' politics, partly because of the South African connections of several England players, but mostly because the West Indies team has managed to inflict a series of humiliating defeats on England during the last few years. At the time of writing, England has not beaten the West Indies in a test for twelve years. Much of the more racist coverage centres on the question of whether the West Indian fast bowling violates either the letter or the spirit of cricket's laws. See E. M. Wellings' 'Government Without Backbone' in *Wisden Cricket Monthly*, March 1985, and coverage of Mike Gatting's nose injury on England's 1986 tour of the Caribbean, *Mirror*, 20.2.86. On the black spectators see the account of the West Indian victory at the Oval, 15.8.84. The *Sun*'s account, 'Mob Rule Triumphs', is the best illustration.

25   *Guardian*, 27.4.84.

26   *Daily Mail*, 16.4.84.

27   *Sun*, 27.4.84.

28   *Hansard* Commons debates, 26.4.84., col. 880.

29   *Guardian*, 23.5.84.

30   *The Times*, 31.5.84.

31   *Daily Telegraph*, 23.5.84.

32   23.5.84.

33   See Jeremy Laurence in *New Society*, 30.6.83, and Ann Shearer's 'The Race Issue must be faced' in the *Guardian*, 26.1.83. Also Jeannette Kupfermann's 'Love is more important than your parents' colour' *Daily Mail*, 14.2.83.

34   Black on Black, Channel 4, 26.2.85.

3   Lesser breeds without the law

In Britain, 'mugging' is, indeed, a form of self-employment (and maybe a primitive form of street-level anti-white politics) that is disproportionately practised by unemployed West Indians (Ian Taylor).

In the Jamaicans, you have a people who are constitutionally disorderly. . . . It's simply in their make up, they're constitutionally disposed to be anti-authority (Sir Kenneth Newman, Commissioner of The Metropolitan Police).

On Tuesday, 19 March 1985, the picture of a young black man with dreadlocks was emblazoned across the front pages of Britain's popular press. Under headlines like 'Lazy Rasta' and 'Cheeky Little Rasta Angers Judge' the papers told a story of conflict between Everton Samuels, a 'pot-smoking rastafarian on the dole for two years'[1] and Judge Michael Argyle. Samuels, dubbed 'Rasta Everton' by the tabloids, had appeared before Argyle on charges of possessing cannabis. When told that the defendant was awaiting the results of a job application, Argyle had apparently offered to help him secure the post. According to the *Sun*, the learned judge adjourned the case so that he could approach the company concerned and speak personally on Samuels's behalf. He spent his judicial lunch-break pleading with the firm's director and eventually obtained a promise that the company was doing everything possible to find Samuels – a trained 'electronics worker' – a suitable position. Argyle went so far as to say that he was prepared to defer sentence if Rasta Everton would 'give the opportunity a spin'.

It was not this generosity by the judge which had put the case on the front pages, but Everton Samuels's refusal of the judge's offer of help. As soon as Argyle made his position clear, Samuels's counsel rose and told the court that it was unrealistic for his client to be expected to take up the job as it would involve at least two-and-a-half hours travel a day. Argyle gave the supposedly ungrateful Samuels a week to find a job for himself. The 'Cheeky Rasta' was reported to have left the court saying: 'If the Judge likes to buy me a car I'll take the job.' He returned a week later and was able to tell Argyle that he had found a job as a van driver. As he handed him a two year suspended sentence on the drugs charge, the judge admonished him with the words: 'You are living in a different world from the rest of
72

us.' Explaining that the publicity attracted by the case had generated a 'flood of hate mail', Argyle continued:

I have to tell you that your attitude has done your own people no good. The court has received a number of letters from fascists and anarchists, all anonymous, which have ended up in the waste bin. Your manner merely feeds the prejudice of those people who think that anybody who is coloured is automatically unfit to be a member of society.[2]

This courtroom drama manifests many of the themes and images central to contemporary racism. It can be used to demonstrate the significance of black criminality in today's racial discourse. The court-room itself has become an important site in which the unity of these discourses can be revealed. The case of Rasta Everton is therefore a useful point at which to commence an archaeology of representations of black law-breaking. It fuses black criminality with an obvious political theme – the rejection of work – which, as we shall see in Chapter 5, has deep roots in the expressive culture of black Britain. The language in which this case appears contains some significant indicators of how representations of black law-breaking have changed during the post-war period.

In the aftermath of the 1984 Carnival in Notting Hill one white reporter, whose tube train had been held up by a group of black youth who 'mugged' each passenger in the carriage in turn, revealed total perplexity that his attackers looked 'so normal' in their 'expensive designer sweat shirts'.[3] Rasta Everton is something of an anachronism in this world where smartly dressed thugs and 'muggers' deliberately disguise their deviancy in the garb of conspicuous elegance, refusing to conform to stereotyped ideas of what young black criminals should look like. Samuels's supposedly criminal character is declared openly in his dress and his sub-cultural affiliation as well as by his black skin. As such, his representation contains the residue of his previous criminal incarnations – the scrounger, the knifeman, the drug dealer. This is what makes him especially interesting. The words 'black youth' do not appear anywhere in the various reports of his court appearances; none of the papers which reported his case felt it necessary to explain what a Rasta was or to tell their readers of the legendary link between Rastafari and drug use. Yet knowledge of these issues is assumed and plays a vital part in drawing the threads of his story together. More important still, the nature of Samuels's original crime and his apparent antipathy to the world of work are linked not just by his blackness but by an inferred definition of the deviant West Indian culture in which these unfortunate traits apparently have their roots.

Samuels's laziness, his drug use, his hat, his locks, his insolence and the later revelation that, two weeks earlier, he had been bound over for two years on the charge of possessing a flick knife, are

73

articulated by his blackness. They become a powerful signifier not just of black criminality, though the folk grammar of common-sense racism would recognize them immediately as the proof of black difference, but of black culture as a whole. When Judge Argyle talks to Samuels about his attitude having done 'your people' no good, the people in question are not black youth, black criminals or Rastas alone, but *all* blacks, or at least all of Afro-Caribbean descent. Standing in the dock, Samuels's crimes, both formal and informal, became *their* crimes, and he was recognized as their representative. Similarly, Judge Argyle and his anonymous correspondents, who are an unacknowledged link with the speeches of Enoch Powell, are positioned in the discourse and the narrative as representatives of the British people, the white British people and their traditional culture, locked in struggle against the disruptive criminal encroachment of the blacks.

The law's majesty, conveyed as much by the judge's kindly efforts as by his power to punish and imprison, has acquired the capacity to show the nation to itself. Where black crimes are made prominent and may even come to dominate public perception of crime as a whole, this has grave implications for the politics of 'race' and racism. This chapter offers some tentative answers to the questions of how and why this has happened.

The ability of law and the ideology of legality to express and represent the nation state and national unity precedes the identification of racially distinct crimes and criminals. The subject of law is also the subject of the nation. Law is primarily a national institution, and adherence to its rule symbolizes the imagined community of the nation and expresses the fundamental unity and equality of its citizens. Beyond this general level, the importance of law and constitution in Britain is understood to be a unique and important cultural achievement. As Britain, stressed by crisis, has moved in the direction of a 'law and order' society, popular politics have infused legality with the capacity to articulate the very core of national identity. This idea has been central to the rise of Margaret Thatcher. Discussion of the vicious conflicts between blacks and the law's agents has been prominent. These conflicts have sometimes been seen as a self-fulfilling prophecy of black externality and alienness which are in turn confirmed increasingly by vivid images of the particular crimes and criminals that are understood to be the anti-social effects of black settlement. In recognition of this and of its role in more authoritarian and populist forms of government regulation and intervention, following Hall *et al.* (1978) it has become commonplace to see the history of 'mugging' as the history of just such a racial category of crime. The moral panics which have attended the deployment of this concept in popular politics are interpreted as evidence that representations of the black presence in terms of its illegality are bound up

74

with the experience of national crisis and decline. They provide at a visceral level contradictory, common-sense explanations, symbols and signs which render the shock of Britain's loss of status intelligible and enable it to be lived out in 'racial' terms. The fundamental process of fragmentation and chaos engendered by the crisis are contained in the images of a disorderly and criminal black population. However, the association of blacks and criminality in political discourse turns out to be more complex than this. The representation of black crime has taken several quite different forms, some of which do not draw on the image of 'mugging' at all. Indeed blacks have not always been thought of as a high crime group in British society. The changing patterns of their portrayal as law-breakers and criminals, as a dangerous class or underclass, offer an opportunity to trace the development of the new racism for which the link between crime and blackness has become absolutely integral.

If the black presence in post-war Britain has been constantly identified as a source of problems, the precise shape and dimensions of these problems have constantly changed, reflecting a shifting balance of political forces in the struggles between black settlers and both institutional and popular racisms. It has been mistakenly argued, particularly in the aftermath of the 1981 street protests, that the identification of blacks with crime is simply a consequence of their membership of a disadvantaged and politically marginal group. This peripheral position is thought to make them more likely to engage in criminal acts. The distinct forms of criminality they practise are both sanctioned by the 'residual ethnic factors' in their inner-city culture and invited by its decaying environment. Their criminality triggers a militaristic police response, creates a white backlash and thereby inaugurates a 'spiral of conflict' in the inner city (Lea and Young, 1982).

This schema, which is not without support on the Labour left, contains a number of propositions which will be challenged below. The extent to which it is empirically demonstrable is not of primary concern here. The argument against it should not be read as a denial of the fact that blacks engage in criminal acts, though there are a number of unresolved questions around the extent of black participation – in particular around the role of official statistics in verifying their involvement. It is no betrayal of black interests to say that blacks commit crime, or that black law-breaking may be related to black poverty as law-breaking is always related to poverty. The possibility of a direct relationship between ethnicity, black culture and crime is an altogether different and more complex issue. It will be examined only as part of my consideration of the growth in new types of racial meaning and racist ideology during the 1970s.

In using the archaeological method this chapter is addressed not to epistemological questions which would seek to evaluate discourses

75

relative to some norm of truth, but to the exploration of the conditions under which the discourse of black crime has become central to contemporary 'race' politics while other discourses have faded out. I am concerned here with the history of representations of black criminality and in particular with the elaboration of the idea that black law-breaking is an integral element in black *culture*.

The next step in the anti-racist argument – an attempt to place these ideas and images on a broader framework or map of social development which reveals not only the changing patterns in racist ideology and practice but also the manner in which these fit into the transformation of British state institutions and political culture at a time of extensive social and economic change is not pursued here but has emerged in the work of other authors.[5] The logic of this approach suggests an agenda for anti-racists in which they forego debating the indices of black criminality and seek to show instead how obsessive concern with black law-breaking has come to sit at the centre of contemporary racist thought. This must be inseparable from the task of producing a strategy for dealing with those forms of racism which look at the black population as a whole through the lens which criminal signs and imagery provide. These same ideas and images inform the policies and practice of various state agencies at both local and national levels. Distinct patterns of political conflict are generated where they are resisted by the blacks whose lives they distort.

I have argued elsewhere that the development of increasingly authoritarian state intervention in the fields of policing and criminal justice has invoked an appeal to the British nation in terms of a common racial sensibility. This has been invoked, not only in the pronouncements of senior police officers who have ventured into the world of popular politics in pursuit of consent and legitimation, but also by government spokespeople for whom the issue of crime and disorder has been a place where a bipartisan approach might be applied. In his Home Office bi-centenary lecture of 1982, for example, James Callaghan argued that on the questions of law and freedom:

There had always to be some approach towards the centre because, whatever their politics, Home Secretaries sprang from the same culture, a culture it was their duty to preserve if the country was to remain a good place to live in.

This view of cultural continuity overriding the narrow considerations of party politics in the area of policing and criminal justice is highly significant. It is precisely this unified national culture articulated around the theme of legality and constitution which black criminality is alleged to violate, thus jeopardizing both state and civilization. Crime in general and black crime in particular disrupt the reverence for law which has been accepted by left and right alike as a fundamental component of Englishness. From the right, law-breaking is

76

seen as an active rejection of national civilization of which law is the most sacred expression. From the left, it is the policies of the authoritarian state and the refinement of oppressive power, especially in policing, which have been identified as being essentially alien to British traditions and destructive of the heritage of freeborn Britons.

Explanations of criminal behaviour which make use of national and racial characteristics are probably as old as the modern juridical system itself. The process in which the nation state was formed in Britain in the eighteenth and nineteenth centuries also provided the context in which modern legal institutions grew and developed. The moral regulation of citizens and their property became a primary object of state intervention. The identification of law with national interests, and of criminality with un-English qualities, dates from this process of state formation and has a long history which remains relevant to the analysis of 'race' and crime today.

The garotting panic which gripped London in 1862 is a well known early example of moral and political alarm about law-breaking which involved focusing the crime on a particular group of people whose deviancy was then conceived in terms of national and cultural differences. Reference was made to the alien, un-English quality which the garotters' activities lent to the areas of the metropolis in which it was practised: 'Highway robbery is becoming an institution in London and roads like the Bayswater Road are as unsafe as Naples.'[6] Once prisoners paroled on 'tickets of leave' were identified as the source of these outrages, the solution to the problem which caught the popular imagination was a revival of transportation abroad beyond the boundaries of the national community. As Jennifer Davis (1980) puts it, once it was concluded that ticket-of-leave men were members of a dangerous and irredeemable class, the liberties of free Englishmen were not to be extended to them.[7]

Sixteen years later, the 'Jack the Ripper' murders in Whitechapel were to provide a second illustration of how particular crimes could be categorized as un-English in inspiration or execution. This time it was a settler community, the Jews of the Spitalfields neighbourhood in East London, who were to be harassed and abused as part of popular outrage against murders which the *Daily News* identified as being 'foreign to the English style in crime.'[8]

Anxiety about the criminal predisposition and activities of the immigrant population inspired demands for the introduction of immigration controls in the first years of this century. When the issue of alien criminality was debated in Parliament, the settlement of Russians, Rumanians and Poles in the East End of London was described by the Tory member Major William Evans-Gordon in military metaphors no less potent than those chosen by Enoch Powell. Though he did not define the entire immigrant population in criminal terms he was firm that a 'considerable proportion of bad characters' were among them and that 'their competition with the home industries extends to burglary and other cognate crimes'. He concluded:

I should have thought we had enough criminals of our own . . . surely the executive government should have the power to deport such persons as were recently referred to by the chairman of Clerkenwell sessions who stated that 'foreign criminals had recently been landing by hundreds in London, formed themselves into gangs and carried on a systematic series of burglaries'.[9]

Historians of Jewish settlement have also identified concern with what were perceived to be the characteristic manifestations of Jewish crime during the Edwardian period. Here concern centred on the involvement of the community in a 'white slave traffic' which involved in the procurement of reputable white women for immoral purposes in cities as diverse as Buenos Aires, Bombay and Constantinople (Holmes, 1979; Gartner, 1973).

In 1912, the Criminal Law Amendment Act introduced flogging for the men of 'almost entirely foreign origin' who were engaged in this vile trade.[10] There was, however, no more general popular panic about the criminal behaviour of the East End Jews. Indeed when the Metropolitan Commissioner and his deputy were summoned to the Royal Commission on Alien Immigration in 1903, the relationship between their force and the Jewish settlers was not discussed as a problem.

The idea that immigrants engaged in higher rates of criminal behaviour and committed crimes which were essentially un-English bears the imprint of a second set of social theories. This tendency has been identified by David Garland (1985a; 1985b) as being central to the development of criminology in Britain and saw the racial deterioration and the criminal propensities of the urban population as related features of moral and physical degeneration which were the consequences of city life.

This association of criminality with urban living is closely connected with discussion of 'race'. It has at various points both supported and provided an alternative explanation to the more obviously biologically based theories. The fact that urban criminals had been identified as a 'race' apart, long before the wave of post-war black settlement, contributes to the potency of today's racial imagery of crime. It may also have strengthened the metaphor for urban crisis and decay which has been provided by black criminality. The appearance of metropolitan criminals with visibly apparent 'racial' characteristics is, in this context, the final proof that earlier anxieties about the effects of urban life had been justified. This is particularly true where, as we shall see below, the racial and cultural characteristics of the black population have been identified as contaminants of their white neighbours.

Anxiety about these harmful aspects of city life was integral to concern about the state of 'national efficiency' which Gareth Stedman Jones and others have argued was widespread in late Victorian and Edwardian England.[11] It endured beyond the 1914–18 war and can be discerned in the language of jungle and tribe with which Cyril Burt described the culture of the Young Delinquent (Humphries, 1981). It reappears not only in the idea of hooliganism as a disease that emerged in discussion of the 'boy labour problem' but in the notion of 'the unfit' that connects discussions of alien criminality in the post-war period[12] with a pathological view of the urban working class which defined the origins of their criminal inclinations in feeble-mindedness and pauperism.[13]

Blacks and crime in post-war Britain

Concern about the criminal behaviour of black settlers in the late 1940s and 1950s assumed a different form, clustering around a distinct range of anxieties and images in which issues of sexuality and miscegenation were often uppermost. Lurid newspaper reports of black pimps living off the immoral earnings of white women were cited by the Home Secretary, Sir David Maxwell Fyfe, in a secret memorandum to the cabinet on 30 January 1954:

Figures I have obtained from the Metropolitan police do show that the number of coloured men convicted for this offence is out of all proportion to the total number of coloured men in London and the police say that the practice is much more widespread than the number of convictions would appear to indicate since the police have not the manpower needed to carry out the necessarily detailed investigations in every suspected case.[14]

His concern surfaced again in a cabinet minute of 9 March which assessed popular feeling on the immigration issue and described increased crime as one of the key anti-social effects of unrestricted immigration:

complaints are becoming more frequent that large numbers of coloured people are living on national assistance or the immoral earnings of white women.[15]

In a similar vein, Sir Harold Scott, Commissioner of London's police between 1945 and 1953, cast white womanhood in a different light by emphasizing the disreputable status of the women involved in these commercial relationships. He criticized the popular tendency to see aliens as the most criminal group in society but restricted his view of their law-breaking to the same small if highly symbolic range of offences:

It is often suggested that aliens are responsible for the bulk of our crimes, but I'm afraid this is wishful thinking. Most of our criminals are home-grown and must be dealt with here. . . . I have put forward the proposal that the law should be amended to enable us to send back to their own countries certain classes of British subjects who are consistent and flagrant law-breakers. Cypriots, Maltese and coloured British subjects are responsible for a disproportionately large part of the offences connected with gaming, living on immoral earnings of prostitutes, and the sale of drugs and liquor (Scott, 1954, p.66).

The absence of street robbery from this list is of course significant, as is the fact that Cypriots and Maltese are listed alongside blacks at an apparently equivalent level of criminality.

The racial discourse of the 1950s and early 1960s tend to dwell on a variety of themes other than crime. Concern over 'the way in which some coloured people acquire tenancies of older property and by their conduct make life difficult for white people living in the same building or area' was also mentioned in Maxwell Fyfe's second minute. It was the housing question which formed the primary focus of popular racist agitation at this time and it broke down into a variety of subsidiary panic issues – shortage, overcrowding, exploitation by black landlords and the role of moneylenders in house purchase by blacks.[16] A full picture of the way these themes meshed together to define the 'race' problem can be found in Elspeth Huxley's *Back Street New Words*.[17]

In a three storeyed house built for one family, with two dark basement rooms, six ordinary rooms and a couple of back passage spaces shared as kitchens or let as 'rooms' to single men, dwelt nine separate families or 'units' comprising twenty-two individuals. (West Indian, Pakistani and Irish; the landlord a Jamaican.) [sic] A single, filthy water-closet; no bath room, everything cracked, peeling, unpainted, down at heel; garbage and discarded household debris (old mattresses, a broken arm-chair, rusty cans, broken bottles, worn-out clothing) littering what had once been a back garden, where now hungry cats prowl; and rents of £3 a room rolling in – £30 weekly net plus extras and perks. (Landlords often fiddle the meter so that the tenant's shilling does not buy a shilling's worth of gas and pocket the difference.) Some of these houses are turned into dormitories for single men and the beds let twice over, day workers and nightshift men taking turns and playing cards together to pass the time at weekends.

Race was thus fixed in a matrix between the imagery of squalor and that of sordid sexuality. In this context, miscegenation, which captured the descent of white womanhood and recast it as a signifier of the social problems associated with the black presence[18] emerged ahead of crime as a theme in the popular politics of immigration control.

A study of West Indian immigration published by the Eugenics Society in 1958 argued that the mingling of races 'runs counter to the great developing pattern of human evolution' and attacked the United Nations for minimizing the 'quite obvious dissimilarities between people and individuals'. Its author also felt that

the positive advantages of miscegenation are hardly to be discerned so far . . . it's easy to mix and impossible to unmix . . . special consideration should be given before immigrants are allowed to enter the country having measurable and largely inheritable, physical attributes below the average for the United Kingdom (Bertram, 1958).

Though the riots of 1958 may have marked a turning point in the history of modern racism, press coverage of the conflict in Notting Hill and Nottingham is notable for the degree to which the crime theme, though present, is again subordinate to other images and anxieties. A racial interpretation of the events was not the dominant one, though concern about black crime was a feature of the debates on immigration control raised by Sir Cyril Osborne later in the year.

Two groups of crime which are causing the police a good deal of anxiety are organised prostitution and the traffic in dangerous drugs. In the London area during the last 12 months, half the convictions for those two groups of serious crime were of what is loosely termed coloured people, including Maltese and Cypriots. That means the tendency for those crimes to occur among coloured people is a hundred times more per person, than among white people in the London area. Surely it is not unreasonable to say that those who are guilty of crimes of that type should be deported.[19]

Osborne's attempt to tie these observations to his account of the origins of the riots seems to have been a failure. Black crime was not frequently cited as being a contributory factor. The main emphasis in newspaper reports fell on the issue of law and order which was identified as the appropriate response to the hooliganism of the Teddy boys who were discovered at the core of the events. Racial definitions and explanations of the conflict had to compete with analyses which located its origins in the irrational and violent behaviour of youth and in the particular urban communities from which they came. These two explanations appear to contradict sharply with one another until it is appreciated that the Teddy boys and their urban community were described almost as a 'race' in their own right. *The Times*, drawing on images of moral and physical degeneration which are clearly derivative of the language of national efficiency discussed above, called the young men 'pallid thugs [who] like the chance of violence without dangerous odds'.[20]

Fyvel's account of the riots is centrally concerned with the rebellious teenage sub-culture inhabited by the thuggish youth. However, he emphasizes its continuity with the culture of their parents by stressing the exceptional nature of the transformation required to turn the typical working-class youth into a violent racist:

81

The riots were started by nine very ordinary working class boys, six of them only seventeen, with previously blameless records . . . upon hearing of the previous race riots in Nottingham, the nine armed themselves with coshes and iron bars and, as if in a dream, they began to walk through the streets of Notting Hill and savagely attack any coloured pedestrians they met, beating them to the ground (Fyvel, 1961, p. 62).

The other major theme in the reporting of the riots was the role played by the Mosleyite Union Movement in fomenting the conflict. *The Times* declared that the 'persistent agitation' of 'fascist' elements to 'Keep Britain White' was 'not to be ignored' because it had an important influence on the 'immature and excitable' residents of the rough areas in which the conflict had broken out.[21]

All these themes took precedence over black crime as explanations of the riots. They defined the racial component of the conflict in terms wholly different from the range of meanings articulated in more recent racial politics. The images of criminal public disorder, so central to today's racist ideology, were confined, where they appeared at all, to the representation of the whites who had set out in pursuit of black victims.

Where concern about black criminality is present it occupies a subsidiary role and is located around offences and criminal acts which are vastly different to the now familiar themes of 'mugging' and street robbery. How are we to account for these profound changes in the signification of black criminality? Fringe concern about black crime persists throughout the period between 1958 and Enoch Powell's 'rivers of blood' speech ten years later. Yet the common-sense wisdom on the subject during this time was summed up by Lord Elton in *The Unarmed Invasion* (1965):

Men who work as hard as do many immigrants are seldom law-breakers. The only serious offence commonly attributed to them by their back-street critics is that of living off immoral earnings, forgery and illegal immigration (p. 77).

Lord Elton's distance from the idea that blacks were more criminal than whites can also be seen from his genuine, paternalistic fear that immigrants would be easy prey for the various racketeers and con men who were lurking ready to exploit their vulnerability.[22] These views were supported by Peter Griffiths, the racist Tory candidate, who had defeated Labour in the 1964 election at Smethwick under the slogan 'If you want a Nigger for a neighbour vote Labour'. His famous triumph over a Labour cabinet minister in an urban, working-class constituency revealed the profound mobilizing power of the race problem and signified, long before 'Powellism' took shape, the importation of racial populism into the official political culture. Yet the crime question played only a tiny part in the portrait of the black problem drawn by Griffiths. In *A Question of Colour* (1966) he dissents from the popular belief in higher rates of black criminality.

Newspaper publicity tends to exaggerate the number of offences committed by coloured people. The race of the offender is reported even when it is completely irrelevant to the case. . . . The totals (for convictions of common-wealth citizens) though considerable especially in the case of West Indian offenders, can hardly be regarded as overwhelming. Certainly immigrants are no more prone to serious crime than our own people (p. 66).

Griffiths's view of the types of crime in which blacks were most active adds crimes of violence (often involving 'hidden knives') to the by now familiar list of fraud, drug trafficking and vice offences. His description of the 'affront to British moral standards' precipitated by the 'mushrooming of brothels in the twilight areas of our immigrant affected cities' is interesting for the mention it makes of female criminals:

From Slough to Balsall Heath . . . come reports of open disregard of the law. . . . In 1958 of the 127 convictions for living on immoral earnings within the Metropolitan police district, forty were of coloured men. During 1962–3 the number of convictions rose to 182 of which 101 were immigrants. . . . In Birmingham all the cases of brothel-keeping by immigrants led to charges against Pakistanis. Living on immoral earnings led to the prosecution of 8 West Indians and 4 Pakistanis while four West Indian women were charged with soliciting.[23]

Griffiths also notes that at this time immigrants were responsible for 33 per cent of all attacks on the police, 20 per cent of public fights and 7 per cent of sexual attacks. There is, however, no mention of 'street crime' here. Besides the themes of housing and miscegenation, an exaggerated concern with the numbers of black immigrants features in the racial discourses of this period. The problems which blacks were thought to represent were depicted in quantitative rather than qualitative terms. Elton was again typical:

Just because it is so constantly forgotten, it cannot be too often repeated that the fundamental problem of immigration is not the colour of the immigrants but their numbers (Elton, 1965, p. 11).

He illustrated the same point with an extraordinary example when the immigration act was discussed in the House of Lords:

If it were known in my home village that the most reverend Primate the Lord Archbishop of Canterbury were coming to live there, we should undoubtedly ring a peal on the church bells. If it were known that five Archbishops were coming I should still expect to see my neighbours exchanging excited congratulations at the street corners. But if it were known that fifty Archbishops were coming there would be a riot.[24]

Interest in the numbers of blacks entering Britain was expressed in the gradual importation of statistics into official discussions of the 'race' problem in all its forms. These were not initially crime statistics but numbers proving the relative ill health of the immigrant population in a way which referred back to the nexus of sexuality and squalor mentioned earlier.

In a 1961 feature on Smethwick, the *Sunday Times*[25] had quoted a social worker who knew Asians 'riddled with VD' who had shunned treatment because 'they want nothing from us at all – except work'. Though passing reference was also made to the typhoid, rickets and leprosy rates of Afro-Asian migrants, the main focus of panic seems to have been supplied by tuberculosis and venereal diseases. An important series of articles in *The Times*, 'The Dark Million', dealt with each in turn:

The best investment that a Pakistani with TB can make is a one way ticket to England. He will be admitted to hospital and get three months there at £25–£30 a week – the normal cost of a bed – and treatment afterwards – at a weekly cost of 10s to £1. He will then be back on assistance for some weeks before he goes back to work. It all adds up to something in the region of £500. . . . There is no proof that this happens, but it is known that they do it. One or two have admitted it.[26]

The learned authority of the *British Journal of Venereal Diseases* was invoked in a quotation which sought to prove that 'Gonorrhoea is reported to be twenty times more prevalent among West Indian Immigrants than among native born citizens.'[27] *The Times* also quoted the results of a survey of 173 clinics in England and Wales which had found that over half their male sufferers from gonorrhoea and a third of those affected by syphilis were immigrants (Chater, 1966). In November 1964 the Dean of the London School of Tropical Medicine warned that air travel from tropical lands was bringing unfamiliar diseases into this country which often could not be diagnosed before they became a danger to the community.[28]

The statistics governing immigrant health were followed by flurries of numbers predicting the size of the black population in years to come, the precise size of the alien population and its fertility rates. 'The Dark Million' series contained a bitter attack on government agencies who were reluctant to compile detailed statistical information on these issues.[29]

The question of immigrant numbers was felt to be so important that the articles took their title from the estimated number of black settlers in the country. The figures they cited put the total number nearer to 700,000.[30] The VD panic had been partly blamed on the high proportion of single male migrants. The birth-rate scare which followed it mobilized for the first time a portrait of whole families. Family units had risen as a proportion of total immigrants in the rush to 'beat the ban' introduced by the 1961 Commonwealth Immigrants Act which came into force in July 1962 (Peach, 1968).

The secretary of the British Medical Association (BMA) in Leamington Spa was quoted in the local paper saying that it was 'virtually impossible' for English women to enter hospital for their first confinements because the beds were occupied by immigrants.[31] Peter Griffiths (*A Question of Colour*, 1966) repeats exactly this claim but attributes the phrase to a Medical Officer of Health from Smethwick. This man went on to explain that the pressure on hospital beds from immigrant mothers was due to the squalid conditions in which they lived. He told this revealing anecdote:

A Leicester midwife attending a coloured confinement found the family in one bed, expectant mother, father and two other children. Just before the birth she managed to get the two children out of the room but the Indian father remained in bed throughout. His excuse? He worked nights!

From quantity to quality – Powellism, piccaninnies and pathology

It is only by looking in detail at the language and imagery of this discourse on 'race' that the extent of changes which followed Enoch Powell's 'river of blood' speech of April 1968 (Powell, 1969) can be appreciated. That speech provides something of a bridge between the older forms and linguistic devices of racism represented in the work of writers like Elton, Griffiths and Pannell (1965), and the recognizably modern forms which identify and address a different range of problems in which black crime is to the fore. If it can be read as a break in the epistemology of contemporary racism, this speech also provides an extended commentary on the way in which legality, the ultimate symbol of national culture, is transformed by the entry of the alien wedge.

Powell first defined the central problem of black settlement as a 'preventable evil' and gave it substance in the fearful notion that 'in fifteen or twenty years' time the black man will hold the whip hand over the white man', an image which derives its potency from a striking inversion of the roles of master and slave, covertly acknowledging guilt while summoning fear. He moves into the main body of the text with a section entitled 'A matter of numbers'. He conceded that 'numbers are of the essence' and specified the proper object of government policy as their diminution by the encouragement of what is called 're-immigration'. However, this is not the main thrust of his argument. The problem introduced by the blacks is not reducible to a matter of numbers, as Elton's archbishop analogy had earlier suggested. The issue is not the volume of black settlement but rather its character and effects, specifically the threat to the legal institutions of the country made concrete by the introduction of new race

85

relations laws. As he puts it: 'If all immigration ended tomorrow . . . the prospective size of this element in the population would be unaffected.'

It is not then a matter of how many blacks there are, but the type of danger they represent to the nation. The rest of the speech is dominated by a polemic against the new race legislation which would afford black settlers the protection of the law where discrimination was proven. It was the contemplation of this bill which lead Powell to compare himself to the ancient Roman with the grizzly vision of the Tiber foaming with much blood. His horror was at the prospect of blacks being afforded limited legal protection and it was this debasement of the legal sanction which appalled him rather than the issue of mass immigration itself.

The letter from an anonymous Briton which comprises the centre-piece of the speech has a double importance. It provides the proof required to legitimate Powell's view of the dire effects of black settle-ment and does so through a discussion of the perversion of the traditional legality which has been the result of the new legislation. Inseparable from this is the identification of young blacks as both a visible political problem in the public sphere and as a metonym for the incompatibility of blacks as a whole with English (city) life. The moment at which crime and legality begin to dominate discussion of the 'race' problem is thus also the moment when 'black youth' become a new problem category, conceived in the combination of youth and 'race'.

The anarchy represented by black settlement is counterposed to an image of England in which Britannia is portrayed as an old white woman, trapped and alone in the inner city. She is surrounded by blacks whose very blackness expresses not only the immediate threat they pose but the bleak inhumanity of urban decay. The letter describing her plight generates racial meanings from an accumulated tension between a series of neat binary oppositions – white/negro, clean/dirty, noisy/quiet. Its racial imagery is also striking for the way in which the conflicting colours are also gendered. The principle character, the aged white woman, is introduced first as 'a white' as if her other attributes are secondary. The word 'negro' is used simi-larly to signify the maleness of those it identifies. Where black people or children are referred to, other words are introduced – immigrants and piccaninnies.

The old woman's house, in the 'once quiet street which has become a place of noise and confusion', is beset early one morning by 'two negroes who wanted to use the phone to contact their employer'. These were the days in which 'negroes' had jobs. Their approach suggests the encroachment not just of alien blacks into the national heartland, but of the public sphere in which blacks are defined as being 'at home' into her private, domestic environment. The intrusion of the immigrants is initially by the threat of violence. She is verbally abused by them for her refusal to let them use the phone even though 'she would have refused any stranger at that hour'. She fears that they may attack her.

Her financial plight eventually forces her to seek replacements for the white tenants who have fled the black takeover of their once respectable street – an allusion to the mother country's post-war need for colonial labour. However, the only lodgers she can find are blacks and she will not accept them. Thus cut off, she begins to feel too afraid to go out and the negroes who have offered to buy her home for a paltry sum gradually institute a campaign of harassment and violence against her. They use their children as weapons in this war.

Windows are broken. She finds excreta pushed through the letter-box. When she goes to the shops, she is followed by children, charming wide-grinning piccaninnies. They cannot speak English, but one word they know. 'Racialist' they chant.

What will become of this woman when the new race relations bill becomes law, wonders Powell's anonymous correspondent? The letter concludes speculatively: 'This woman is convinced she will go to prison. And is she wrong? I begin to wonder.'

The national tragedy described by the letter hinges on the transformation of English legality. The innocent are to be consigned to prison after being found guilty of racialism while the really guilty ones – the blacks who push excreta through letter-boxes and know just one word of English – are left to roam free. The inversion echoes the transposed master/slave image which opens the speech. The national constitution is distorted and destroyed by the presence of the alien blacks. They are the criminals, not the old woman, and their criminality is the central expression of their alien status. It expresses their distance from the authentic Englishness signified in the life which the law-abiding old woman was able to enjoy before their noisy arrival.

Legality is the pre-eminent symbol of national culture and it is the capacity of black settlement to transform it which alarms Powell rather than the criminal acts which the blacks commit. The discursive frameworks and textual strategies which define the new racism are all present in Powell's speech. The basic images and signs recur time and again in subsequent debate and commentary on 'race'. The portrait of white female vulnerability, the noise, the shit through the letter-box, endures into the 1980s as imagery for the effects of black settlement. It continues to connote immigration long after immigration ceased, and rests on the stain of illegality which has expanded to encompass a more detailed account, even a theory, of black propensities towards crime and disorder. Powell's wide-grinning piccaninnies were soon to grow up, and with the onset of their adolescence, the image of young black muggers stalking mean inner-city streets in pursuit of the old and infirm entered the syntax of British racism.

At one level, Powell's intervention merely expanded the hole in official political culture through which Peter Griffiths had first introduced a genuinely populist politics of 'race' to dramatic effect. The political language of Powellism that followed, secured the crucial link between 'race' and nation by focusing attention on the issue of legality and then on the violation of the constitution by blacks. The debate over the effects of the race relations legislation led directly into anxiety over black crime, and Powell played an integral role in the transition from one to the other.

By the time in 1976 when he declared 'mugging' to be a racial crime,[32] a complex combination of common-sense definitions and explanations of the 'race' problem had become fully operative. The history of these and of the initial stages of the panic surrounding 'mugging' is recounted elsewhere and need not be repeated here.[33] It is important, however, to emphasize that the 'mugging' label did not arrive here initially as an expression of the deterioration in relations between blacks, particularly young blacks, and the police. There is plenty of evidence to substantiate the view that this conflict emphatically preceded both the use of the 'mugging' term and the official view of blacks as a high crime group in the population (Humphry and John, 1972; Hunte, 1965).

The 1971–2 session of the Home Affairs Select Committee on Race Relations and Immigration chose to inquire into the issue of 'Police/Immigrant Relations'. Their report (HMSO, 1972) refers to the relations between police and young blacks as 'difficult and explosive' and quotes a spokesperson from the West Indian Standing Conference who had said:

To state that a sizeable proportion of the West Indian Community no longer trust the police is to confer a euphemism upon a situation which, for many, has reached a level equal to fear.

He continued:

The Conference is convinced that if urgent action is not taken to give effect to the grave issue at hand, violence on a large scale cannot be ruled out. The solution rests largely in the hands of the police.

Another witness identified among police 'a tendency . . . to consider that because a man was black he was a potential criminal'.

These perspectives seem familiar today but the arguments with which the police answered them show that any resemblance to more recent views of conflict between blacks and the police is only superficial. Evidence from the Police Federation, the rank and file police officers' 'union', concluded with the view that 'there was no serious problem in police/immigrant relations', but warned that the position of 'vociferous militants' in the black communities would be strengthened unless more was done to improve education and employment prospects for immigrants.

The Metropolitan Police evidence noted that: 'We often find that although we are prepared to talk to some of them [immigrant communities] they do not seem willing to talk to us.' Both submissions stated their opposition to the idea that blacks were naturally, socially or constitutionally disposed to higher levels of criminal behaviour than whites. The Federation said that 'if [a man] does a gas meter it is because he wants money, not because he has a black skin', while the Met. went so far as to endorse a view of the relationship between the environment and crime which had gained currency as a result of the publication of John Lambert's *Crime, Police and Race Relations* in 1970: 'There was not so much a problem of immigrant crime as of crime in over-crowded areas, where immigrants tended to live.'

The overall view which emerged from the committee's report swings between the idea that blacks were less criminal than whites and the idea that they were more or less similar in their criminal habits. The former position was propounded by the Chief Constables of Sheffield and Leeds who respectively stated that 'the crime ratio is far less with the immigrant people that it is with white people' and 'the immigrant areas are less of a problem to us from the police point of view than the skinheads or the crombies'.

The Chief Officer from Leeds identified a 'special difficulty', though not a criminal offence, in the 'number of West Indian girls leaving home and sleeping rough for one or two days at a time'. In spite of this, he added, prostitution problems with coloured girls were 'far less' than with white ones. One Metropolitan Police division, covering Notting Hill and Notting Dale, submitted a special comparative study of black and white crime statistics to the committee. Although the black population of the district was estimated at around 12 per cent, some 30 per cent of the callers at Notting Hill police station were revealed to be black.

This survey, together with similar, less detailed figures from Wandsworth, drew attention to the apparently disproportionate involvement of young blacks in robbery. Yet this observation is remarkable for its distance from the stereotype of the 'mugging' which was to follow it.

Immigrant crime rates were, if anything, a little lower than those for the indigenous population. The only exception to this was robbery. Of 38 robberies in Notting Hill in 1971, 30 involved coloured people, mainly teenagers. These robberies were not organised or premeditated, but were usually things such as snatching handbags . . . the coloured population does not feature largely in the drug scene (HMSO, 1972, p. 23).

Where the crimes, which were to become known as 'muggings', were identified, they were seen as a minor issue which was insufficient to dent the fundamental belief that immigrant criminality was low. Similarly, this report was written long before the phrase 'black youth' had acquired its fearsome contemporary power to signify disorder and national decline. Where West Indian youths are recognized as constituting 'special difficulties' for the police this is a result of their homelessness rather than their lawlessness.

Though the first stirrings of an explanation of black family life in pathological terms are undoubtedly present, the main reason given in the report is the parental insistence that by 15 the (male) youth should be able to support themselves by the fruits of their own work. The overcrowding of family homes was also mentioned as a contributory factor.

The gulf between this report and subsequent theories of 'race' as the effect of separable, antagonistic national cultures cannot be overemphasized. West Indians, it explained, were 'British in way of life, language and laws: only their culture and colour [are] different.' This is an interesting formulation because it excludes 'way of life' from the definition of culture which is being used. The content of this cultural difference is not revealed, but the suggestion that ethnic cultures amount to a complete discontinuity if not conflict between 'racial' groups is nowhere to be found. The same view emerges from the report's discussion of West Indian shebeens and noisy parties, a subject deemed important enough to be the first of the special difficulties listed. The committee began by denying that 'noisy parties are necessarily more attributable to black than white people'. They do, however, go on to criticize one particular type of party.

The shebeen was identified by police witnesses as a 'thorn in the flesh' of the force in various urban areas. These self-made leisure institutions were identified as a problem for the police but again there was no attempt to connect the patterns of consumption and recreation of which they are part to any idea of a characteristically West Indian culture or way of life. The fulcrum of official anxiety in this area is the suggestion that licensing laws are being broken as a matter of routine.

More significant for future common-sense theorizations of black criminality was the report's grasp of the political problems which lay beneath the surface of the black communities and its sense that conflict with the police was guided by a form of political antagonism rooted in the American ideology of 'Black Power'. The evidence submitted by the Police Federation had sought to turn the official mind towards consideration of the Black Power and Black Alliance movements which were thought to be recruiting among the young unemployed. There is no suggestion that these groups and movements were either representative of the community as a whole or of any innate West Indian predisposition to disorder. The Metropolitan Police evidence admitted that the force was 'worried' about the rise of isolated local pockets of militance but not 'unduly worried about it'. Young people were again identified as being 'ripe for plucking' by older, more experienced agitators. No direct connection between the rise of Black Power and unemployment was apparent to the committee.

A Police Federation representative from Coventry expressed concern about the publication of literature inciting young West Indians to violence and identified 'back street organizations . . . composed of coloured ex-students who are maoists and revolutionaries' as the culprits. Where the two themes of youth and militancy come together in this way it was the role of the militants which caused the greater alarm.

These representations of criminality were centred primarily but not exclusively on the West Indian communities. The problem of Asian criminality was presented around different themes, particularly illegal immigration, which was also identified by the committee as a special difficulty. The traffic in illegal immigration was viewed as a minor but none the less significant problem for police forces, particularly as it offered a gateway into other important areas of criminal activity, such as blackmail and forgery. Significantly, the need to circumvent immigration control was not viewed as anything to do with Asian culture, family size, or a distinct way of life. The report concluded: 'in general legal immigrants are as opposed to it [illegal immigration] as anyone else'. The distinction drawn here recalls the gas meter example cited above. It separates criminals from the law abiding, the disreputable from the respectable, in a manner which makes no concessions to the idea that blacks are a priori criminals, or even the suggestion that their patterns of criminal behaviour are culturally determined.

The governmental response to the committee's report was published in late 1973. It persists with the view of black criminals and disorderly types as a minority within an overwhelming majority of solid citizens. The immigrants, it begins, 'are not in themselves a problem for the police' (HMSO, 1973). The white paper went further than the committee document by suggesting that the truculence and disorderly behaviour of black youth might originate in their frustration at not being 'accepted on the same terms as others regardless of colour'. As I have pointed out elsewhere (CCCS, 1982) the paper contextualizes discussion of the policing problems presented by black youth with an extended reference to the problems which police have had with other groups of (white) young people. The open acknowledgement of youth subculture and style as expressions of disorderly orientation is offered as the key to interpreting the behaviour of the 'small minority of young coloured people . . . apparently anxious to

91

imitate the behaviour amongst the black community in the United States' (HMSO, 1973).

These views of the relationship between 'race' and crime recede rapidly in the period between the arrival of the 'mugging' concept and the 'long hot summer' of 1976 which hosted the most bitter confrontations to date between blacks and the police.

Those years saw the definition of blacks as a low crime group turned round 180 degrees. They also witnessed the formation of a politicized roots culture among the black populations of the inner city, which will be examined in detail in Chapter 5. What is important here is the extent to which that culture's political expressions, symbols, themes and modes of organization are themselves bound up with the new definition of blacks as a law and order problem. When the Metropolitan Police returned to the House of Commons Home Affairs Select Committee to give evidence in the 1975–6 session, their submission not only sought to withdraw the mistaken impression they had given five years earlier in suggesting that blacks were a low crime group but also identified the malevolent activities of

'certain individuals, organisations and journals' which 'consistently demon-strate their antipathy to the police and . . . signal their intent to sabotage police/community relations . . . continued editorial vilification of the police and other social agencies, distorted accounts of court proceedings, and repetition and exaggeration of unsubstantiated and one-sided complaints of police "brutality" which forms the sterile basis of a number of ethnic news-papers and periodicals, have a cumulative effect on the state of police/black relationships, and provide a false justification for extremes of group behav-iour' (HMSO, 1976, p. 182).

These activities were denounced by the police as attempts to politicize the merely criminal actions of a disorderly and youthful minority. The phrase 'West Indian Community' was used in quotation marks, presumably intended to be ironic in tone. These sentences in the police submission conceal a commentary on the growth of articulate antagonism towards the police and detailed criticism of their practice. The ironic reference to the West Indian community can be read as an acknowledgement of the degree to which the community was being defined and organized politically around the policing question during this period. A series of well-publicized cases in London and elsewhere had provided disturbing evidence of the degree of conflict which had developed as well as the degree of organization in the black communities around the policing theme.

If the 1970 conflict around Notting Hill's Mangrove restaurant and the subsequent trial on charges of riot and affray fed anxiety about the role of 'Black Power Militants' in the growth of crime and disorder, the tone of panic in the mid 1970s was set by a sequence

92

of bitter confrontations in and around other black cultural institutions – the dance-halls and clubs where the bass-heavy beat of the sound systems pumped righteous blood to the political heart of the community.

Predictably concern was greatest where 'black youth' were involved and the first of these confrontations also took place in Notting Hill at the Metro youth club in August 1971. The confrontations which followed are noteworthy not only for the consistency with which they originate in institutions which were cultural and recreational rather than formally political but for the new types of political organization and struggle which were constructed as part of the various campaigns to defend those who had been arrested. While the law was recognized as a repressive force there was no reluctance to use what constitutional and democratic residues it contained. The strategy which was devised sought to reveal and then exploit the political dimensions of the legal process by using the dock as a platform for the critical perspectives of the defendant while combining this legal struggle with popular, local agitation and organizing of community support. Those campaigns were aimed at maximizing mobilization rather than membership of the various organizations involved.[35]

This combination of tactics and the synchronization of protest inside and outside the law, provided a model which has become central to the political repertoire of black activism up and down this country.[36] The detail of the cases in Birmingham, Leeds and all over London cannot be examined here, though the manner of their passing into the folk memory of black Britain is one of several points of interest, signalling the decisive role of culture in the reproduction of black political sensibility. Most are remembered not by the names of those arrested, nor by the police officers who abused them, nor even by the districts in which the confrontations took place. The clubs and cultural events at which the arrests were made are what fixes them in history – the Metro 4, the Swan Disco 7, the Burning Spear Club 6.

The best known examples of this type of protest are provided by the large-scale cultural events of the community which drew national and regional rather than merely local support: the Bonfire Night riots in Chapeltown, Leeds, in 1973, 1974 and 1975; the running battle between police and youth at Brockwell Park in Brixton and, most famous of all, the Carnival riots of 1976, 1977 and 1978. Of these, the Notting Hill Carnival riot of 1976 will be examined in detail later, as a watershed in the history of conflict between blacks and the police and in the growth of the authoritarian forms of state planning and intervention during the 1970s.

It is important to remember that these major visible confrontations were exceptional only in their scale. By this time both police and black community sources agree that smaller conflicts were becoming routine events on the pavements of inner-urban areas. The Metropolitan Police's 1976 evidence to the Home Affairs Select Committee confided that 'the potential for conflict' was inherent in every law enforcement situation between police and West Indians (HMSO, 1976), and admitted that forty incidents between police and black youth with the potential for large-scale disorder had occurred in the twelve months before March 1976. Given the concentration of these events in the summer months, this total amounts to almost one major incident each week. The minor confrontations are not listed, but five incidents are cited and summarized in the report as typifying the broader problem. Of these, two originated in West Indian parties and the rest in a reggae festival, a youth club and a local fair. All involved attempts by a crowd to release blacks who had been arrested and three of the five feature struggles over a black presence in public space which was thought to be illegitimate because of its size or character. Incident 2, for example, originated from a group of black teenagers who were thought by officers to be obstructing the entrance to a railway station. Incident 3 was provoked by forty black youths milling about in the road outside a club, and incident 4 by a group of blacks who were standing on the pavement outside a party.

The police memorandum observed that 'members of London's West Indian community do appear to share a group consciousness'. In each of the examples of black disorder listed, a cultural context is instrumental in establishing the extent and character of this collective, oppositional identity. Violence is seemingly formed by or in relation to, specific cultural institutions and events and identity is reproduced or transmitted by attacks on the police. Culture secures the link between the criminal minority and the mob who spring to their defence. Thus attacks on the police are also gradually seen to be expressive of black culture.

The Met. presented elaborate statistical proof of its revised thesis that blacks were after all disproportionately more criminal than whites. Their evidence dates their change of opinion from 1974 when 'concern began to grow . . . about the degree of involvement by black youth in robbery and theft [from the] person offences in some areas' (HMSO, 1976). It concluded: 'Our experience has taught us the fallibility of the assertion that crime rates amongst those of West Indian origin are no higher than those of the population at large.'

The adequacy of the statistical material presented by the Met. can be questioned on a number of grounds. The compound 'circumstantial' category of robbery and other violent theft was used to lump together fundamentally different types of offences: the violent (robbery) and the non-violent (theft) across the lines which the law had set between them. This had the effect of inflating the total. The new category rapidly became a synonym for 'mugging' (GLC, 1986).

No information as to the 'race' of victims was included, thus inviting the conclusion that blacks were robbing whites rather than other blacks. The various 'non-white' groups were added together to produce a single 'racial' category. Most significantly, the figures were based on arrests and victims' perceptions of the assailant rather than any figures for convictions. These objections are not central to the argument here but they have been the focus of a long political and criminological controversy which was rekindled after the Met. again issued 'racialized' statistics of this type as part of their response to the Scarman Report on the Brixton riots and the criticism of the police which had greeted it. Joe Sim (1982) has argued that the decision to issue the statistics and the manner of their release can be interpreted as a political intervention by the Met. designed to undermine what were felt to be the unacceptable contents of Scarman's report. If this instrumental and calculated purpose is a plausible analysis of the 1982 figures, such an explanation could also apply to the release of identical figures in 1976. The political chemistry of the earlier moment had little in common with the post-riot atmosphere of 1982 when policing was enjoying an unprecedented level of public scrutiny and debate. However, there are several reasons to suggest that the release of the figures was a part of the Met.'s political strategy at that time.

First, the emphasis on brute and basic images of black criminality and on crime rather than politics as the motivation and the primary characteristic of black law-breakers must be set in the context of the London Spaghetti House siege of September 1975. The restaurant was held up and members of staff taken hostage by armed black activists who identified themselves as politically inspired. Robert Mark, the Met. Commissioner, described the episode in his autobiography as 'the most difficult and potentially explosive of all the various problems which I had to deal with in my 20 years as a chief officer of police' (Mark, 1978). He continued: 'From the outset it was rightly assumed that this was a simple armed robbery that had gone wrong . . . any attempts . . . to represent it as a political act were received with the derision which they rightly deserved.'

It is conceivable then that this political initiative around the theme of black crime, coming, after all, from the Yard's most senior officers, was part of a plan to offset the possibility that other similar political criminality might develop. The emergence of the Police Federation on to the stage of national politics is a second important background factor. The Federation's 'Law and Order' campaign had been launched in the autumn of 1975. Black crime was again a major issue and may have provided common ground between the force's developing rank and file voice and the views of its senior officers. This agreement, which cemented unity inside the force across the divisions of rank and bureaucracy, was matched by a populist politics. Mark had tried, in his own words, to engage the police service in 'the moulding

95

of public opinion and legislation' (Critchley, 1978), and imagined a situation in which the force could draw a direct mandate from the population partly through more sophisticated use of the media. He had earlier referred to the relationship between his force and the press as an 'enduring if not ecstatically happy marriage'[37] and he proved to be an effective communicator, politicizing his office in an unprecedented manner, particularly through television.

The political potential of the 'race' issue was readily apparent by this time and the Met. acknowledged as much when they admitted that their 1976 memorandum to the Select Committee 'will be taken by some people and used as racist propaganda against the black community' (HMSO, 1976). I am not suggesting that they intended to stir up racial sentiment for its own sake, but rather that the emphasis on black crime became a useful means to bolster the standing of the police, enhancing support for the organization at a difficult moment and winning popular consent which could no longer have been simply taken for granted.

Yet if the release of the racial statistics and the new emphasis on the problem of black crime was a tactical ploy, the emphatic defeat of the Met. by 'howling mobs' of black youth during the 1976 carnival in Notting Hill suggested that it was an unpredictable and unreliable one. The aftermath of the riots saw the popular press extremely critical of the policing of the festival. An editorial in the *Evening Standard* was typical of some of the criticism expressed.

It would be less than fair to aver that the police were in the right. All the reports suggest that Scotland Yard was far too heavy-handed on Monday. It should not have sent 1500 uniformed men to police the Carnival in the Notting Hill area. A force seven times as large as the one that attended last year's festivities must surely have contributed to the tension in a part of London in which, as the Yard knows very well, the police are regarded by many inhabitants as the natural enemy. The whole exercise was an error of judgement.[38]

The picture of black criminals being seen to get the upper hand was not, in the short term at least, a productive image for the police. The quality of their leadership was called into question and there was an increasing level of demand that something should be done.

Press reports of the carnival are interesting for what they reveal about the new conceptions of black crime and disorder. As in the Met. evidence of 1976, the carnival explosion was presented as the result of the crowd becoming involved in rescuing or preventing the arrest of black criminals out of some sense of racial solidarity. One police spokesman told the *Daily Mirror:* 'It's the same old story, a lot of West Indians who intervened and attacked our men did so without bothering to inquire why we were trying to arrest other coloureds.'[39] The rioters were described in several papers as the 'calypso mob' or 'calypso rioters'. This underlines the importance of the cultural dimension in creating the forms of racial solidarity which induced the mob to side with their criminal 'race' peers against the forces of law and order. The *Mirror* described the almost magical transformation which had occurred: 'suddenly the joyful smiles on the faces of the calypso revellers disappeared. They were replaced by an angry army of black youths'.[40] The *Financial Times* reported that the mob had been said to be heading towards Notting Hill police station which had been placed on siege alert. The *Daily Telegraph* invoked the memory of 1958 by pointing out that it was eighteen years to the day since the earlier conflicts. Alone among the press, that paper branded the disturbances 'race riots', suggesting that as far as the national race problem was concerned, nothing had changed in the intervening period. On closer inspection the meaning of the term 'race riots' in the *Telegraph* report is quite different from the conventional meaning of the words which are usually understood to refer to violent clashes between different racial groups. The 1976 riots were racial events for the *Telegraph* not because they involved racial conflict but because they expressed the 'race' of the blacks who had created them:

Fierce race riots broke out in London's Notting Hill last night at the end of the three-day Caribbean carnival. At least 95 policemen were injured as coloured men in screaming groups attacked them with bottles and bricks. Several policeman were stabbed.[41]

Mark's autobiography compared the carnival riot to the 'sordid celebrations attending the hangings at Tyburn tree' and explained the unfavourable press coverage which his force had received by referring to the mendacity of newspaper reporters whom he identified as part of a stratum of politically motivated people urging 'a kind of black saturnalia in the interests of good race relations' (Mark, 1978). His final report as Commissioner of the Met. denied that the riots had been 'racist in nature' (HMSO, 1977), but indicated the direction of future police strategies in relation to race and crime in its declaration that there would be no 'no-go areas in London'. This comment betrayed an enhanced sense of the spatial and geographical dimensions to policing which became a feature of police practice in London as part of the response to the Notting Hill defeat. The pockets of black settlement in which the disorderly minority were thought to reside were subjected after the carnival riot to what can be described as a policy of containment. Runnymede Trust research into the use of the 'sus' law carried out during this period revealed that the law was not used uniformly, even within inner London, and that appearances on the charge were concentrated in courts serviced by police officers working in the West End of the city. If there were to be no no-go areas for the Metropolitan Police their practice suggests that they were keen to impose restrictions of this type on the freedom of movement enjoyed by 'black youths' (Demuth, 1978).

The containment policy identified certain neighbourhoods as high crime areas and proved this by reference to comparative statistics for 'muggings'. Special squads of anti-mugger police were set up in some areas.[42] The attempt to informally exclude blacks from certain central districts was matched by intense and aggressive policing in their home territory. The Special Patrol Group (SPG) was used in several of these operations, and particularly in South London and Hackney became the focus of community antipathy to the police.[43]

The story of street level conflicts between the various black communities and the police would fill a chapter on its own and has been recorded by other writers. It is not the principal issue here. The extension of containment policy under Sir David McNee's commissionership is important not for the local conflicts which resisted it but for the manner in which it marked a departure from a policing strategy based on the need to combat particular types of crime – burglary or 'mugging'. Instead, the direction shifted towards area-based strategies which assume that any inhabitant of a high-crime district could be treated as a criminal. We shall see below how ideas like these have been refined and brought into the mainstream of police thinking under the leadership of Sir Kenneth Newman, the present Met. Commissioner.

In the 1976–8 period they were still in a preliminary stage and the concept of 'mugging' was still centrally featured as a part of the justification for differential police practice between areas.[44] However, 'mugging' was not the only mode of criminal behaviour which was used to prove the disorderly character of London's criminal areas. The growth of neo-fascist political activity during this period provided the context for an important encounter between the anti-police proclivities of black youth and those of white anti-fascist 'extremists' who attempted to smash the National Front and its associates off the streets wherever they organized public demonstrations. The right-wing organizations rapidly developed the tactic of marching in a provacative manner through black districts. In recognition of its populist power and its congruency with their belief in black inferiority, concern about the level of black criminality was prominently featured in their propaganda. The counter-demonstrations instituted by the emergent anti-racist movement were joined in London and elsewhere by large numbers of black youth. In Lewisham and Ladywood in 1977 and in Southall as part of the run-up to the General Election in 1979, black protesters attacked both 'fascists' and the police who provided them with protection. Their resistance gave credence to the view of the decaying inner-city areas as rough and violent places, where anti-police attitudes were commonplace.

The black mob, either on its own or allegedly manipulated by white 'outside agitators', thus opened a new chapter in the lexicon of racialized crime imagery. Pictures of blacks collectively engaging in disorder began to confirm the suggestion that this type of behaviour had something to do with what made aliens distinct. Violence made the link between the blackness and disorder more complex and more profound.

The shift towards a plural collective image rather than the lone and isolated figure of the 'mugger' reflected the partial de-racialization of the mugging concept which had followed once white 'muggers' had begun to be caught. It also reflected the need to explain the public order problems which had become routine in the inner areas. Groups of blacks engaging in disorder and moving to defend the criminal minority against arrest were seen as expressing the culture of the whole community: their cultural distinctiveness. Where the ethnic politics of community self-organization were also discernible, in a variety of guises: Black Power, Rastafari, or Asian militancy – they too acquired the taint of criminality. I have described the entry of the Rastas into official explanations of black deviancy and pathology elsewhere (CCCS, 1982). It is important to remember that between 1975 and 1981 the symbols and rhetoric of that movement achieved a mass character in Britain's black communities, triggering official alarm in proportion to the degree to which they were adopted as a reference point by many people who did not choose to signify their allegiance or interest by wearing locks or colours.

The riots in Bristol during 1980 signalled that the containment strategy would not, on its own, be sufficient to deal with the problems of a disorderly black population. Containing a community successfully depended on an overall grasp of which communities and areas were volatile. The burning of St Paul's conveyed the message that bitter confrontations could erupt anywhere where blacks were settled, regardless of whether there had been any previous history of conflict with the police.

Fred Emery put it thus in *The Times:* 'No one at Westminster would have . . . shortlisted Bristol as the potential powder keg.'[45] The much-publicized involvement of white residents in the protest, notably the participation of white pensioners in the looting of the supermarket, further complicated the picture. One local paper described the riot as '50–50 whites and blacks',[46] but the events were rapidly racialized with the theme of black culture as the catalyst of disorder becoming more and more dominant. Emery continued: 'It is no good pretending that "this was not in any sense a race riot" when there is, as Mr Merlyn Rees put it, "particular needle" between West Indian youth and the police.' The *Star* picked up this theme under its headline 'Race Mob Runs Riot'. The *Mirror* and the *Sun* made no overt reference to the 'race' of the rioters in their respective headlines

'Mob Fury' and 'Riot Fury'. The *Daily Telegraph* quoted a white bystander who identified the origins of the riot in 'a question of authority and the reaction to authority', but this observation was perversely used to confirm the special role of blacks in the events. By now, anti-authoritarianism was also being identified as a black cultural trait.

As the explanatory narrative of the events unfolded, the lawless character of the St Paul's area was traced back to its black settlers and their ways of life which had apparently rubbed off on their white neighbours. Black sociologist Ken Pryce was summoned to provide proof of this claim. He explained to the *Sunday Times* that 'ganja' (marijuana) which was alleged to have been sold at the Black and White cafe, the community institution with the usefully symbolic name where the riot had begun, was, in fact, a 'most important life-style trait' in the area.[47] Criminal use of drugs was revealed then not only as a means of recruitment of whites into this way of life, but as a tangible link between the riots and the culture of the black Bristolians whose inability to live without their weed expressed their difference from true Britons. Ganja also linked their superficially different types of criminality. It made explicit the connection between the private and usually petty lawbreaking of the pot smoker and the expressive public disorder which had been symbolized most powerfully in St Paul's by the burning of the local Lloyds bank.

Pryce also drew attention to the role of ganja in the Rastafarian religion. Drug use has been a background theme in the representation of blacks as a criminal group for a long period. It was reflected in another drugs case in June 1982. This saw pupils at Eton, one of the country's most famous public schools and a symbol of the ruling class in its own right, detained by police. The *Daily Mail* reported the story prominently and sought to make the most of the contradiction between the popular image of Eton as a bastion of traditionalism and the tale of black-inspired drug use there. The transformation of the pupils and their descent into criminality was achieved by a Rastafarian who had sold them not only ganja but apparently his lifestyle too:

Inquiries by housemasters have uncovered stories of boys as young as 14 smoking cannabis and reggae parties where cigarettes were handed round. . . . [A] boy said that there were three sources for the drug . . . a house owned by a Rastafarian in Slough and London streets dealers in the Railton Road area of Brixton and All Saints Road, Notting Hill. He claimed that . . . up to 10 boys would gather in a room to listen to Bob Marley records and roll hashish cigarettes.[48]

This example is less trivial than it might initially seem. It confirms first, the ubiquity of the threat to British life which is represented by the activities of black criminals; second, the power of that group who are able to secure entry into a secure and protected educational environment; and third, the pleasures involved in forsaking the duties and obligations of British discipline and replacing them with an idle and hedonistic lifestyle. The headmaster of Eton, Dr Eric Anderson, concludes the piece by warning that 'cannabis is a national problem among young people'. The relationship between white youth and black culture suggested in this story will be explored more fully in the next chapter.

Hedonism and dangerousness are very closely entwined in imagery of the black criminal. We have already seen how black parties and shebeens were gradually identified as sources of anti-police violence rather than simply places in which the licensing laws were being broken. The most significant recent example of the fusion of these two themes in discussion of 'race' came in the reporting of a ten-day party which ended in injuries to six police officers when the mob who had been taking their leisure inside 'surged out' and attacked the police.[49]

The papers reported that the party had been a source of fear not only for the police but for local white residents who had had to sleep 'in their kitchens at the back of the house with the doors barricaded'. Officers who had been dispatched to quell the party after a reported ten days of continuous noise reported that as soon as the mob erupted into violence shouts of 'white bastards' and 'white pigs' were heard. The *Sun* which gave the duration of the party as only eight days, reported that the riot had ensued when 'West Indian party-goers thought the police were going to call time on their fun'.[50] The *Daily Mail*, which listed the party's length as nine days, referred to the mob as 'guests' at the party and claimed that the trouble had flared as police had gone to investigate a reported assault. Music from the party, claimed the *Mail*, was 'shaking houses nearby' and it warned that if disruption like this was allowed to continue then 'worried people will take the law into their own hands'. Later, the *Mail* continued, a 'knife was found in a nearby garden'.

The party was alleged to have run throughout the period between Christmas and New Year without a break. This context is significant because it is the tension between how 'normal' English people spend the holiday period and the way that the blacks have fun which forms the point at which their respective cultures can be seen to diverge and become antagonistic. The shouts of abuse from the party suggest that the police attempt to 'call time' had been interpreted by the blacks as a racial act, and the activity of the police seen to be expressive of whiteness, further cementing the view of the party as expressive of black culture and blackness.

The law, embodied in the police, erects a barrier, not just of respectability but of racial culture or ethnicity. The reports establish a supportive relationship between the police and the local white residents harassed by the noise. This image of the law intervening to contain and suppress black culture and disorder is very different from the portrait of law in the 'rivers of blood' speech examined earlier. The threat of blacks, specifically of black youth, appears essentially the same, but the thirteen years have seen the representation of law and legality in the popular politics of race turned right around so that the police were now acting not in favour of the blacks but against them.

1981–5 street crimes and symbolic locations

It was a different party, almost exactly two weeks later, which was to provide the next important staging post in the history of representations of black criminality. The death of thirteen young blacks in a mysterious fire in Deptford, south-east London, was to hang over the race politics of Britain for the next few months like a pall of thick acrid smoke. The reporting of the fire must also be taken into consideration because the absence of interest or concern from Fleet Street was itself to become a significant factor. The tragic deaths set in motion a sequence of events which lead directly to the explosion in Brixton in April 1981, and provided a means to galvanize blacks from all over the country into overt and organized political mobilization. Whether the Deptford inferno was the result of a fascist attack is not of concern to us here. What matters is the fact that the dimensions of the loss were not sufficient to summon the interest of the news media until the controversies surrounding the police investigation developed a momentum of their own, and until black protest aimed directly at the institutions which manufacture news had drawn attention to the deaths and the official silence by marching through central London.

The disinterest of the press is, I believe, inexplicable without reference to the kind of signifier that 'black party' had become. Of course, the ten-day party that ended in a riot may have been fresh in the minds of editors, who, in any case may have been less interested in the deaths *because* the dead were black. My point is rather that the 'black party' had become such an entrenched sign of disorder and criminality, of a hedonistic and vicious black culture which was not recognizably British, that it had become fundamentally incompatible with the representation of black life and experience in any other form.

The multiple deaths of black youth at a party in an area renowned for its disorderly history – the deaths took place just a few yards from the sight of the Lewisham riot of 1977 – could not become news because the tragedy and the connotations of black culture in which the party was steeped somehow cancelled each other out.

A national march of blacks to protest against the handling of the investigation and the non-reporting of the media was organized by a group lead by the *Race Today* collective. The demonstration, which attracted between 15,000 and 20,000 people, assembled in Deptford on 2 March. It had a twofold aim: to strengthen the local campaign by a display of solidarity on the streets of South London's black neighbourhoods; and to dramatize the power relations involved in the struggle around the fire, by taking the march past some of the key political institutions and state apparatuses which had been seen to be suppressing the truth about the fire and had been implicated in the oppression of the black working class in general. The march moved up Fleet Street, home of the British newspaper industry, past the Courts of Justice, in a gesture of defiance to the racially partial versions of justice which they offered, and finally to Speakers' Corner in Hyde Park, the celebrated shrine of British free speech and tolerance of minority opinion.

The route reflected its organizers' sense of the important symbolic dimensions to effective urban political action. However, their understanding of the relationship between social and spatial dimensions of urban protest was not lost on the police who interrupted the march and attempted to end it prematurely as it reached the Thames. It was this intervention by the police which precipitated the violent conflict.

Some of the marchers who walked the 8-mile journey carried placards which read 'Jill Knight we want to rave tonight', a reference to the disparaging comments made about the 'ten-day party which ended in a riot' by the local MP, a right-wing Conservative.

The Policy Studies Institute survey of the police in London contains an account of how the fire and its aftermath were viewed from inside the force. Their report reveals how the fire 'had the effect of focusing racialist attitudes within the Met.' (Smith and Gray, 1983), rapidly becoming an object of humour between officers at street level.

1st PC   Do you know what they've renamed Deptford?
2nd PC   No, what have they renamed it?
1st PC   Blackfriars.

One officer described the march as 'hundreds of rampaging niggers'; another

made it clear that the march had been a 'defeat' for the police, 'though I managed to hit a nigger in the mouth' (holding out his hand to show a small mark) 'This is where the nigger's teeth went in'. Someone else commented, 'I hope you've had your tetanus jab' to general laughter. The discussion ended with the officers agreeing that 'they' were 'animals' and that 'they should be shot'. . . . There was . . . further talk about blacks being 'animals' and 'bestial'.

103

When one of the researchers registered 'gentle disagreement' with these views, a Chief Inspector said:

The American, when they were dealing with their, what they call little banana republic, they had to invent the Colt. 45 because that's the only thing that would stop a spade. If a nigger's coming straight at you, you can put a .38 straight through him and he'll keep coming'.

These images and arguments are an interesting insight into the distinct types of racist ideology and reasoning which inform the occupational culture of rank and file police work. For our purposes, they are also important because they establish a link between black political protest and the bestial qualities of blacks as perceived by police. The link between black crimes and black protest is secured not by reference to the cultural criteria characteristic of the new racism but by the importation of vulgar biological ones. The effect is essentially the same: blacks are a distinct group which expresses its obvious differences in acts of violence. These occasionally claim a spurious justification in ethnic politics.

Whether or not intended by police as a direct response to these protests and the 'defeat' which they may have represented, it was only shortly afterwards that 'Swamp '81', the mass 'stop and search' operation that immediately preceded the Brixton riots of 1981, was launched. Ten squads of police were involved in the operation which began four days before the first outbreak of rioting. During this period 943 people were stopped and searched before the first outbreak in the Brixton area. Of these, seventy-five were charged, one for robbery. It is impossible to discover how many suspects were eventually tried and found guilty.

The content of the riots and their inspiration, particularly the extent to which they may have been motivated by antipathy towards the police, cannot be evaluated here. This chapter is only concerned with the images and representations of black criminality which they generated and reproduced. Lord Scarman's report in the first phase of the riots in Brixton is a crucial document in the history of this discourse on the black community. It set the official seal on a definition of the origins and extent of black crime and tied these to what were felt to be distinct patterns of politics and family life, characteristic of black culture.

Scarman's discussion of the black community in the Brixton area (HMSO, 1981), begins with a section on the family which reproduces the stereotyped image of black households beset by generational conflict and torn asunder by antagonism between authoritarian parents, who are inclined towards Victorian-style discipline and their British-born children who operate with a more permissive set of mores. The pathological character of these households is established in the text by a discussion of the effects of male absence and of male
104

presence which is 'supportive but seldom dominant'. According to Scarman, the resulting 'matriarchy' undergoes 'destructive changes' under the impact of British social conditions and the disintegration of this basic structure of life is part of the chain reaction which ended in the Brixton riot:

Without close parental support, with no job to go to, and with few recreational facilities available, the young black person makes his life in the streets and in the seedy commercially run clubs of Brixton. There he meets criminals, who appear to have no difficulty in obtaining the benefits of a materialist society.

The process described by Scarman can be summarized in Figure 1. It is important because it forms a significant junction between the forms and images of 'common sense' or folk racism and the sociologically credible accounts of black life which have emerged from scholars in the sub-discipline of 'race relations'.

The intensity at which this cycle operates is determined by poverty, and in some of the more sophisticated versions of the theory, by racial discrimination and prejudice as well (Lea and Young, 1984). Scarman views riotous protest and violent criminal behaviour as alternative solutions to the political and economic problems encountered by young blacks.

The accumulation of these anxieties and frustrations and the limited opportunities of airing their grievances at national level in British society encourage them [black youth] to protest on the streets. And it is regrettably also true that some are tempted by their deprivations into crime, particularly street-crime – robbery, car theft and pick-pocketing offences: in other words, some of them go 'mugging'. They live their lives on the street, having often nothing better to do; they make their protest there: and some of them live off street crime. The recipe for a clash with the police is therefore ready-mixed.

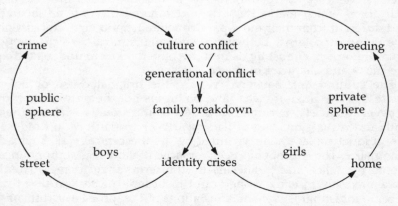

Figure 2 The cycle of pathological and deviant black culture

Although he retreats from the view that these circumstances can be called causes of the riot, he emphasizes that they constituted a set of social conditions 'which create a pre-disposition towards violent protest'. Crime and protest are viewed as alternative responses but there is an area of overlap identified between them and this is where Scarman's discussion of the role of Rastafarians is located.

He repeats the old charge that the 'outward signs of the faith' have been appropriated by 'young hooligans' to the point at which the minority of genuine, spiritual adherents risk being 'overwhelmed by the wild and the lawless'. The degree of legitimate protest represented by the 'essentially humble and sad' Rasta who is occupied by nothing more than 'his aspiration – the return to Africa from exile in "Babylon" ' is corrupted by the encroachment of these 'imitators' who, externally indistinguishable from the authentic cultists, commit wrongs in their name. It is the external symbols of Rastafari – 'the dreadlocks, the headgear and the colours' – which allow or encourage this ambiguity to persist, cementing the fundamental idea that the acts of criminality which are identified as objects of concern are somehow representative of cultural tendencies.

Scarman concludes that 'there was a strong racial element in the riots'. The meaning of his phrase is not completely clear but it seems to signify something more than the skin colour of the rioters. It suggests that the 'outburst of anger and resentment by young blacks against the police', in which the origins of the riot can be identified, was in itself somehow 'racial'.

The report reveals that, in the immediate area of the disturbances, blacks are some 30 per cent of the overall population and 50 per cent in the 19 to 21 age group. This points to the conclusion that the deprived social conditions of the area were shared by many who were not Afro-Caribbean by descent and who did not opt to express their 'anxieties and frustrations' by means of riotous protest. It is only 'race' which marks those who detonated the riots as separate and different from their more passive white neighbours. The distinctive cultural patterns, both expressive and familial, which emerge from the report, almost by default, become the key to understanding the cause and character of the conflicts.

The cultural link between crime – the original cause of police interest in the Brixton area – and politics is not the only connection between them. Their common context – 'the street' – defines them both and reveals their essential similarity. Scarman's report indexes the gradual replacement of 'mugging' as the central sign for black criminality. The concept has been replaced in more recent pronouncements by police and politicians by the term 'street crime'. This is used precisely to elide robbery and disorderly protest so that they become indistinguishable manifestations of the same basic difficulty: a black population.

I have already identified the tendency to move away from simple offence-based categories towards an analysis of urban crime which is based on the idea of criminal areas. The concept of 'street crime' fits neatly into this departure and draws together the previously competing images of the isolated black 'mugger' and the disorderly black crowd into a single shorthand term with greater explanatory power than either of its constituent elements.

The need to be seen to respond to the scale of social and economic problems described in Scarman's report involved the Met. in an attempt to construct a more systematic and strategic relationship with other governmental agencies and institutions. This initiative was pioneered by Sir Kenneth Newman who succeeded Sir David McNee as Met. Commissioner in October 1982. It has been conducted under the heading of 'multi-agency policing' and is clearly more compatible with an area-based approach in which the high-crime neighbour-hoods or parts of neighbourhoods could be targeted and subjected to particularly intense forms of police surveillance and control. Stat-istics for 'racial' offences still played a part in the means of identifying these high-crime areas and the idea that they were also areas in which street disorder could break out at any time is very much the product of the post-Scarman period. Multi-agency tactics were therefore combined with the development of an increased militarized capacity and a tighter grip on the flow of information relating to public order 'flashpoints' as they became known. In October 1984, the Commissioner described the effects of this new policy to Westminster Chamber of Commerce:

During the summer this year there were many mini-riots which had the potential to escalate to Brixton 1981 proportions. But they were quickly and effectively extinguished. So effectively indeed that they hardly rated a mention in the press.[51]

Elsewhere, he identified the reasons why this militarized capacity had been introduced. Images of black crime and disorder were again prominent: 'It is the rough, difficult and potentially violent aspects of multi-ethnic areas that oblige police units having a more robust capability' (Newman, 1983a). The multi-agency strategy was prem-ised on a view of police and other social agencies working side by side in pursuit of what Newman has repeatedly called 'social control'. The disparate activities of the various agencies involved are linked along a continuum of professionalism and can be synchronized by police leadership and common responsibility for the enhancement of social order.

Policing is merely a sub-system of the total system of social control. The Departments of Education, Health and Social Services, Environment and Manpower Services are the most obvious agencies capable of making an impact on the quality of social control. . . . Perhaps we should use the expression 'Social Control' in a benign sense, to provide a unifying concept within which the activities of police and other agencies can be co-ordinated. Each component of the social control system should examine its policies and operations and order its priorities towards a unified strategy for addressing the worst aspects of social disorganisation, particularly those associated with crime and the fear of crime.

The image of disorderly and criminally-inclined black youth was introduced yet again to demonstrate the common interests of police and other governmental agencies. If their common purpose was 'social control', it was a version of that control which was, in public discourse at least, to describe black youth as its primary object.

Many agencies are equally responsible for the communal good and find themselves similarly locked in conflict with black adolescents. I am sure that solutions lie in the sharing of perceptions not only with these agencies but, more vitally, with those who have managed to gain the trust of the black teenager (HMSO, 1984, p. 47).

Newman has also specified the scope and type of threat to social order which these young people represent. His analysis of them marks the end of our archaeological inquiry because it departs radically from the patterns of the past. Unlike his predecessors, he does not locate the source of the threat blacks pose in the criminal acts which they commit. These are accepted as a problem but are allocated a subsidiary role. The substantive danger which emanates from inner-city pockets of disorderly values and street protest arises not from 'mugging' or riots but from the symbolism of these areas; in particular, their negative symbolism for popular ideas of police capacity and power. These areas have become symbols of opposition which are counterproductive in the police campaign to 'create an ethos in society which makes crime unacceptable':

Throughout London there are locations where unemployed youth – often black youth – congregate; where the sale and purchase of drugs, the exchange of stolen property and illegal drinking and gaming is not uncommon [sic]. The youths regard these locations as their territory. Police are viewed as intruders, the symbol of authority – largely white authority – in a society that is responsible for all their grievances about unemployment, prejudice and discrimination. They equate closely with the criminal rookeries of Dickensian London (Newman, 1983b).

The existence of these areas comprises a threat which is less to do with any immediate lawlessness they contain than with their capacity to convey the limitations of police power and to signify the fragile nature of the order which police are able to impose:

If allowed to continue, locations with these characteristics assume symbolic importance a negative symbolism of the inability of the police to maintain order. Their existence encourages law breaking elsewhere, affects public

108

perceptions of police effectiveness, heightens the fear of crime and reinforces the phenomenon of urban decay.

Newman is doing more than just recognizing the gap between the actual (instrumental) struggle to impose order at street level and the (symbolic) struggle over representations of crime, authority and disorder. He is arguing not only that these two dimensions of policing do not directly correspond to each other but also that the struggle over signs and images, particularly those which involve blacks, has become more important for the maintenance of order than the actual law-breaking that they denote.

His words contain an acknowledgement of the centrality of black criminality to perception of the urban crisis in general as well as a recognition of the potency which the image of the black law-breaker has now acquired. This is a potency which now threatens to undermine the authority of the police who have brought it into the centre of popular politics. He is perhaps striving to close the Pandora's box which the race–crime theme has become. Black crime and disorder must be extinguished not because they effect change, social or political instability, or even because they diminish the quality of life in the inner-city areas where neighbourliness supposedly evaporates under the burden of high-crime rates, but because they signify the limits to the order of public authority with which police are identified.

Conclusion

This examination of the imagery of black criminality is necessary to the overall argument of this book not simply because the antagonism between blacks and the police has been a consistent and primary factor in the process of 'race' formation which has shaped black settlers in Britain into a political community. The idea that blacks are a high crime group and the related notion that their criminality is an expression of their distinctive culture have become integral to British racism in the period since the 'rivers of blood' speech.

I am suggesting that the view of the blacks as innately criminal, or at least more criminal than the white neighbours whose deprivation they share, which became 'common sense' during the early 1970s, is crucial to the development of new definitions of the black problem and new types of racial language and reasoning. As culture displaced anxiety about the volume of black settlement, crime came to occupy the place which sexuality, miscegenation and disease had held as the central themes and images in the earlier discourses of 'race'. Crime, in the form of both street disorder and robbery was gradually identified as an *expression of black culture* which was in turn defined as a cycle in which the negative effects of 'black matriarchy' and family pathology wrought destructive changes on the inner city by literally breeding deviancy out of deprivation and discrimination. To plead that this is recognized is not to deny that blacks have sometimes been identified as the perpetrators of crimes which resemble the stereotyped image of the 'mugging'.

What must be explained is the durability of these images and their remarkable ability to act both as a focus for popular anxiety about crime in general and as a sign for national decline, crisis and chaos. The element of blackness is crucial to how they work.

Sir Kenneth Newman's distinction between the actual crimes which blacks commit and the symbolism with which the representation of these crimes has become endowed is highly significant. It points to the autonomy which the ideology of racism has acquired from the reality measured by levels of recorded crime in which blacks are either perpetrator or victim. The manner in which anxiety about black crime has provided hubs for the wheels of popular racism is an extraordinary process which is connected with the day to day struggle of police to maintain order and control at street level and, at a different point, to the political conflicts which mark Britain's move towards more authoritarian modes of government intervention and social regulation (Gilroy and Sim, 1985) during the 1970s and 1980s. It cannot, though, be reduced to either of these tendencies and must be examined in detail on its own as well as in its relationship to them. The 'thin red line' of troops in the colonial front line, standing between us and them, between black and white, has been translated into the 'thin blue line' of police, personifying the law. Black transgressions of it become further evidence of their alien character and their distance from the substantive, historical forms of Britishness which are the property of white culture.

As with the theme of 'race' and nation examined in the previous chapter, part of what makes this form of racism novel is its ability to unite and transcend the conflicting positions of formal politics. The ideas that black crime is expressive of black 'ethnicity' and that black crime can be used to illustrate the problems of crime in general have recently been featured in analyses which announce themselves as socialist as well as those which shelter under the banner of conservatism. The balance between biological and cultural factors in determining ethnicity is, of course, weighed differently, but where culture or sub-culture is defined as a fixed and impermeable property of human life these are differences of degree rather than any fundamental divergence.

The populist potential of the black crime theme is another factor which has made it attractive to sections of the left, particularly those who appear to regard the Conservatives' apparent monopoly of the law and order issue with jealousy and resentment (Birley and Bright, 1985).

The discourse of black criminality has been articulated not just by the police who have sought to mobilize popular support for the increase of their resources and the expansion of their powers, but by the extreme right who have organized marches and protest against the levels of black crime and sought to link these fears to the argument for repatriation. The readiness and speed with which these links have been made and reproduced should, therefore, contain a note of warning to those who would seek to use anxiety about black crime as a means to renovate Labour's political relationship with disenchanted white voters in inner-city areas.

The racial connotations of these images and their concrete attachments to the languages, aims and organizations of overtly racist groups will not simply evaporate while socialists struggle to hitch the law and order issue to their own political purposes. They are more likely to remain and drag the political energies of the white working class down into the depths of racism and reaction.

Notes

1 *Sun*, 19.3.85
2 *Standard*, 25.3.85.
3 *Observer*, 2.9.84. See also the report of the criminal activities of the 'Killerman Gold Posse' (a South London gang) in the *Daily Mail*, 8.3.86.

London's young blacks picked up the word [posse] from Western films which often feature posses of men on horseback gaining strength from numbers, thundering out of town to wreak revenge. Police in high-crime areas such as Brixton say that virtually every black male between the ages of 13 and 24 now belongs to a posse. They give them exotic names which they daub on the walls of their housing estates.

The 'Killer Man Gold Posse' was not an all-male gang. Sixteen-year-old Debra 'Styler' Read, so named because of her expensive taste in clothes, called the female judge a bitch as she walked from the courtroom.

4 Michael Foucault describes the archaeological approach at the beginning of his *The Order of Things*

. . . such an analysis does not belong to the history of ideas or of science: it is rather an inquiry whose aim is to rediscover on what basis knowledge and theory became possible; within what space of order knowledge was constituted; on the basis of what historical a priori, and in the element of what positivity, ideas could appear, sciences be established, experience be reflected in philosophies, rationalities formed, only, perhaps, to dissolve and vanish soon afterwards (Foucault, 1970, pp. xxi-xxii).

5 Hall *et al.*, *Policing The Crisis* and the CCCS volume, *The Empire Strikes Back*, are the texts I have in mind here.

6   *Spectator*, 19.7.1862, quoted by Jennifer Davis (1980, p. 199).
7   Davis (1980), p. 203.
8   *Daily News*, 11.9.1888.
9   House of Commons *Hansard*, 29.1.1902, col. 1278.
10 House of Commons *Hansard*, 1.11.1912, cols 768–99.
11 Stedman Jones, *Outcast London*, chapter 6.
12 Cyril Osbourne MP, House of Commons *Hansard*, 5.12.1958, col. 1552.
13 *The Times*, 2.10.1911.
14 Public Records Office (PRO) CAB, 129/65,C (54) p. 34.
15 PRO CAB, 129/66, C (54), p. 94.
16 *Guardian* 1.12.65.
17 Published by Chatto, London 1964, pp. 50–1.
18 *Picture Post*, October 1954.
19 House of Commons *Hansard*, 29.10.58, cols 198–9.
20 *The Times*, 3.9.58.
21 *The Times*, 4.9.58.
22 *The Times*, 28.1.65.
23 Leslie Frewin and Co. (London 1966).
24 House of Lords *Hansard*, 12.3.62, cols 71–2.
25 ibid. p. 97; see also Norman Pannell's contribution to *Immigration. What is The Answer? Two Opposing Views*, N. Pannell and F. Brockway (Routledge, London 1965).
26 *The Times*, 20.1.65.
27 *British Journal of Venereal Diseases* 39 (1965), pp. 214–24. See for a different view, which laid the blame on white women rather than black men, British Medical Association, *Report of The Working Party on The Medical Examination of Immigrants* (BMA, 1965).
28 *The Times*, 20.11.64.
29 *The Times*, 28.1.65.
30 *The Times*, 18.1.65.
31 *Leamington Spa Courier*, 16.4.65.
32 *Daily Telegraph*, 12.4.76.
33 Most notably in *Policing The Crisis* and *The Empire Strikes Back*.
34 HMSO, 1972, Select Committee on Race Relations and Immigration *Police/Immigrant Relations Vol.1.* (471–1).
35 *Race Today*, October 1976.
36 The cases of the Bradford 12, the Newham 7 and the Newham 8 provide the best examples here. In each case a vigorous community campaign was pursued hand in hand with a critical legal strategy which was aimed not merely at securing acquittals but at raising political issues in the courtroom.
37 This phrase apparently comes from a speech which Mark gave to the Institute of Journalists on 30 November 1971. It is quoted by Robert Reiner in *The Politics of The Police* (Harvester Press, Brighton 1985), p. 139.
38 *Evening Standard*, 26.4.78.

39   *Daily Mirror*, 31.8.76.
40   *Daily Mirror*, 31.8.76.
41   *Daily Telegraph*, 31.8.76.
42   *Evening Standard*, 26.4.78.
43   The best sources here are The Institute of Race Relations' 1979 pamphlet *The Police Against Black People*; The Hackney CRE report *Policing In Hackney. A record of HCRE's Experience 1978–82* (1983), and *The Final Report of The Working Party into Community/Police Relations in Lambeth* (London Borough of Lambeth, 1981).
44   *Evening News*, 25.9.78.
45   *The Times*, 5.4.80.
46   *Bristol Evening Post*, 3.4.80.
47   *Sunday Times*, 6.4.80.
48   *Daily Mail*, 4.6.82.
49   *Daily Mirror*, 3.1.81.
50   *Sun*, 3.1.81.
51   *Guardian*, 17.10.84.

4 Two sides of anti-racism

In so far as contemporary movements in industrial societies do not take the forms predicted by an analysis of nineteenth century capitalism, the left has not tried to understand these movements, but rather has tended simply to disapprove of them. The wrong people have mobilized, for they are not truly the industrial proletariat. Or they haved mobilized around the wrong organizational and political strategies. The movements of the people disappoint the doctrine, and so the movements are dismissed (Frances Fox Piven and Richard Cloward).

'To hell with the US Army colour bar! We want our coloured sweet hearts!' shouted hundreds of English girls who tried to break into an American army camp at Bristol when coloured troops, who recently arrived in this country from Germany, were about to embark for America. British police officers had to be called to protect the coloured soldiers from being mobbed by the hysterical girls, whose ages ranged between seventeen and twenty-four. Kissing and embracing went on for hours until, with a special reinforcement of military police, the couples were separated and the negroes forced back to their barracks (George Padmore).

The previous chapter looked at the ideological content of the new racism and in particular at the representations of legality and law-breaking which exist at its core, tying the political problems which originate in the surveillance and control of disorderly black populations in urban areas to the imagery of a nation beset by chaos and crisis.

This chapter examines recent political organizations and movements which have defined themselves as anti-racist. This is necessary for two main reasons. First, to show that the content of 'anti-racism' has not always been a direct response to the ideologies and practices of racism, and second, to look at the relationship between anti-racist politics and political formations more readily identifiable as expressions of class antagonism and consciousness.

This chapter will argue that the link between the language and practice of anti-racist politics and those of class politics is a tenuous one but that anti-racist politics have, at key points during the last ten years, articulated a means of representing class outside of the categories in which it has been constructed and reproduced by means of 'race'.

114

The process by which concern about crime displaced other themes and became the central sign for the problem of 'race' is an important reminder that 'race' politics has no givens, no essential meanings or preferred images which establish its continuity beyond the limits of history and struggle. Like the gradual synonymity of 'race' and nation which betrays the genesis of ethnic absolutism and its new racism, postponing and mediating the effects of national crisis, it underlines the point that the political conflicts which give 'race' substance can change significantly from one historical period to the next. To explore these arguments further, this chapter will address two periods in the recent history of anti-racism in Britain, comparing the different understandings of 'race' and anti-racism which have been expressed by organizations and movements which have declared themselves to be primarily anti-racist in their orientation.

Their political languages and some of the strategic and tactical questions raised by them and by the contrast between them will be examined. The more formal and institutionally-based politics of anti-racism which emerged in the interventions of Labour local authorities, particularly the Greater London Council (GLC) in the aftermath of the 1981 riots have been chosen to represent one pole of political activity. The anti-racist mass movement of the late 1970s, specifically Rock Against Racism (RAR) and the Anti Nazi League (ANL), comprises the other. These have been selected because each has a clear and substantial commitment to the cultural dimensions of struggle, moving beyond the confines of formal politics into the realm of popular discourses, and because each articulates in a different way with a class politics.

The first is associated with the institutions and agencies of socialist local governments and the second was directly influenced by the practice of far left groups, particularly the Socialist Workers' Party (SWP) which sought to incline the anti-racist movement in the direction of class consciousness and solidarity through developing a strategy guided by the slogan 'Black and White Unite and Fight'.

It is immediately necessary to emphasize that in looking at anti-racism as a political phenomenon, I will not be concerned with the self-organization and independent struggles of the black communities. The history of their struggles requires a broader and more detailed analysis than can be conducted under the heading of anti-racism. Political organization and struggle which have identified and promoted themselves as anti-racist are of more interest here not only because they have received virtually no attention from other writers, but because the commitment to a practical anti-racist politics necessarily generates an interesting commentary on and negotiation of actual relationships between black and white people.

The autonomous organization of blacks deals with these issues only intermittently and cannot be either analysed or described as an

115

expression of 'anti-racism'. This is not to deny that the struggles of blacks in this country may be anti-racist in that part of their effect may be to oppose and dismantle racist institutions and ideologies. However, as we shall see in the next chapter, the aim and inspiration of these struggles has not usually been identified as anti-racism by those who have developed and organized them.

We will also see in the next chapter that where the aims and objectives of black struggles are made clear, they are both more extensive and more modest than the anti-racist label suggests. More modest because these struggles define themselves by their relationship to the everyday experience of their protagonists and the need to address and ameliorate concrete grievances at this level; more extensive because an elaborate and sophisticated critique of social structure and relations of contemporary capitalism has been a consistent if not a continuous feature of the 'racial' politics and culture from which these struggles have sprung. These two tendencies shape each other and their reciprocity dissolves the old distinction between reformist and revolutionary modes of political action. The elimination of racism is only rarely announced as the primary object of these struggles. The concrete settings in which racial subordination is experienced may shape the patterns of discontent which precede protest so that they do not progress beyond the immediate circumstances in which spontaneous resistance or accommodation are the most likely responses. People do not encounter racism in general or in the abstract, they feel the effects of its particular expressions: poor housing, unemployment, repatriation, violence or aggressive indifference. Where the experience of these and other concrete manifestations of exploitation and oppression which work by means of 'race' does develop into an abstract conceptualization capable of relating diverse and contradictory experiences into a unified whole, there is no reason why this understanding of social and political power relations should be contained at the level of 'race'. If the various sites in which oppression is felt are linked by a concept of racism, understood not as a separate or external feature of society but as an integral element in a system or process, the limits to a 'racial' explanation may be readily visible. Indeed the attempt to make 'race' always already a meaningful factor, in other words to racialize social and political phenomena, may be itself identified as part of the 'race' problem.[1]

It is not that the people who are actually affected by racism are incapable of thinking abstractly about the character of the oppression which determines their lives, but rather that the understanding of it, revealed in their expressive culture at least, is both too sophisticated and too practical to be diverted into the belief that 'race' is a simple cause rather than a complex effect of the underlying problems they face.

116

This chapter turns away from these issues to look instead at movements and patterns of political organization in which 'anti-racism' rather than black liberation has been advanced as the primary object of struggle. Organizations of this type have directed their efforts and their appeal more towards whites than blacks. They have been concerned not directly with the enhancement of the power of the oppressed or disadvantaged groups but with the development of racially harmonious social and political relations.

Before we look at these struggles in detail it is necessary to grasp that black liberation and anti-racism are two quite distinct orientations which get regularly confused in British racial politics. They are not the same and may actively conflict. Tension may exist, for example, between an anti-racist pluralism which allocates 'race' the status of a substantive difference but seeks to detach it from the stigma of domination and subordination, and other anti-racist positions which deny that 'race' has any effectivity of its own. This is often part of a commitment to the idea that either or both class and gender are more profound and more important.

Anti-racism in the 1970s

Blacks have been actively organizing in defence of their lives and communities ever since they set foot in Britain. Several writers have looked at these patterns of self-organization in greater detail than is possible here (Hiro, 1971; Abdul-Malik, 1968; Pryer, 1984; Sivanandan, 1982). Their histories have also occasionally drawn attention to the anti-racist organizations and struggles created during the 1950s and 1960s, which brought black and white together and formed a significant counterpart to the movements for black liberation in Britain and in its colonized countries.

The rise and demise of organizations such as the Co-ordinating Committee Against Racial Discrimination (CCARD) formed to oppose the 1961 Commonwealth Immigrants Bill and the Campaign Against Racial Discrimination (CARD) inaugurated in February 1965 after a visit to London by Dr Martin Luther King and dedicated to campaigning for the elimination of discrimination in civil society and in the immigration legislation, are important subjects for further research (Glean, 1973). Yet the anti-racisms of the 1970s are even less well known. That decade contained a series of qualitative shifts in the racial politics of Britain. The 1971 Immigration Act brought an end to primary immigration and instituted a new pattern of internal control and surveillance of black settlers. It was paralleled by a new vocabulary of 'race' and crime which grew in the aftermath of the first panic over 'mugging'. These developments are two of the most important from the point of view of black self-organization. However,

117

the expansion and consolidation of organizations of the extreme, neo-fascist right was also to transform decisively the meaning of anti-racism. Dilip Hiro points to the existence of street level harassment and other activity by extreme racist groups including the British Ku Klux Klan as early as 1965, two years before the National Front (NF) was formed. Threatening letters to the London secretary of CARD had promised 'concerted efforts against West Indians, specially those living with white women' (1971). It was the entry of these groups into the process of electoral politics which acted as a catalyst for the creation of anti-fascist/anti-racist committees as an outgrowth of the organized labour movement in Britain's major towns and cities during the early and mid 1970s.

The NF had enjoyed its first party political broadcast during the February 1974 election and had fielded fifty-four candidates, a substantial increase from 1970 when only ten had stood. The party's journal, *Spearhead*, told its readers in January 1974 that 'It need hardly be said that our election campaign now takes absolute priority over everything else.'

In the second election of that year, the Front fielded ninety candidates who obtained 113,844 votes. In the local government elections of May 1974, the NF averaged nearly 10 per cent of the poll in several districts of London (Fielding, 1981), and in a by-election at Newham South, beat the Conservative candidate and took 11.5 per cent of the total votes cast.

In June 1974 the anti-fascist forces organized a march and picket of a National Front meeting at Conway Hall in Red Lion Square. The resulting confrontation between demonstrators and the police ended with the death of one protester, Kevin Gately, who had been part of the International Marxist Group's contingent on the demonstration (Scarman, 1975; Clutterbuck, 1978). The fascists had been using the hall for meetings during the four years before 1974 and anti-fascist pickets of these meetings had begun in October 1973. Gately was claimed as something of a martyr to the re-born cause of anti-fascism. His death was seen as proof of the destructive nature of the extreme and anti-democratic forces which had been reconstituted on British streets, twenty-nine years after the war which had been fought to free Europe of fascist tyranny.

Trades Unionists of the older generation were doubly shocked when reaching for their newspapers on the 16th June 1974. Firstly they learnt of the tragic death in a central London street of a young man, Kevin Gately. Then they read deeper to discover the circumstances of his death. They were to find that the ugliest and most brutal of twentieth century movements – fascism – which they had dearly hoped was buried forever in 1945, had returned to plague us anew (Nicholson, 1974).

These words begin a pamphlet issued by the Transport and General

Workers' Union which set out to alert its members and other trades unionists to the growing danger of British neo-fascism. Jack Jones's introduction to the pamphlet was clear about why the fascist groups should be opposed but the reasons he cites are unconnected with the experience of black settlers, make no mention of Britain's black population and contain no acknowledgement of the problem of racism as something distinct from, though connected to, fascism: 'Although they may deny it the "National Front" is the modern version of the Fascism of Hitler, Mussolini and Mosley.'

This definition of British neo-fascism exclusively in terms of the fascisms of the past against which the British had enjoyed their finest hours in battle, recurs again and again in the politics of anti-racism during the 1970s. Jones's words betray the central tension in the politics of the anti-racist struggle, namely the tendency to conceive of neo-fascism and racism as distinct and unrelated problems and to make the popular memory of the Second World War the dominant source of images with which to mobilize against the dangers of contemporary racism.

It is almost as though the activities of the National Front and similar groups only become a problem when they threaten democracy by their participation in its electoral system and only visible where a sham patriotism is invoked. Their record of racial violence against black individuals and communities remained either unseen or was not thought to have a place in the development of a socialist anti-fascist politics.

An informal and locally-based network of anti-fascist/anti-racist committees grew in the period between 1973 and 1976. It is during this period that the emergent anti-fascist movement began to express itself as a self-conscious political formation and to create its own organs for communication and debate. Though its primary audience lay in the black communities rather than among anti-racists, the journal *Race Today* (hijacked from the Institute of Race Relations and re-oriented by its activist editorial collective) had an important role in these discussions. The magazine's central place in the struggles between blacks and the police, around education and housing in the East End of London and in the attempt to build links between black political organizations in different parts of Britain as well as between British blacks and radical struggles elsewhere in the world, all made considerable input into what anti-racism was to mean.

Race Today posed a consistent challenge to the idea that black liberation was reducible to 'anti-racism' and to the related fallacy that the struggle against racism could be contained by the need to oppose the neo-fascist groups. At the opposite pole of the embryonic anti-racist movement was the anti-fascist magazine *Searchlight*. It had been founded in February 1975 with the aim of consolidating the anti-fascist forces so that they could challenge the electoral and popular

119

success of the NF. The magazine's first editorial took its cue from the slogan of the anti-fascist movement of the 1930s, 'They Shall Not Pass'. This motto was used as a caption for the magazine's front cover, a photograph of a young male neo-fascist with dark glasses, leather jacket and quiff, rather incongruously holding a Union Jack. The mandate for a new anti-fascism announced by the magazine derived from the need to defend democracy from the encroachments of the extreme right. *Searchlight* combined detailed information on the activities and histories of the extreme right groups with coverage of fascist violence and race related stories from mainstream and local press.

Though the network of local groups developed and the need to combat the growth of neo-fascist organizations was more widely accepted as the Nazi backgrounds of the NF leadership were gradually revealed, anti-fascist organizing remained locally-oriented and essentially small scale. A move towards anti-racist rather than anti-fascist politics was initiated by the conflict between blacks and the police which grew steadily after 1973 and culminated in the 'Long Hot Summer' of 1976 when London's young blacks defeated the Metropolitan Police at the Notting Hill Carnival and major confrontations with the police took place in Southall and in Birmingham. The neo-fascists had organized a 'March Against Mugging' in September 1975 under the slogan 'Stop The Muggers. 80% of muggers are black. 85% of victims are white.' This was significant not simply for its open defiance of the laws on incitement to racial hatred and the new tactic of provocative marches through black areas but for the convergence it represented between the official, respectable politics of race signalled by the authoritative official crime statistics and the street level appeal of the neo-fascist groups who had seized the issue of black crime and begun to refine it into a populist weapon which could prove the wisdom of their distinctive solution to Britain's race problems – repatriation.

The process in which anti-fascist and anti-racist activism became a movement rather than an aggregate of uneven and disparate local groups significantly had its origins outside the realm of politics. It relied for its development on networks of culture and communication in which the voice of the left was scarcely discernible and it drew its momentum from the informal and organic relationship between black and white youth which sprung up in the shadow of 1970s youth culture.

Rock Against Racism (RAR) was formed by a small group of activists in or around the Socialist Workers' Party (SWP) in August 1976. Its founders wrote to the music press inviting support for an antiracist stance in answer to the racist pronouncements of rock stars like Eric Clapton,[2] who had expressed his admiration for Enoch Powell on several occasions, and David Bowie,[3] who had not only said that Britain was in need of a right-wing dictatorship but declared Hitler to be 'the first superstar'. The image of Bowie beside Hitler and Powell was to recur in RAR's visuals. The SWP had made anti-fascist organizing a major priority during the summer of 1976 and the original RAR letter was heavily derivative of their analysis and political style. It called for black and white to unite and fight along the fundamental lines of class. However, it deviated sharply from this traditional leftism in its insistence on the autonomous value of youth cultures and on the radical potential of 'rock' and its offshoots. This position seems to have been part of a wider argument about the value of populist struggle. 'Rock was and still can be a real progressive culture, not a packaged mail-order stick on nightmare of mediocre garbage. Keep the faith, black and white unite and fight.'[4] Following this intervention, the RAR group produced the first issue of its fanzine *Temporary Hoarding* for the 1977 Mayday celebrations at the Roundhouse in London (Huddle, 1978). The appearance of RAR coincided precisely with the growth of punk and the two develop-ments were very closely intertwined, with punk supplying an oppo-sitional language through which RAR anti-racism could speak a truly populist politics. The first issue of *Temporary Hoarding* made this relationship explicit and asserted the fundamental commitment to music which characterized the early RAR output. 'We want Rebel music, Street music. Music that breaks down peoples' fear of one another. Crisis music. Now music. Music that knows who the real enemy is. Rock against Racism. Love Music Hate Racism.' This kind of appeal was later to be expressed in slogans which made an even more overt plea for a non-sectarian transcendance of the various sub-cultural styles and identities and asserted a vision of the musics and the styles they had created in a pluralist coalition: 'Reggae Soul Rock and Roll Jazz-Funk and Punk Our music' read RAR's poster/broadsheet. The first issue coupled practical advice for the organizers of RAR gigs with some powerful photomontages and a short, didactic article 'What is racism?' by David Widgery. He coupled an overview of the development of racism in Britain's crisis with an important political argument which showed that from the start RAR was fighting for its corner in an anti-fascist/anti-racist movement which was reluctant to face the novelty of the forms in which racism was expressing itself.

The definition of racism proposed by Widgery and expanded in RAR's practice over the next three years stressed that racism linked the activity of the neo-fascists directly to the actions of state agencies, particularly the courts, police and immigration authorities.

The problem is not just the new fascists from the old slime a master race whose idea of heroism is ambushing single blacks in darkened streets. These private attacks whose intention, to cow and brutalise, won't work if the

121

community they seek to terrorise instead organises itself. But when the state backs up racialism it's different. Outwardly respectable but inside fired with the same mentality and the same fears, the bigger danger is the racist magistrates with the cold sneering authority, the immigration men who mock an Asian mother as she gives birth to a dead child on their office floor, policemen for whom answering back is a crime and every black kid with pride is a challenge.

The strategic consequences of this position can be spelled out. Racism was there to be smashed, and the activity involved in smashing it was neatly counterposed to the passivity of sitting back and watching it unfold. The central problem perceived by this approach was the absence of adequate organization. The new stucture which RAR was creating would fill the gap. Just as *Sniffin' Glue*, the punk fanzine, included a couple of chord diagrams and then told its readers 'now go and form a band', *Temporary Hoarding* included a blueprint for doing RAR's political work. It would be implemented with the guidance and assistance of experienced and sympathetic SWP members and supporters. Yet the defeat of racism was not to be accomplished in the name of youth or even of a common class position though both were implied. The hatred of racism and its organic counterpart – the love of music – were enough to hold together a dynamic anti-racist movement of young people. RAR's audience, the anti-racist crowd, was conceived not only as consumers of the various youth cultures and styles but as a powerful force for change which, in its diversity, created something more than the simple sum of its constitutive elements.

This anti-racism drew attention to the complex race politics of all white pop music and grasped the importance of the black origins of even the whitest rock as a political contradiction for those who were moving towards racist consciousness and explanations of the crisis. The third issue of *Temporary Hoarding*, published to coincide with the 1977 Notting Hill Carnival, contained an obituary for Elvis which, though seemingly at odds with the punk orientation of the rest of the magazine, made these very points:

What Presley did in music was stunning. Everyone down in Memphis – which was the heart of the new South – 50% black population – stayed on their own side of the tracks or across the airwaves. Presley took the two and hurled them together. Black soul, hillbilly insistence. His fusion changed everything. It accelerated the Civil Rights movement. It jerked a dead generation alive. It changed the future. Sinatra symbolised a generation, Presley created one.[5]

Punk provided the circuitry which enabled these connections to be made, rendering, as Hebdige (1979) has argued, the hitherto coded and unacknowledged relationships between black and white styles an open and inescapable fact. Drawing on the language and style of roots culture in general and Rastafari in particular, punks produced not only their own critical and satirical commentary on the meaning and limits of white ethnicity but a conceptual framework for seeing and then analysing the social relations of what *Temporary Hoarding* called 'Labour Party Capitalist Britain'. The dread notion of 'Babylon System' allowed disparate and apparently contradictory expressions of the national crisis to be seen as a complex, interrelated whole, a coherent structure of which racism was a primary characteristic, exemplifying and symbolizing the unacceptable nature of the entire authoritarian capitalist edifice.

If the language and symbols of black culture provided the melody and harmony from which RAR would improvise its two-tone tunes, the key of its performances and the register of the movement was influenced by the general political mood of the period. Novel combinations of ethnicity, 'race' and national consciousness had emerged in popular celebrations of the Royal Silver Jubilee. This brought festivities – street parties, school holidays – and an explosion of monarchist memorabilia which pushed the icons and symbols of a royalist and patriotic definition of Britishness and the British nation to the fore.

The explosion of popular nationalism provided the punks with images of Britishness from which they could disassociate themselves and against which they could define their own, alternative definitions of the nation: past, present and future. No less than the upsurge of neo-fascist activity in the 1976–7 period, the Royal Jubilee formed the immediate context in which the relationship between racism and nationalism could be revealed and new forms of anti-racism created which were equally opposed to both.

The punks' assault on the central icons of patrician British nationalism, particularly the Queen's face (transformed by safety pins on the cover of the Sex Pistols' 'God Save The Queen' which was the number one record in Jubilee week), was an important symbolic manifestation of this element in their sub-culture. The ultimate talismans of the national culture they were rejecting – the Union Jack and the Royal visage – were used to generate a new political ideology which Hebdige has described as a 'white ethnicity' (1979). This both paralleled and answered the proscriptive blackness of the dread culture to which it was a cryptic affiliation.

Whether or not these strands within punk warrant the term ethnicity, they signify that the encounter with black culture in general and Rastafari in particular had changed the terms on which black and white young people engaged each other. From now on, 'race' could no longer be dealt with as a matter for private negotiation in the shadows of the ghetto blues dance or the inner-city shebeen where a token white presence might be acceptable. The rise of an articulate British racism, often aimed squarely at the distinct

123

experiences and preoccupations of the young, destroyed the possibility of essentially covert appropriations of black-style music and anger which had been the characteristic feature of the mod and skinhead eras. 'Race' had to be dealt with, acknowledged as a primary determinant of social life and, in the same breath, overcome. If contact with black culture was to be maintained, then a disavowal of whiteness was called for, not by the blacks themselves but by punk culture's own political momentum. This drew selectively on the input of RAR activists and supporters.

Some recognition of the persistent slippage between British and white was also required. Rather than constituting a wholly alternative Britishness which could justly be named an ethnic culture, these parts of punk were articulating a satirical commentary on the limits of ethnicity and 'race', on the very meaninglessness of whiteness which both neo-fascists (explicitly) and popular nationalism (implicitly) alike sought to endow with a mythic and metaphysical significance.

This was a struggle over the meaning of the nation and over the meaning of punk. It was to continue long after the heyday of the movement. In the March 1981 issue of the National Front journal, *Spearhead*, Eddie Morrison, an NF activist, argued that 'Punk rock and its attendant new wave style' were worthy of support from racial nationalists because they were 'totally white in origin' and 'carried a message of the frustration of the masses of White working-class youth'. He continued, 'Electronic music and New Waves Bands is [sic] a new style of White Folk music.'[6]

There were crucial ambiguities in the punk anthems which dealt directly with 'race' and sought to make a connection between the position of dispossessed whites and the experience of racism. The Stranglers' 'I Feel Like a Wog' and the Clash's 'White Man in the Hammersmith Palais' both featured almost continually in the Rock Against Communism chart in *Bulldog*, the paper of the Young National Front. They held the number one and number two positions as late as September 1982.

The attack on the Queen's portrait and on the Union Jack was as much a direct gesture to the neo-fascists as it was a reworking of the ideological themes and signs which had, in an earlier period, defined 'Swinging London' and turned Carnaby Street into a mecca for subculturalists from all over the overdeveloped world. The Sex Pistols' lead singer, John Lydon, pronounced frequently and at length on the subjects of 'race', nation and Britishness. He told one American journalist:

There's no such thing as patriotism any more. I don't care if it blows up . . . England never was free. It was always a load of bullshit. I'm surprised we [the Sex Pistols] aren't in jail for treason. . . . Punks and Niggers are almost the same thing . . . when I come to America I'm going straight to the ghetto . . . I'm not asking blacks to like us. That's irrelevant. It's just that we're doing something they'd want to do if they had the chance (Young, 1977).

Punk's leading musicians cemented their appropriation of black style and their hostility to both racist nationalism and nationalist racism in several records which recast reggae music in their own idiom. The similarities and the differences between punk and black styles were pinpointed. The best example of this is the Clash version of 'Police and Thieves', a tune which had been a roots hit in 1976 for Junior Murvin and which had blared out from a speaker dangled from an upstairs window when anti-fascist demonstrators attacked the National Front march in Lewisham during August 1977. It thus acquired a special place in the cultural history of the anti-racist movement of this period, symbolizing in itself the coming together of black and white in opposition to racism.

Another record, similarly created as a dread commentary on the state of Jamaica after Michael Manley's election victory of 1976 but masquerading as a mystical invocation of the apocalypse, was seized by the punks and given a central place in their cultural cosmology. This was 'Two Sevens Clash' by the roots vocal trio 'Culture', and like 'Police and Thieves' it became something of a punk anthem.

Though many punk bands refused to play reggae, the music remained a constant point of reference and a potent source of their poetics. It should also be remembered that the genesis of punk coincided with militant action by young blacks in the 1976 Notting Hill Carnival riot. The imagery of black, urban insurgency was particularly visible as the nation reflected on the carnival explosion and the defeat of the Metropolitan Police by mobs of stone-throwing youths. Understanding why black youth had turned on the police was, as we have seen in Chapter 3, now inseparable from reckoning with the cultural context in which the riot had occurred. The cultural backdrop to black combativity was important to punks also, though for rather different reasons. The street carnival, with its bass-heavy sound systems pumping out the new militant 'rockers' beat of reggae as the half bricks and bottles flew overhead, demonstrated to the punks the fundamental continuity of cultural expression with political action. The two were inextricably interwoven into a dense and uncompromising statement of black dissent which was a source of envy and of inspiration to a fledgling punk sensibility. This envy and its creative consequences were spelled out by the Clash in their song 'White Riot', described by one writer as the after-effect 'of being caught in the racial no-man's land between charging police and angry black youth at the Notting Hill Carnival riots of 1976' (Coon, 1977).

125

Black men have got a lotta problems
But they don't mind throwing a brick
But white men have too much school
Where they teach you to be thick
We go reading papers and wearing slippers

White riot I wanna Riot
White Riot A Riot of My Own

All the power is in the hands
of people rich enough to buy it
While we walk the streets
too chicken to even try it
And everybody does what they're told to do
And everybody eats supermarket soul food

White Riot I wanna Riot
White Riot A riot of My Own

The intimate political and ideological connections embodied in this musical relationship were given substance by RAR's efforts to put on gigs up and down the country in which black and white bands and their audiences could combine. The organization put on 200 events in just over one year. In these, the emphasis was on the creation of an experience in which the emptiness of 'race' could be experienced at first hand and its transcendance celebrated. The Clash were to maintain a link with RAR throughout its early years and were the main attraction of the RAR/ANL Carnival in East London in May 1978.

The effect of punk on RAR's ability to function effectively was not confined to its pronouncements on 'race' and nation. Punk style, like its anti-authoritarian ideology, was also borrowed, used and developed by RAR. It became an integral part of the movement's capacity to operate in a truly popular mode, a significant component in its ability to be political without being boring at a time when the NF was identified as being 'No Fun'. This can be seen most clearly from an examination of the visual design of RAR broadsheets and magazines. In breaking from what was felt to be a dour and therefore self-defeating leftist approach, almost as devoid of fun as drab fascist propaganda, RAR's designers, Ruth Gregory and Sid Shelton, David King, Roger Huddle, Red Saunders, Andy Dark, Rick Fawcett and others laid great emphasis on the visual appeal of their publications.

Huddle has described the design of early *Temporary Hoardings* as 'sometimes unreadable' but stressed that they were 'a genuine attempt to create some kind of media of pop imagery that would relate on a big scale'.[7] He continues:

We used to have arguments about how far you could push the style before it became unreadable, how many laws you could break. . . . Apart from using typewriters and felt tip pens, we could do a lot of things we couldn't do before. We tried to be free, which was also a problem because we had no audience feedback to discipline us.

The sense of infringement described by Huddle draws directly on punk aesthetics. *Temporary Hoarding*'s pages appropriated elements of what has been called the 'anti-design'[8] of the punk fanzines. Something of the same spirit guided the work of 'MINDA' the design duo responsible for the appearance of CARF – the pre-ANL paper of local anti-racist and anti-fascist groups – which had been produced bi-monthly from May 1977 onwards.[9]

Making the RAR broadsheet look good, exciting and powerful did more than just dent the left's obsession with the power of the written word. It went hand in hand with the idea that once it had been read, and its political content savoured and digested, the broadsheet would not be mere waste paper like any other periodical which had outlived its time.

The early issues of *Temporary Hoarding* were either folded so that they opened into a poster, or contained a pull-out sheet across their large centre spread. Issue 3, for example, opened into a montage calendar of authoritarian developments and popular resistance in Britain during the preceding twelve months. Images from RAR, the National Abortion Campaign, Soweto, Grunwick, punk, the Hull prison riot. Anti-Front demonstrations, the occupation of the Elizabeth Garrett Anderson Hospital for women, Northern Ireland, and the Agee and Hosenball campaign were blended and intercut beneath the slogan used by Michael Manley in his election campaign of the previous year 'A Year Under Heavy Manners'.

At the foot of the poster, Trotsky, Mao, Lenin, the Clash, Bob Marley, Bernadette McAliskey, Polly Styrene, Big Youth, Angela Davis, Arthur Scargill, Muddy Waters and other famous faces were grouped around the cut up slogan 'We shall be Free' and the RAR logo. A second montage on the other side of the paper celebrated the Lewisham anti-NF protest of 13 August and made the link between the neo-fascists and the state concrete by rewriting the name of the Metropolitan Police Commissioner McNee as McNFE.

Other issues also contained montages, many featuring the black and white musicians who had given RAR their labour, together with the catchphrases and mottos of the anti-racist mobilization: 'Love Music Hate Racism' and 'Black and White Unite and Fight'.

The inclusion of communication at this level and in a visual rather than verbal form was a highly significant aspect of RAR's success. It recognized and sought to address the fundamental component of consumption in pop culture, giving *Temporary Hoarding*'s readers not just a political position to reckon with but an object to use, treasure and retain. The broadsheets reasserted the use value frozen inside

127

Figure 3   RAR Montage,1977

the commodity form, and its political effect could endure beyond the necessarily ephemeral scope of RAR's other activities. More important still was the designers' commitment to the power of looking, rather than reading, as a source of political feelings and consciousness. The fractured form of the montages in particular reproduced the fragments of RAR's own contradictory constituency while conveying the discontinuity and diversity of the complex social and political process in which a growing British authoritarianism was being generated. In the visual and verbal rhetoric of both RAR and the punks, racism was now more than a symbol.

I have not intended to suggest that the *Temporary Hoarding* designers hijacked a given or pre-existing punk style culled from the pages of cheap fanzines like *Sniffin' Glue* and *Guttersnipe*. The spirit of punk combined with the constraints of limited time and money to create the preconditions for the emergence of the new style. This was itself taken up, not just within punk but inside design orthodoxy. It is impossible to account for RAR's achievements without acknowledging the visual dimension of their political appeal. Their designs
128

and montages allowed for the communication of complex and at times contradictory ideas in a condensed yet exhilarating form which contrasted sharply with the dry, didactic pronouncements of their fascist rivals in the struggle for young hearts and minds. We shall see below that some figures on the left were to attack RAR's methods and activities for their 'lack of politics' (Weightman, 1978).

The new forms of communication created in the encounter of RAR and punk accommodated and encouraged precisely the anti-authoritarian and anti-state politics which tied RAR's anti-fascism to its anti-racism and its anti-nationalism. The organization might not have been successful if it had been called Rock against Royalty, Rock against Patriotism or Rock against the Nation, but in these early days those were the contradictions on which it grew and reproduced. Somehow, racism stood for and expressed the unacceptable inner workings of all these and more.

The definition of racism which guided RAR's practice was not narrow but extensive. It recognized that racism had become a condensed sign for all the unacceptable social relations of 'Krisis Time 1977' and 'Labour Party Capitalist Britain'. It is necessary to explore this a little further and to look at how RAR's constituency rather than its ideologues took up and expanded this conception. In its editorial, the fourth issue of RAR's paper described the mood of its readership and the way in which Rocking Against Racism had 'caught the time':

Everyone wants stickers, everyone wants badges, everyone wants posters, everyone wants T-shirts, everyone wants to tell us their experiences, their fave local band, their ideas about how to fight racism, about their bigoted families, about mates beaten up, about anger and frustration, about their town, about racism in their street, their block of flats, about fear . . . helplessness. All understand that racism isn't some mystical shit that makes up life in Labour Party Capitalist Britain. Krisis Time 1977. Racism is political. Fighting it is extra – political cause you can't stop NF thugs intimidating and petrol bombing people just by holding a dance.

The editorial sheds further light on the complex way in which the consumerist impulse of pop culture was rearticulated around radical ends. It stresses the fragmented and heterogeneous ways in which racism was 'lived out' in the diverse corners of Britain. It makes racism central to radical or revolutionary sentiment not because it was the most important dimension to life in the declining UK but because it was a moment in the process of social and political struggle where the system as a whole was vulnerable, where its irrationality, bias and brutality could be demonstrated to exist. It was the proof that everything that the left had said about capitalism in general and Britain in particular was true.

Temporary Hoarding consistently devoted a large proportion of its available space to the letters, poems and articles sent in by its readership. These provide a wealth of insights into what racism meant to RAR's diverse constituency. A powerful letter identified as 'our best' in *Temporary Hoarding* 4 told the personal history of a young white woman in the Cheshire area who was 'dating a coloured man' against the wishes of her parents. This experience was used as the key to opening up the whole tangled issue of racism and fascism in the north-west and among young, unemployed whites in general. The woman pleaded to join RAR and offered to lend her labour towards putting on some gigs in her area. She felt that this could be a valuable contribution in the struggle to move potential fascist supporters among white youth towards an anti-racist position. *Temporary Hoarding* received letters from the six counties of Northern Ireland which made connections between the experience of blacks and that of Catholics in the statelet[10] or argued that Ireland was undergoing the British crisis at its most intense and profound. 'The kids here really know the meaning of racism and boredom.' The 'Love Music Hate Racism' slogan concluded several of the letters and bound together statements from young people all over the country. A young Welshman calling himself 'Soul Brother Brillo' from the Kingsmead estate in Hackney sent a cheque for ten badges and announced that he was proud to be the only white inhabitant of his tower block; Gary Glickman, 'a Jewish punk' also from Cheshire, wrote asking for 'a newsheet/badge/poster/sticker/and info about the movement'; Craig J. Wilson (15) and Rita (Twink) Mingaye (16) from Havant, Hants, also wrote asking for information and declaring themselves to be opposed to 'the discrimination against Homo/Bi-sexuals and women and Jews that the fascists would bring about if they came to power'.

Other letters discussed policing, fear, abortion rights and the local situation in various other parts of the country. The articles in the issue amplified and developed several of these obviously political themes. A long interview with the Tom Robinson Band was sandwiched between a piece on the death of Steve Biko and a photomontage pull-out poster illustrating the words of a Tom Robinson song with pictures of Ascot, street riots, neo-fascists marching and health workers demonstrating against the cuts. Other contributions dealt with sexuality, the music scene in the GDR. Interviews with Polly Styrene and a reggae toaster and record shop proprietor made up the rest of the magazine. At this stage RAR claimed to have sold 12,000 badges.

Anti-Nazi or against racism?

The fourth issue of *Temporary Hoarding* came out in late 1977. The Anti Nazi League (ANL) was launched on 10 November that year. It was to change and re-direct RAR's politics and orientation. The League was launched as a broad initiative, drawing together sponsors from right across the spectrum of radical politics with a variety of show business personalities, academics, writers and sports people. The League's founding statement drew attention to the electoral threat posed by the NF and their associates. The danger they represented was once again conveyed by reference to the Nazism of Hitler.

Like Hitler with the Jews, the British Nazis seek to make scapegoats of black people. They exploit the real problems of unemployment, bad housing, cuts in education and in social and welfare services. . . . In these months before the General Election the Nazis will seize every opportunity to spread their propaganda. During the election itself, National Front candidates might receive equal TV and radio time to the major parties. The British electorate will be exposed to Nazi propaganda on an unprecedented scale.

The League's sponsors sought to 'organize on the widest possible scale' and appealed to 'all those who oppose the growth of the Nazis in Britain [to unite] irrespective of other political differences'. As the League's name suggests, its aims were simpler and more straightforward than RAR's heterogeneous concerns. It was a single-issue campaign modelled on the Campaign for Nuclear Disarmament (CND) and centred on electoral politics whereas RAR's critique of Labour had fused with punk's anarchic and cynical analysis of parliamentarism.

What we must examine now is the degree to which the ANL deliberately sought to summon and manipulate a form of nationalism and patriotism as part of its broad anti-fascist drive. The idea that the British Nazis were merely sham patriots who soiled the British flag by their use of it was a strong feature of ANL leaflets. This inauthentic patriotism was exposed and contrasted with the genuine nationalist spirit which had been created in Britain's finest hour – the 'anti-fascist' 1939–45 war. The neo-fascists wore the uniforms of Nazism beneath their garb of outward respectability and it is hard to gauge what made them more abhorrent to the ANL, their Nazism or the way they were dragging British patriotism through the mud. The League's leaflets were illustrated with imagery of the war – concentration camps and Nazi troops – and were captioned with the anti-fascist slogan 'Never Again'. One leaflet, 'What would life be like under the Nazis?' warned potential NF supporters that 'The NF says they are just putting Britons first. But their Britain will be just like Hitler's Germany.' Another, 'Why you should oppose the

131

National Front' made a more direct challenge to the quality of NF patriotism: 'They say they are just patriots. Then why does Chairman Tyndall say: "the Second World War was fought for Jewish, not British, interests. Under the leadershop of Adolph Hitler, Germany proved she could be a great power".'

In the *Guardian*, ANL spokesperson Peter Hain described the NF brand of patriotism as a 'masquerade'.[11] Above all, the popular memory of the anti-fascist war was employed by the ANL to alert people to the dangers of neo-fascism in their midst. Pictures of the NF leaders wearing Nazi uniform were produced as the final proof that their Britishness was in doubt. How could those who secretly aped the fascistic antics of Britain's sworn enemies then pose as guardians of national culture and interests, asked the League? Its resources were channelled into materials which could be used in anti-fascist campaigning for local polls and the anticipated general election.

The attempt to impose the elimination of Nazism as a priority on the diverse and complex political consciousness crystallized by RAR was a miscalculation. The narrow definition of the problem of 'race' – as a product of fascism – matched by a rapid broadening of the campaign against it drew on RAR's momentum, punk and the residues of anti-Jubilee sentiment. However, this shift imposed a shorter life and more limited aims on the movement. The goals of anti-racism were being redefined. The Rasta-inspired pursuit of 'Equal rights and Justice' was being foresaken, in the ANL if not RAR. It was replaced by the more modest aim of isolating and eliminating the fascist parties at the polls. The exposure of fascist leaders as Nazis was rapidly taken over into Fleet Street, broadening support still further and increasing popular hostility to those who would threaten democracy, but the exclusive identification of racism with Nazis was to create problems for anti-racism in the future.

RAR co-operated with the ANL in organizing several large demonstrations, 'Carnivals', in different parts of the country. The first of these, in London during May 1978,[12] attracted 80,000 people, most of whom marched across the city, through the NF strongholds of the East End to a celebratory concert in Victoria Park, Bethnal Green. The ANL input into these events was smaller than RAR's contribution. The format was devised from a tried and tested blend which had made RAR's local gigs successful. The national publicity which the League could command provided a counterpart to the grassroots activities of RAR, and young people were still the major target group of both campaigns. Yet the gradual switch to anti-Nazism from anti-racism which had been precipitated by the growth of the League, marked the beginning of a concerted appeal to older voters, and involved a direct appeal to their memories of anti-fascism in the

132

1930s and 1940s. Ernie Roberts, a member of the League Steering Committee, described this shift in emphasis:

The success and strength of the league is based on the old who remember fascism and the 1939–45 war; on the young who see fascism as a menace to their freedom, culture and future and on the women who know the inferior position which fascism forces them to accept.[13]

Where the ANL did direct its message towards the young, it was heavily reliant on the strategies and political languages of both RAR and punk. One of its leaflets prepared for circulation among school children, for example, brought together the anti-fascist views of John 'Rotten' Lydon, the Sex Pistols' singer, and Brian Clough, the football manager, under the heading NF = No Future.[14]

The League's appeal to older people was accompanied by further changes in its organizational strategy. The most significant of these was the creation of a host of sectoral mini organizations which were to carry the anti-Nazi struggle out of the dance-halls and away from street corners into the workplace and thence supposedly into mainstream working-class politics. Teachers Against the Nazis, Rail Workers, Dockers, School Kids, Hunt Saboteurs, Bikers, Architects, Vegetarians and Football fans all emerged, and their very plurality began to fracture the fragile unity which had been created by shared cultural opposition to the nationalism, fascist violence and police harassment which RAR had identified as the content of racism and the key symptoms of the national crisis.

Rocking Against Racism had allowed space for youth to rant against the perceived iniquities of 'Labour Party Capitalist Britain'. The popular front tactics introduced by the ANL closed it down. Being 'Anti-Nazi' located the political problem posed by the growth of racism in Britain exclusively in the activities of a small and eccentric, though violent, band of neo-fascists. Though they were more than usually visible in the 1976–9 period, and regardless of whether they would have been able to make serious inroads into the traditional allegiances of working-class voters in the inner cities, Tyndall, Webster, McLaughlin and their cohorts were only a small and subsidiary part of the political concerns which had fired RAR youth.

Temporary Hoarding's coverage of Front leader Webster's lone patriotic demonstration through Thameside in Manchester was inflamed by outrage against the connection between his fascism and the support action of the racist state. This continuity was manifest as hundreds of uniformed police escorted the solitary flag-bearing figure on his way through the anti-fascist protest. In sharp contradiction, the ANL made more and more of the relationship between these fascists and the ones which had been vanquished by Britain in her finest hour. No matter how much energy the League could muster

133

for the task of 'kicking out' the Nazis from wherever they lurked, even the most racist Britons did not necessarily recognize themselves as Nazis or identify their ideas about alien culture, mugging or repatriation, as being derived from the teachings of Hitler or Mussolini.

The League emphasized the Nazi character of neo-fascist and racist politics to the exclusion of every other consideration. This may have lead to the electoral defeat of the NF, British Movement and their allies but this was achieved ironically by reviving the very elements of nationalism and xenophobia which had seen Britannia through the darkest hours of the Second World War. This patriotism, temporarily articulated to the anti-Nazi cause, was an unstable foundation. It could begin to detach itself from the anti-fascist forces as soon as the NF and the other similar groups began to shrug off accusations of Nazism and started to present themselves credibly as nothing more than concerned British patriots.

The formation of a mass anti-racist movement in this country has passed largely unacknowledged by left writers. It is important to appreciate that at the time when both RAR and the ANL were at their height, considerable adverse comment was passed on their activities by socialist observers. It was felt that the tactics of the League were wrong, giving, for example, insufficient importance to the issue of organizing workers' self-defence squads (RCG, 1978) or, more significantly, that anti-racism was and could not be anything more than an intermediate stage in the development of a substantive and complete variety of political consciousness and organization. Typifying this position, Tariq Ali, then one of the leaders of the International Marxist Group (IMG), a Trotskyist group whose members were active among supporters of the ANL, described the Victoria Park Carnival which had drawn 80,000 people together under the banners of RAR and the ANL with these words: 'Lots of people will come along for Rock Against Racism today and see that it should be Rock Against the Stock Exchange tomorrow.'[15] The activities and organizational strategies adopted by the extreme right in the post RAR/ANL period were clearly influenced not only by the tactics which anti-racism had used to mould a mass movement but by an appreciation of the importance of pop culture in forming the political outlook of young people. This had no parallel on the left. *The Young Nationalist*, youth organ of the British National Party, told its readers:

The record and cassette is [sic] more powerful than the TV or newspapers where youth is concerned. Disco and its melting pot pseudo-philosophy must be fought or Britain's streets will be full of black-worshipping soul boys (Barber,1979).

The NF's youth paper *Bulldog* consistently devoted column inches to pop culture and is still trying unsuccessfully to initiate a 'Rock Against Communism' campaign along the lines of RAR.[16] In recognition of the power which black music has as a transmitter, not merely of black culture but of oppositional and anti-authoritarian values, extreme right groups have waged their own informal campaigns against local radio stations which have in their opinion played too much black music thereby diluting the national will. London's Capital Radio, for example, was hit by an organized campaign which bombarded their switchboard with calls protesting at the fact that a third of the station's music is by black artists. It was reported that up to thirty such calls were being logged each day. A Capital spokesperson said: 'The callers sound as if they are reading from a script and using the same expressions like "you're pandering to the latter day immigrants instead of serving the traditional cockney".'[17]

The first phase of the ANL mobilization drew to a close with the Conservative election victory of 1979. RAR continued its activities, championing the 'two-tone' styles and bands even as its mass support gradually shrank. The organization continued to put on gigs all over the country and *Temporary Hoarding* looked at the activities of local groups in different areas. A 'Dance and Defend' tour was organized in support of the anti-fascist demonstrators who had been arrested and assaulted during a police riot at an NF election rally in Southall.[18] One ANL activist was killed by police and several RAR workers who had also been involved in a local community and music centre – 'People Unite' – received gross injuries when the building was stormed by officers from the Met.'s militarized squad, the Special Patrol Group (SPG). The tenth issue of *Temporary Hoarding*, in November 1979, featured articles on the Southall events, mods, two-tone, ska, immigration controls, Northern Ireland, teenage sexuality and the violence of night-club bouncers. It contained reports from RAR groups in Reading, Hull, Dublin and Stevenage as well as London. The incoming Conservative administration had played the race card as part of its own populist electoral strategy. This altered the configurations of racial politics, further de-emphasizing the role of the neo-fascist parties. Anti-racism therefore acquired a party political connotation. The League's single issue orientation became harder to sustain and looked out of place when the Prime Minister elect made remarks about British people 'feeling rather swamped'. Destroyed at the polls, the neo-fascist groups adopted a lower profile, stepped up their work with youth using many of RAR's ideas and adopted what they called a strategy of tension which placed a greater stress on physical intimidation and harassment of blacks. As part of a belated answer to this, unsuccessful attempts were made to revive the League during the spring of 1981.[19]

Municipal anti-racism

The abortive attempt to revive the League preceded the first outbreak of street protests in Brixton by only a few weeks. It is to the after effects of these events that we now turn. The riots of 1981 cannot be examined in detail here, but they are important to the history of anti-racism in Britain because they forced attention away from the marginal antics of the neo-fascists. The riots reasserted a definition of racism as something intrinsic to the political processes of Britain in crisis. Political debate about what anti-racism might be shifted and settled briefly on the systematic discrimination and disadvantage as well as the ruthless and coercive forms of policing to which the black areas where protest erupted had been subjected.

The subsequent racialization of the riots, which were labelled as black events expressive of the disorderly cultural and political traditions of their un-British protagonists, could provide raw material for an additional study of the languages of racial politics in contemporary Britain. The official explanation of the events was presented in the Scarman Report, and used the particular experience of Brixton to illuminate the national dimensions of the disorders, even where this was inappropriate. Less than a third of those arrested during the disorders had been 'of an ethnic appearance other than white'[20] yet the issue of 'race' dominated the popular memory of the events and cast the typical rioter as an unemployed, young Afro-Caribbean male living in an inner-city neighbourhood (Fielding and Southgate, 1982).

The extent to which these patterns of disorder actually grew out of the distinct experience of inner-city blacks is not important for the moment. Their capacity to represent the race problem being experienced by Britain as a whole is more important. The problem acquired substance in the account of black pathology which was given an official imprimatur by Scarman's report and 'race' duly emerged as a primary causal factor in his narrative of the riots. The Labour administrations elected in the metropolitan counties during the spring of 1981 were quick to institute a range of special agencies and programmes of work charged with the task of addressing the ethnic minority needs to which the burning and looting had given a supposedly inarticulate expression.

Scarman's clumsy denial that 'institutionalized racism' existed in Britain, however plausible within his own definitions, fuelled the anti-racist fervour of his new critics. They not only challenged his view but argued that the riots were proof that racism was not only endemic but a potent, corrosive force in society.

The initial strategy of the new Labour local authorities emphasized the need for them to put their own houses in order as a precondition

136

for the credibility of broader campaigning around anti-racist objectives. This 'internal' struggle to transform or at least adapt local authorities required a distinct range of tactical manoeuvres tailored to the shape and character of local state bureaucracies. The anti-racist tactics which emerged inside these agencies and institutions have not been easily transferable to the struggle against racism outside their walls, on the streets and in popular politics. The attempt to apply what can be called the institutional/bureaucratic model of anti-racist strategy as if it were a general, universal blueprint rather than a specific plan adapted to the peculiarities of local government, forms the central contradiction in the discussion of municipal anti-racism which follows. However successful these initiatives have been in addressing the issue of black disadvantage inside the institutional structures of local authorities and the voluntary bodies they fund, the overall structure of the bureaucracies, their formal rationality, hierarchical mode of organization and the coercive powers they enjoy as a result of their role as providers of money, all point to the specificities of their anti-racist strategy and indeed to the narrow definitions of anti-racism being pursued.

The role of anti-racist policy, for example, may be rather more significant in organizations of this type than it would be in more popular and less structured bodies, or agencies in which a political consensus is harder to create. The forms of anti-racist training most appropriate, for example, to work in the housing department of a Labour local authority may carry fewer guarantees when applied to the experience of manual workers, nursery staff or security guards in the same organization let alone those whose employment does not provide a legitimate opportunity for the development of anti-racist policy.

Programmes for equality of opportunity for staff within the local authority structures were introduced. The bureaucracies which perpetuated a racial division of labour confining blacks to the lowest levels in the hierarchy came under official scrutiny from a new cadre of professional officers and advisers mandated for the elimination of racism. Committees were set up consistent with the formal structure of the local authorities which could highlight the needs of ethnic minority groups and organizations. Finally, new programmes for the financial support of ethnic minority cultural and political work were introduced. By April 1984 sixteen London boroughs, both Labour and Conservative, had taken at least some steps along this road. The hub of this municipal anti-racism was provided by the Labour Greater London Council (GLC). The leader of that authority, Ken Livingstone, signified the priority attached to the issue of 'race' by assuming the chairpersonship of the newly created Ethnic Minorities Committee himself. In 1982–3, the first year in which the committee had a budget for grants, over 300 applications were received for the annual budget of £850,000. The following year the committee's grants budget had risen to approximately £2.5 million (GLC, 1985).

The motives behind these developments were diverse. Pressure on the authority from specialized community relations agencies coincided with the growth of black political activism inside the Labour Party. The group of blacks, which also organized itself around the demand for a black caucus or section within the party, issued warnings that the electoral allegiance of black populations in urban areas could no longer be taken for granted by Labour. To other analysts who had suggested that the riots represented the formation of an alienated or dissident urban underclass, the growth of specialized anti-racist initiatives was a vehicle for the reincorporation of these marginal elements into the rituals of the political system.

The centrepiece of the GLC's anti-racist strategy was the declaration of London as an 'anti-racist zone' and the announcement that 1984 was to be an anti-racist year in which the struggle against racism would be a continual and primary focus of the council's work. These commitments took the council into the realm of popular politics, and relied on public awareness campaigning marshalled through billboards and press advertisements. Early in 1984 the Ethnic Minorities Committee approved an initial budget of £310,000 for this purpose. Later in the year a further £552,000 was approved in principle for an extension of the campaign until March 1985 (GLC, 1984b).

Local counterparts to this strategy were supplied by borough councils which engaged in a parallel programme of popular anti-racist activity that included the same elements as the GLC along with more concrete popular initiatives such as the renaming of streets and estates to highlight the contribution made by blacks to world history as well as the multi-ethnic composition of neighbourhoods. Lambeth's Rhodesia Road was renamed Zimbabwe Road, and so on.[21]

It was, however, the GLC's billboard advertisements which formed the core of this campaign. The first posters produced in the campaign occupied large roadside hoardings and featured stark anti-racist slogans and exhortations against a plain white background. Typical of these was the following: 'Nearly a million Londoners are getting a raw deal – simply because the other 6 million let it happen. Let's kick racism out of town.' Another poster bearing the question 'Where would Mrs Thatcher have got to if she had been black?' was also distributed at this stage. No images were featured on these first posters and their textual form invited written comment. The question about Mrs Thatcher was answered by one graffito with the words, 'To the front of the housing queue'. This answer encapsulates a deeper problem which lay in the strategy that generated these posters, namely the tendency to assume that readers had a general perception of blacks as a disadvantaged group which could be drawn upon as the basis of an anti-racist sensibility. Related to this misplaced assumption was the idea that at this level of political communication, the concept of racism required no elaboration, but would be recognized immediately as a negative and unwholesome political trait. The poster provided no apparent link between the assertion that some Londoners were getting a bad deal and the political solution being suggested: 'Let's kick racism out of town'.

On one site in North London, the word racism was crossed out and the word 'blacks' written in its place. Leaving aside for the moment the issue of whether the effects of racism are felt 'simply because whites let it happen' (a proposition which either makes the struggle against racism appear facile or denies that whites have an active role in perpetuating the institutions and structures which reproduce it) the idea that racism adds up to a 'raw deal' for its victims suggests a fundamentally pluralist understanding of racial conflicts in which the structural aspects of racial politics are minimized. When the problems raised by racism are seen in this way, the solution to them becomes the provision of an unspecified 'better deal'. This can be seen counterproductively as a form of special treatment. Furthermore, by the manner in which the poster separates the discussion of interaction between people from the injunction 'Let's kick racism out of town' it creates a view of racism as an autonomous ideological force, readily extricable from other dimensions of social life. Who will do this kicking out? Where will those people or ideas thus kicked relocate themselves? The choice of the verb 'kick' raises obvious additional problems in that its connotations of physical brutality may not be wholly compatible with the task of winning broad popular support for the struggle against racism, particularly where blacks are already seen as a volatile and violent group. The stress on numbers of blacks and whites conveyed by the poster suggested that these numbers were, in themselves, significant when presumably an anti-racist position would be the same whether the number of oppressed blacks in London was 500,000 or 50,000.

The posters which followed were not placed on large advertisement hoardings though they were targeted at a similarly wide audience through newspapers and magazines. In these, images ere introduced to support the text and a more elaborate form of argument began to emerge. One showed a photograph of a white iced gateau with a piece of chocolate cake of different dimensions inserted into it where a slice had been removed. The picture was captioned 'Which slice of the cake are you getting? In the majority of cases Ethnic Minorities do not receive their equal share of the capital's resources. Stamp Out Institutional Racism now.' The two different types of cake crammed together on the same plate, provided in fact a striking image for the fundamental incompatibility of blacks and whites whose obvious differences were reproduced in displaced form among

139

Figure 4   GLC poster, 1983

the crumbs. The slice of chocolate cake which represents black settler population, calls to mind the Powellite image of the 'alien wedge' with complete precision. It is manifestly out of place, an unnatural intrusion into the body of the white cake, iced with buildings and decorated to suggest relative prosperity and economic privilege. Again, the final injunction 'Stamp out institutional racism now!' was given no explicit content by the images chosen or the supporting text. If the GLC was responsible for administering and distributing the capital's resources, a bewildered reader of the poster might ask, why don't they give things out more equitably?

By locating the problem of racism in this relationship between the council as custodian of the resources/cake and its incongruous black minority slice, the white reader is abandoned by the text, appearing instead as a spectator on the margins of a private conversation. The poster's question 'Which slice of the cake are you getting?' suggests that it was aimed at both black and white readers, allowing or even encouraging each 'racial' group to extract its own lessons from the cake image. Yet this anti-racist logic constructs the black reader as the primary audience and the poster becomes an exhortation to blacks to support the council's strategy for 'stamping out institutional racism' rather than a challenge to racist ideology and explanation.

Another poster which sought to address the politics of 'race' in a popular form is particularly interesting because it contained a commentary on the anti-racist poster campaign itself. Four whites, two of each sex, are depicted walking past a GLC anti-racist hoarding on which is printed the slogan: 'If you're not part of the solution then you're part of the problem. You've got the power to challenge the damaging effects of racism, use it.'

Each figure holds a folded newspaper up between their own face and the message on the hoarding. The final injunction in this case is 'Racism, better off without it'. Whether the figures are simply shielding their eyes from the ideological glare of the poster or whether their stance is intended to suggest the role of the popular press in reproducing racist ideology is not clear nor particularly important. It is more significant that the imagery chosen to represent the struggle against racism is provided by the GLC anti-racist campaign itself. Here, of course, white readers are the primary audience and are invited to recognize themselves in the actions of the white figures who will not look up at the message which the poster within a poster bears. The white reader who does look at the poster thereby puts themself in a different category from those (the racists) who will not look. Thus the poster suggests that by the act of looking at the slogan and absorbing its message, anti-racism is created and racism itself abolished. Consuming the poster becomes, in the terms of its text, part of the solution rather than part of the problem. The 'power to challenge the damaging effects of racism' of which the

141

Figure 5   GLC poster, 1983

poster speaks is defined as the power to look at a GLC poster. We may as the poster tells us, be better off without racism but the images and text do not make racism intelligible or concrete except in the refusal to consume anti-racist posters.

The problems of definition and strategy which arise from this brief discussion of the GLC anti-racist posters can be pursued further elsewhere in the council's anti-racist output. At every stage of the anti-racist campaign and the anti-racist year programme the council's underlying political and philosophical positions were spelled out in pamphlets and other supporting documents. For example, after the council ran a series of advertisements in national newspapers bearing the question, 'What is this thing called racism?'[22] readers were invited to write in to the Ethnic Minorities Unit for a booklet which would tell them the answer and suggest what might be done about it. The text of the ads continued:

You may hear a lot about it [racism]. But you may not understand how it affects you and your life in London. So, send for our booklet 'What Can I Do To Challenge Racism?' It's surprising, it's alarming and helpful. And it's Free.

The sixteen-page booklet combined general definitions of racism and anti-racism with what was presented as practical advice as to what could be done about its particular manifestations of racism in discrete areas of social life – the church, employment, the arts, media, education, housing, the health service and policing. The first page asserts the political importance of racism and argues that it is a ubiquitous presence. This was one of the recurrent themes in GLC statements on 'race': 'Racism directly affects us all. We are either the victims or the perpetrators.' The formula which reduces the complexity of racism to these two positions seems to argue against the possibility of anti-racism at all. Where does anti-racism come from? How is it possible to cease being a perpetrator, and cease being a victim? Is their any traffic between groups? If so, how does it operate? The booklet does not tell us. Following on from this, it provides a definition of racism which presumably guided the GLC's own practice and anti-racist strategy.

Racism is normally defined as prejudice plus power where prejudice is an unfavourable opinion or feeling formed beforehand or without knowledge, thought or reason, often unconsciously and on the grounds of race, colour, nationality, ethnic or national origins. Power is the ability to make things happen or prevent things from happening. Thus racism is having the power to put into effect one's prejudice to the detriment of particular racial groups.

Several critical points can be made about this definition. It appears to endorse the idea that racial groups are real in the sense of being fixed and exclusive. Race is presented as preceding racism and having the same status as 'national origins'. Race is differentiated from the question of colour (phenotype) but what it is remains unspecified. It is presented as an unproblematic common-sense category. Its existence can be taken for granted and the political problems which attend it are reduced to the issue of prejudice. This in turn ties the definition to observable human action denying implicitly the salience of structural and ideological factors which cannot be grasped through the concept of prejudice and its consequent behavioural focus. As an adjunct to this, power is seen as a possession rather than a relationship in the classic manner of the 'zero-sum game'. The basis on which this view of power is maintained is revealed once the discussion turns in the direction of strategy. 'In order to eliminate racism, there has to be a twin challenge aimed at the institution where power is located and at people's behaviour which is too often conditioned by racially prejudiced attitudes.' This is less of a definition than a justification for the GLC's own strategy which combined, as we have noted, an internal programme of equal opportunities policy with a public awareness campaign. One moment power is a property of individual relationships which involve prejudice between different races, the next it is located in institutions which have no discernable relationship to individual behaviour. How these two distinct objects of the GLC strategy relate to each other is not explained even though it is inferred that their relationship is functionally important in the reproduction of racism.

To its credit the booklet does, by comparison with the posters, emphasize that people can act against racism in all its diverse forms. Its definitional page ends with a prescription of how they can act and of the manner in which an anti-racist commitment comes into being: 'by being deeply aware of all forms of oppression and by taking action personally and collectively to end all oppression'. This vague, semi-religious language conveys a complete inability to locate what is specific to racial oppression and therefore to anti-racism.

Rather than tie the anti-racist project to a distinct and recognizable range of themes and political priorities as RAR had done (nationalism, fascism, policing, racial violence) this municipal anti-racism allows the concept of racism to ascend to rarified heights where, like a lost balloon, it becomes impossible to retrieve. This induces a strategic paralysis which is further encouraged by the allocation of a pre-eminent if not monopolistic role in the defeat of racism to the council's own agencies and activities. The council becomes the primary site of anti-racist struggle whether the racist object being kicked out of town is made up of the racist institutions which the council manages or the racist opinions of the public which only the council is equipped to challenge. The general task of advancing anti-racism is thereby collapsed into the specific strategic priorities of the GLC, a model which regardless of its in-house effectiveness, is not universally applicable to anti-racist politics in noninstitutional settings but which is none the less offered up as a general blueprint.

In this operation, the would-be anti-racist is abandoned in a political vacuum. Overdue attempts to fill it are made in the practical instructions which follow. These urge concrete action appropriate to tackling the various manifestations of racism in different areas of life. The action proposed is, however, disappointingly vague and general. For example, those concerned about the racism in the field of 'arts and recreation' are urged as an initial move to 'write to the chairperson of your local council's arts and recreation committee. Find out how many black and other ethnic minority people the arts and recreation department itself employs . . .'. Local government institutions are not just being presented as the primary source of anti-racist action and sentiment. In this model, the politics of anti-racism exists entirely within the circuit between them. The practical suggestions for furthering the struggle against racism in the media, a set of institutions over which local governments have no control, is exactly the same. Anti-racists are encouraged by the booklet to write or ring their protest in to the Independent Broadcasting Authority, programme controllers and editors. As far as health is concerned the advice is the same, though this time the letters are to be sent to the District Health Authority, the Family Practitioner Committee and the Minister of Health. The tactics are constant, only the target of the letters changes from issue to issue, institution to institution.

The unevenness of racism, its different forms in different institutional contexts and the correspondingly different forms of organization, tactics and modes of action required to attack it are simply not acknowledged to be significant. There are no priorities and no genuine strategic calculation. In this fight against racism, it would seem that any target is as valid as any other. Racism covers all society's institutions like a thick blanket of snow. Deprived of any overall direction and purpose anti-racists are invited to dig away into its frosty crust anywhere that tickles their fancy. A few carefully-aimed letters and an abstract commitment to redress all forms of oppression are all the tools which are apparently required. This definition of anti-racism offers its recruits a choice between the mystical and the mundane. Unlike RAR, whose anti-racist vision was premised on the collective transcendence of 'race' in concrete settings and the continued celebration of that transcendence in politically infused forms of pleasure, the GLC's tactics relied on isolated and individualized acts. It is highly significant that writing letters and contemplating oppression in general are essentially solitary activities. The problem of what connects one anti-racist to the next is not recognized as a substantive political issue. Municipal anti-racism solved it by providing signs, badges and stickers through which individuals could convey their affiliation to others without having to

145

negotiate through collective activity the extent to which definitions of anti-racism were actually held in common. These products may have created a form of solidarity between the atomized individuals who consumed them. But the basis of that solidarity and the subsequent content of their anti-racism remains obscure and fixed at the individual level. Anti-racism is for this model a personal quest.[23]

I am not suggesting that writing letters or embracing the contemplation of oppression in general have no place in the struggle against racism, but rather raising the question of whether these forms of political action, which are among the more traditional options available, address the formation and reproduction of racism in the ideology, culture and structures of contemporary Britain. More fundamentally still, I am suggesting that these tactics have originated in a version of anti-racism which identifies racism, the object which it sets out to challenge, only in discrete institutional settings. The struggle against it within those institutional walls is then represented as the primary and sometimes the only worthwhile form in which bona fide anti-racism can develop. At its worst, this tendency can lead to the analysis of racism as if it were only a problem because its irrationality creates an obstacle for the development of rational government intervention rather than because of the power relations which it organizes and legitimates. This is precisely the message of another GLC advertisement placed in a variety of journals and magazines during 1984 and 1985.[24] This ad featured a photograph of an open card index. The letters which make up the word racism are visibly protruding from the cards where the alphabet would usually be seen. The immediate caption for the picture reads 'When racism stops you from being efficient are you doing your job?'; beneath this is a paragraph arguing in favour of equal opportunity policies which ends with the sentences: 'If you're not providing equal opportunities, you're probably breaking the law. In a multi-racial society, you're certainly not doing your job.' The image of racism in the form of well-ordered, uniform cards in a neat index is only too expressive of the definition spelled out in more detail in the anti-racist pamphlet. The cards which appear to be blank are neat, clean and barely used suggesting the efficiency which becomes the primary issue in the supporting text.

Anti-racism is defined as both efficiency and good management practice and the supporting text mixes factual statements – 'A black school leaver will find it three times as hard to get a job as a white school leaver' – with questions – 'What percentage of your staff are black?' The effect of this ad is to suggest that racism and anti-racism are issues which can be tackled in terms of administration and management.

The text assigns no causal priorities. Racism and inefficiency appear simply to coincide. Is racism bad because it makes firms

WHEN RACISM STOPS YOU FROM BEING EFFICIENT ARE YOU DOING YOUR JOB?

Finding the right person for the job is never easy. And mistakes are always costly. But how many employers let racism narrow their choice?

A black school-leaver will find it three times as hard to get a job as a white school-leaver – with the same qualifications and experience. Is your firm recruiting on real merit? Unemployment levels among black people are twice those of the country as a whole. What percentage of your staff is black? Black and other ethnic minorities are concentrated in the lowest paid manual jobs. Are you promoting staff according to ability and performance?

The 1976 Race Relations Act made racial discrimination unlawful – yet it goes on, blatantly, in too many firms. How many of the rest are actively preventing it? By the firm's policy? By advertising vacancies in ethnic media? By monitoring recruitment? By ensuring that no employee suffers racial harassment?

If you're not providing equal opportunities, you're probably breaking the law. In a multi-racial society, you're certainly not doing your job.

For further information contact: Ethnic Minorities Unit, GLC, Room 686ᴀ, County Hall, London SE1 7PB.

LONDON AGAINST RACISM

You've got the power to challenge the damaging effects of racism. Use it!

Figure 6   GLC advertisement, 1984

and governmental institutions inefficient? Will making them more efficient make them less racist? The ad remains silent and ambiguous on these points. Again racism is represented as a tidy and regular process or event. The moral and political dimensions of the struggle against it are subsumed by the suggestion that it must be done away with because it is inefficient and in any case illegal.

Towards a new anti-racism

Having explored contrasting definitions of anti-racist politics and drawn attention to some of their respective strengths and shortcomings, it is possible to identify some pointers towards what might be the basis of a more adequate conceptualization. Without adopting a programmatic tone or intent, I will now summarize what I think these might be.

The contradiction between understandings of racism based on the need to combat neo-fascism and those which have emphasized anti-racism of a more diffuse nature focused on state agencies and popular politics remains at the heart of racial politics today. We have seen that RAR and the ANL diverged around this point, setting different priorities for their work as a result. In the above discussion of their achievements I have tried to suggest why the second, primarily anti-racist rather than anti-fascist, orientation provided the more appropriate route. These two different approaches to anti-racist politics should not be over-polarized. Yet they do indicate different modes of action, in particular, different positions on the role of state agencies in controlling neo-fascist groups and the violence they create. There are additional dangers in an anti-racist commitment which declares itself first and foremost an anti-fascism. Not least of these is the nationalist resonance which anti-fascism has acquired in this country (Barnett, 1982). But, at a more fundamental level, the emphasis on neo-fascism as the most dangerous embodiment of contemporary racism inevitably pulls discussion of 'race' away from the centre of political culture and relocates it on the margins where these groups are doomed to remain. To exaggerate the importance of their activities and allow them to become dominant in the definition of racism risks the suggestion that racism is an aberration or an exceptional problem essentially unintegrated into the social and political structure. The National Front and similar groups become seen, not at one end of a continuum of political sentiment but as an embarrassing excrescence on the otherwise unblemished features of British democracy. They become a problem which can be dealt with effectively through the mechanisms which that democracy has provided in terms of policing and legal intervention. To pose the issue of racial politics in a way which gives these groups a disproportionate significance is also to reduce the analysis of racism to a debate over the extent of the continuity which ties their new fascism to its brown and blackshirted antecedents. This renders anti-racism vulnerable from the moment that John Tyndall, Patrick Harrington or whoever it is in the anti-fascist searchlight, begin to deny that they are not Nazis but plain, if over-enthusiastic, patriots.

The experience of the GLC campaigns examined above suggests that the pursuit of a general theory of anti-racist politics may itself be a misplaced and fruitless activity. Anti-racism will be deformed and discredited where it tries too rapidly to generalize a tactical or strategic orientation which has developed out of specific determinate conditions. Equal opportunities policies, for example, may be a necessary element in the formation of anti-racist initiatives inside the kind of bureaucratic agency in which an overall policy can be introduced and used as a baseline for political reform. However, these policies are not a sufficient precondition for the emergence of a substantive anti-racism in organizations of this type. The methods and strategy which they promote may be completely inappropriate in organizations which enjoy a less centralized or less rational structure. The abandonment of a general theory of anti-racist practice also requires the sacrifice of crude definitions of racism in the prejudice plus power formula quoted earlier. This may fit well into the rational bureaucratic conception of anti-racist politics but it is unable to account for expressions of racial classification and structuration which are not behavioural or attitudinal or which rely on a populist response from the white subjects they bring into being.

Races are political collectivities not ahistorical essences. 'Race' is, after all, not the property of powerful, prejudiced individuals but an effect of complex relationships between dominant and subordinate social groups. If whites have shared the same job centres, schools, police cells, parties and streets with blacks in what sense can we speak of them having additional power? The very complexity of these relations and the extent of difference which exists between the meanings and structures attached to 'race' in different social formations are additional factors which undermine the possibility of a general theory of race relations and the sociologically inspired attempt to elevate that concept into an analytical rather than merely descriptive term. Even within a single social formation at a particular phase of its development racism will not be an unbroken continuous presence. It will be unevenly developed. Even where it is diffuse it will never be uniform. The different forces which form 'races' in concrete political antagonisms will operate at differing tempos and in contrasting ways according to immediate circumstances. Racial attacks may be higher in one area than the next. The manner in which racist sentiment is expressed may vary, for example, according to the extent and character of black settlement; in relation to the composition of a black community, its position in the contradiction between capital and labour, its gender, age structure or even its ability to communicate with the dominant group and the degree of cultural overlap which exists between white and black.

If, as has been suggested, the 'race' issue has been seen from the vantage point of sympathetic liberalism as a matter of policy rather than politics (Hall, 1978), the tasks of a more sustained and thorough-going anti-racism must include an attempt to show how administration of institutional reforms (policy) can be articulated to a sound grasp of extra-institutional politics.

The development of anti-racist policy around which these reforms can cohere should be a cautious exercise. If they are to be credible outside the institutional settings in which they were dreamed up, anti-racist policies must not have the effect of appearing to reduce the complexity of black life to an effect of racism. This is a real danger when racism is presented sweeping all before it and the power relations involved are caricatured as an eternal tussle between victims and perpetrators. I have already argued in the introduction to this book that the role of victim is articulated into contemporary British racism. What anti-racism must do if it expects to be taken seriously by the black settlers in whose name it claims to act is to transcend this sociologism and move towards the longer-term aims of demonstrating the historical dimensions of 'race' and bringing blacks fully into historicity (Touraine, 1977), as actors capable of making complex choices in the furtherance of their own liberation. Finally anti-racism must negotiate, as RAR did, the political priorities which emanate from the defensive struggles and negotiations of racially subordinate groups. No meaningful anti-racism can ignore the content of these conflicts for it constitutes the raw material used to establish the meaning and limits of 'race'. These struggles may be both political and cultural and the manner in which these instances combine may result in new kinds of political practice which defy Eurocentric categorization.

The GLC's attempts to develop popular anti-racism tended to lack the active participation of large numbers of black people. However, on one occasion during its reign, the council did inadvertently blunder into an area of activity which was capable of generating massive interest among black youth, supposedly the most marginal of social groups. The Hip-Hop Jam of 9 September 1984 attracted over 30,000 predominantly, though not exclusively, black young people to a GLC event. The jam brought together for the first time all of London's most celebrated rappers, dancers, DJs, mixers and graffitists on the South Bank site in the shadow of County Hall.

Never before had so much talent and potential gathered on one stage. And never before could so much have been achieved. . . . Bambaataa (leader of the Bronx's original Zulu Nation) had sent a personal message. . . . A message of peace and love and respect for one another.[25]

The event, which had cost the council £5000 and had been planned around an estimated crowd of 5000, degenerated into a mini-riot after an ill-disciplined steward became aggressive and hit a member of the audience. Police were brought in to control the crowd and in the mêlée which followed the GLC was itself discredited in the eyes of many of these young people. It is impossible not to wonder what might have happened if their culture had been given some place in the council's definitions of anti-racist activity. The style of the campaign and its posters might have been very different. The expressive culture of the black community will be considered in detail in the next chapter.

Notes

1 This point comes across strongly in the speech by Haile Selassie which forms the basis of Bob Marley's song 'War'.
2 *Melody Maker*, 9.12.78.
3 *Evening News*, 20.9.77.
4 *Sounds*, 28.8.76.
5 Michael Gray, 'Elvis', *Temporary Hoarding*, no. 3, 1977.
6 *Searchlight*, May 1981.
7 See the interview with Roger Huddle in *Camerawork*, no. 24, March 1982.
8 Don Slater, 'David King', in the same March 1982 issue of *Camerawork*.
9 See MINDA's own account of their work in *Photography Politics One* (eds), Terry Dennett and Jo Spence (Photography Workshop, London 1979).
10 There were four such letters in issue 4.
11 20.10.78.
12 The second RAR carnival took place on 24 September 1978 in Brockwell Park, Brixton.
13 See p. 41 of the *Revolutionary Communist*, no. 9, 1979.
14 Clough said, 'Nazism is just as much a disease as cholera, leprosy or smallpox and it must be treated to stop it spreading. I believe the Front must be removed from the life of this country and I will play my part in whatever way I can.' Rotten said 'I despise them. No one should have the right to tell anyone they can't live here because of the colour of their skin or their religion or the size of their nose. How could anyone vote for something so ridiculously inhumane?'
15 *Leveller*, 16.6.78.
16 *Leveller* 31.10.79. For evidence that RAC is still struggling on see *New Dawn*, no. 2, 1986.
17 *Broadcast*, 29.3.85.

18   See the NCCL's *Southall 23 April 1979. The report of the Unofficial Committee of Enquiry* (London, 1980).

19   *New Musical Express*, 7.3.81.

20   *Home Office Statistical Bulletin*, 20/82, 13.10.82.

21   *Daily Mail*, 1.7.85.

22   1.4.85

23   This point has been made as part of critiques of Racism Awareness Training. See, for example, Ahmed Gurmah's, 'The politics of Racism Awareness Training', *Critical Social Policy*, **11**, 1983.

24   The advertisement appeared, for example, in *Police*, the subscription-only magazine of The Police Federation.

25   See Tim Westwood's account of the Jam in *Blues and Soul*, no. 416, 23.9.84.

5   Diaspora, utopia and the critique of capitalism

The Times of November 1857 contains an utterly delightful cry of outrage on the part of a West-Indian plantation owner. This advocate analyses with great moral indignation – as a plea for the re-introduction of negro slavery – how the Quashees (the free blacks of Jamaica) content themselves with producing only what is necessary for their own consumption, and, alongside this 'use value' regard loafing (indulgence and idleness) as the real luxury good; how they do not care a damn for the sugar and the fixed capital invested in the plantations, but rather observe the planters' impending bankruptcy with an ironic grin of malicious pleasure, and even exploit their acquired Christianity as an embellishment for this mood of malicious glee and indolence (Marx, *Grundrisse*).

There is a very great deal in the world which Europe does not or cannot see: in the very same way that the European musical scale cannot transcribe – cannot write down, does not understand: the notes, or the price of this music (James Baldwin).

So far, this book has placed an implicit emphasis on the exclusionary effects of racism. This position must be modified, for though blacks are represented in contemporary British politics and culture as external to and estranged from the imagined community that is the nation, those representations are, like the 'racial' essences on which they rely, precarious constructions, discursive figures which obscure and mystify deeper relationships. These images of black alterity are phenomenal forms produced in a series of political and ideological struggles. As such, they are neither uncontested nor completely efficient. They lack the capacity to suppress the whole historical process of which they are part. Deconstructing and contextualizing them is important for the development of anti-racism, not least because they have been unable to block or even interrupt the long-term organic processes which have articulated blacks into British society. The manner in which blacks have been incorporated may be incomplete, uneven and provisional but they are none the less part of this country. Despite their obvious viciousness and political charge, today's racisms must not be allowed to mislead. Racial subordination is not the sole factor shaping the choices and actions of Britain's black settlers and their British-born children. The racial nationalist portrait of blacks as fundamentally alien must not be accorded too much power. It is only one theme in the antagonism which forms and disorganizes today's English working class. It is not a complete analysis, but a common-sense construction and must therefore compete with other alternative explanations which make life intelligible.

The examination of black cultures which forms the bulk of this long chapter is necessary for several reasons. It shows something of the richness of cultural struggle in and around 'race' and demonstrates also the dimensions of black oppositional practice which are not reducible to the narrow idea of anti-racism. The cultural forms examined below and the autonomous institutions in which they have been created are simultaneously sites of both 'race' and class formation. The complexity of the relationship between these two processes is habitually unseen by analysis which falsely abstracts 'race' and class from one another. It is, however, clearly evident in the black expressive cultures which spring up at the intersection of 'race' and class, providing a space in which the competing claims of ethnic particularity and universal humanity can be temporarily settled.

It bears repetition that 'race', ethnicity, nation and culture are not interchangeable terms. The cultural forms discussed below cannot be contained neatly within the structures of the nation-state. This quality can be used to reveal an additional failing in the rigid, pseudo-biological definition of national cultures which has been introduced by ethnic absolutism. Black Britain defines itself crucially as part of a diaspora. Its unique cultures draw inspiration from those developed by black populations elsewhere. In particular, the culture and politics of black America and the Caribbean have become raw materials for creative processes which redefine what it means to be black, adapting it to distinctively British experiences and meanings. Black culture is actively made and re-made.

Racisms generate and have to struggle against countervailing ideological tendencies some of which, as the last chapter has shown, have their origins outside the orbit of formal politics in the sphere of cultural creation. The conversation over the meaning and significance of 'race' which has taken place in and around youth cultures and 'sub-cultures' since their formation can be identified as an important illustration of this process. It precedes the RAR movement which tried to systematize it and anchor it in leftism. It can be heard in the strained, cover versions of Afro-American rhythm and blues tunes recorded by white, British performers from the Beatles to Paul Young. It can be seen in the movements of black and white dancers in the studio crowd on the 1960s television pop magazine programme 'Ready Steady Go'. It can be deduced from analysis of the multi-racial composition of insurgent, inner-city mobs in urban disorders which are later designated 'racial' events. Its voices present not so much a phantom history of post-war 'race relations' (Hebdige, 1979), but a substantive history of its own – a history that shows the necessarily complex relationships which have existed between blacks and the cultural and political institutions of the white, urban working-class communities that are transformed and reoriented by their presence.

This chapter introduces the study of black cultures within the framework of a diaspora as an alternative to the different varieties of absolutism which would confine culture in 'racial', ethnic or national essences. It suggests some of the elements required for the analysis of recent black history in Britain. It looks at aspects of the organic relationship between blacks and whites which has developed, unevenly, over a considerable period of time in the leisure institutions of urban Britain. It explores the manner in which the black elements in these 'two-tone' encounters have drawn on the cultural politics of black struggles in the US and the Caribbean, and finally focuses on the critique of capitalism enunciated by and immanent within the expressive cultures of black Britain.

As black styles, musics, dress, dance, fashion and languages became a determining force shaping the style, music, dress, fashion and language of urban Britain as a whole, blacks have been structured into the mechanisms of this society in a number of different ways. Not all of them are reducible to the disabling effects of racial subordination. This is part of the explanation of how the youth cultures discussed above became repositories of anti-racist feeling. Blacks born, nurtured and schooled in this country are, in significant measure, British even as their presence redefines the meaning of the term. The language and structures of racial politics, locked as they are into a circular journey between immigration as problem and repatriation as solution, prevent this from being seen. Yet recognizing it and grasping its significance is essential to the development of anti-racism in general and in particular for understanding the social movements for racial equality that helped to create the space in which 'youth culture' could form. The contingent and partial belonging to Britain which blacks enjoy, their ambiguous assimilation, must be examined in detail for it is closely associated with specific forms of exclusion. If we are to comprehend the cultural dynamics of 'race' we must be able to identify its limits. This, in turn, necessitates consideration of how blacks define and represent themselves in a complex combination of resistances and negotiations, which does far more than provide a direct answer to the brutal forms in which racial subordination is imposed.

Black expressive cultures affirm while they protest. The assimilation of blacks is not a process of acculturation but of cultural syncretism (Bastide, 1978). Accordingly, their self-definitions and cultural expressions draw on a plurality of black histories and politics. In the context of modern Britain this has produced a diaspora

155

dimension to black life. Here, non-European traditional elements, mediated by the histories of Afro-America and the Caribbean, have contributed to the formation of new and distinct black cultures amidst the decadent peculiarities of the Welsh, Irish, Scots and English. These non-European elements must be noted and their distinctive resonance must be accounted for. Some derive from the immediate history of Empire and colonization in Africa, the Caribbean and the Indian sub-continent from where post-war settlers brought both the methods and the memories of their battles for citizenship, justice and independence. Others create material for the processes of cultural syncretism from extended and still-evolving relationships between the black populations of the over-developed world and their siblings in racial subordination elsewhere.

The effects of these ties and the penetration of black forms into the dominant culture mean that it is impossible to theorize black culture in Britain without developing a new perspective on British culture *as a whole*. This must be able to see behind contemporary manifestations into the cultural struggles which characterized the imperial and colonial period.[1] An intricate web of cultural and political connections binds blacks here to blacks elsewhere. At the same time, they are linked into the social relations of this country. Both dimensions have to be examined and the contradictions and continuities which exist between them must be brought out. Analysis must for example be able to suggest why Afrika Bambaataa and Jah Shaka, leading representatives of hip-hop and reggae culture respectively, find it appropriate to take the names of African chiefs distinguished in anti-colonial struggle, or why young black people in places as different as Hayes and Harlem choose to style themselves the Zulu Nation. Similarly we must comprehend the cultural and political relationships which have lead to Joseph Charles and Rufus Radebe being sentenced to six years imprisonment in South Africa for singing banned songs written by the Birmingham reggae band Steel Pulse – the same band which performed to London's RAR carnival in 1978.[2]

The social movements which have sprung up in different parts of the world as evidence of African dispersal, imperialism and colonialism have done more than appeal to blacks everywhere in a language which could invite their universal identification (Sheppard *et al.*, 1875). They have communicated directly to blacks and their supporters all over the world asking for concrete help and solidarity in the creation of organizational forms adequate to the pursuit of emancipation, justice and citizenship, internationally as well as within national frameworks. The nineteenth-century English abolitionists who purchased the freedom of Frederick Douglass, the distinguished black activist and writer, were responding to an appeal of this type.[3] The eighteenth-century settlement of Sierra Leone by blacks from England and their white associates[4] and the formation of free black communities in Liberia (Geiss, 1974) remain an important testimony to the potency of such requests. The back-to-Africa movements in America, the Caribbean and now Europe, Negritude and the birth of the New Negro in the Harlem Renaissance (Perry, 1976; Berghahn, 1977) during the 1920s all provide further illustrations of a multi-faceted desire to overcome the sclerotic confines of the nation state as a precondition of the liberation of blacks everywhere (Padmore, 1956).

Technological developments in the field of communication have, in recent years, encouraged this desire and made it more powerful by fostering a global perspective from the memories of slavery and indenture which are the property of the African diaspora. The soul singers of Afro-America have been able to send 'a letter to their friends' in Africa and elsewhere.[5] The international export of new world black cultures first to whites and then to 'third world' markets in South America and Africa itself (Wallis and Malm, 1984), has had effects unforeseen by those for whom selling it is nothing other than a means to greater profit. Those cultures, in the form of cultural commodities – books and records – have carried inside them oppositional ideas, ideologies, theologies and philosophies. As black artists have addressed an international audience and blues, gospel, soul and reggae have been consumed in circumstances far removed from those in which they were originally created, new definitions of 'race' have been born. A new structure of cultural exchange has been built up across the imperial networks which once played host to the triangular trade of sugar, slaves and capital. Instead of three nodal points there are now four – the Caribbean, the US, Europe and Africa. The cultural and political expressions of new world blacks have been transferred not just to Europe and Africa but between various parts of the new world itself. By these means Rastafari culture has been carried to locations as diverse as Poland and Polynesia, and hip-hop from Stockholm to Southall.

Analysis of the political dimensions to the expressive culture of black communities in Britain must reckon with their position within international networks. It should begin where fragmented diaspora histories of racial subjectivity combine in unforeseen ways with the edifice of British society and create a complex relationship which has evolved through various stages linked in different ways to the pattern of capitalist development itself.

The modern world-system responsible for the expansion of Europe and consequent dispersal of black slave labourers throughout Europe and the new world was from its inception an international operation. Several scholars have pointed to its uneasy fit into forms of analysis premised on the separation of its economic and cultural sub-systems into discrete national units coterminous with nation states

157

(Wallerstein, 1979, chapter 13; Robinson, 1983). The social structures and processes erected over the productive and distributive relations of this system centred on slavery and plantation society and were reproduced in a variety of different forms across the Americas, generating political antagonisms which were both international and transnational in character (James, 1938; 1985). Their contemporary residues, rendered more difficult to perceive by the recent migration of slave descendants into the centres of metropolitan civilization, also exhibit the tendency to transcend a narrowly national focus. Analysis of black politics must, therefore, if it is to be adequate, move beyond the field of inquiry designated by concepts which deny the possibility of common themes, motives and practices within diaspora history. This is where categories formed in the intersection of 'race' and the nation state are themselves exhausted. To put it another way, national units are not the most appropriate basis for studying this history for the African diaspora's consciousness of itself has been defined in and against constricting national boundaries.

As the international slave system unfolded, so did its antithesis in the form of transnational movements for self-emancipation organized by slaves, ex-slaves and their abolitionist allies. This is not the place to provide a full account of these movements or even of the special place within them occupied by ideas about Africa. However, that continent has been accepted by many, though not all, who inhabit and reproduce the black syncretisms of the overdeveloped world as a homeland even if they do not aspire to a physical return there. Ties of affect and affiliation have been strengthened by knowledge of anti-colonial struggles which have sharpened contemporary understanding of 'race'. These feelings, of being descended from or belonging to Africa and of longing for its liberation from imperialist rule, can be linked loosely by the term 'Pan Africanism' (Geiss, 1974; Padmore, 1956). The term is inadequate as anything other than the most preliminary description, particularly as it can suggest mystical unity outside the process of history or even a common culture or ethnicity which will assert itself regardless of determinate political and economic circumstances. The sense of inter-connectedness felt by blacks to which it refers, has in some recent manifestations become partially detached from any primary affiliation to Africa and from the aspiration to a homogeneous African culture. Young blacks in Britain, for example, stimulated to riotous protest by the sight of black 'South Africans' stoning apartheid police and moved by scenes of brutality transmitted from that country by satellite, may not feel that shared Africanness is at the root of the empathy they experience. It may be that a common experience of powerlessness somehow transcending history and experienced in *racial* categories; in the antagonism between white and black rather than European and African, is
158

enough to secure affinity between these divergent patterns of subordination. As Ralph Ellison pointed out long ago:

. . . since most so-called Negro-cultures outside Africa are necessarily amalgams, it would seem more profitable to stress the term 'culture' and leave the term 'Negro' out of the discussion. It is not culture which binds the people who are of partially African origin now scattered throughout the world but an identity of passions (Ellison, 1964, p. 263).

These matters need not occupy us further here. Though it should be noted that the struggles to which they refer, have, since the very first day that slaves set out across the Atlantic, involved radical passions rooted in distinctly African history, philosophy and religious practice. Passions which have, at strategic moments challenged the political and moral authority of the capitalist world system in which the diaspora was created. The ideologies and beliefs of new world blacks exhibit characteristically African conceptions of the relationship between art and life, the sacred and the secular, the spiritual and the material (Mbiti, 1969). Traces of these African formulations remain, albeit in displaced and mediated forms, even in the folk philosophies, religion and vernacular arts of black Britain.

The struggle to overcome slavery, wherever it developed, involved adaptations of Christianity (Bastide, 1978; Cone, 1985; Palmer, 1975; Harding, 1969; Genovese, 1979) and politically infused music and dance (Cone, 1972) which, in DuBois's phrase, comprised 'the articulate message of the slave to the world' (DuBois, 1969). This message, however articulate, was also heavily encoded. Frederick Douglass describes it coming out 'if not in the word(s) in the sound . . . as frequently in the one as in the other' (Douglass, 1974). It existed beyond words, and where words were used, their meanings within the dominant culture were strategically inverted, often twisted inside out (Mitchell-Kernan, 1972; Gates, 1984b). The 'sorrow of the heart' which Douglass heard in the slaves' songs, conveying the horrible character of slavery, was so profound yet carefully concealed that whites who heard it were able to speak of the 'singing of the slaves as evidence of their contentment and happiness'. There is an important warning here for those who seek to analyse the politics of these black cultures exclusively through their overtly committed content. These cultures have been produced over a long period of time in conditions of the most terrible oppression. They have been created inside and in opposition to the capitalist system of racial exploitation and domination, by those who experience subordination at its most vicious and degrading. Nor are these cultures mere aggregations of oppositional statements directed at that system, which once decoded will be easily translated into the political vocabularies of other historically specific traditions of radicalism. Their protests are synchronized with an affirmation of particularity. Afro-centric spirituality and conjure

159

(West, 1982; Reed, 1972; 1973) as well as the linguistic tropes which negotiate the boundaries of insubordination and insolence in slave cultures denied legitimate access to literacy, have all bequeathed distinct political legacies which may not, for example, have immediate equivalents in the epistemological repertoire of contemporary Marxism or social democracy. These cultural forms contribute to a dynamic movement which has required them to become impermeable or at least unrecognizably political as a necessary precondition of their effectiveness. They have initiated forms of 'meta-communication' where 'surface expression and intrinsic position diverge' (Cooke, 1984). These issues have been explored by scholars and activists primarily in relation to the literary culture of Afro-America where blacks have sought dialogue with the white majority (Baker, 1984; Gates, 1984a; Ellison, 1964; Baraka, 1984). There has been less analysis of the more popular traditions of cultural creation – music and dance – where engagement with white audiences, culture and society has been more recent and less widespread. In an attempt to address this absence, the rest of this chapter presents a history and exposition of the musical cultures of black Britain and their attendant social relations of consumption. The political character of these expressive cultures will be examined by reference to their forms as well as any overtly critical or interventionist content. The idea that the spaces in which cultural consumption takes place provide locations in which racial politics can be erased or dispersed by lived and formed relations based on gender, age, class and locality will also be looked at. The expressive cultures will be shown to articulate with patterns of political organization and action.

Black and white on the dance-floor

In July 1949, a *Picture Post* feature article by Robert Kee on 'The British colour bar' was illustrated by a photograph of a young couple and their child. The man was black and the woman was white. The caption beneath their picture was headlined, 'a marriage that can lead to difficulties'. It revealed that the man, Herman McKay, was earning a living running a dance-band. In fact, the picture shows his wife helping him into his stage costume. The caption explained that he had been forced to adopt the pseudonym 'Alfonso Perez' as an essential part of this musical venture. This picture and its accompanying narrative vividly illustrate the way in which, from the beginning of post-war settlement, blacks were an ambiguous presence inside the popular culture of the 'host society'. Mr McKay was acceptable in the persona of 'Perez' the bandleader. He was welcome as a musician, as a producer of that culture, but the article implies that the informal but widespread colour bar would have excluded

160

him as a customer from many of the places in which he worked as a performer.

The gradual transition from migrant to settler status involved a progression through a medley of different cultural forms. The early settlers were comparatively few in number (Peach, 1968) and beyond the British educations which were their colonial inheritance, they lacked a single cohesive culture which could bind them together. They set about creating it from the diverse influences which were available and which corresponded to their predicament. The dances, parties and social functions in which students, ex-service people and workers enjoyed themselves, reverberated to black musics drawn from the US and Africa as well as Latin America and the Caribbean. They jived and jitterbugged, foxtrotted and quickstepped, moving from one cultural idiom to another as the music changed. Class and occupational conflicts among the settlers as well as ethnic differences and the gender ratio[6] contributed to a degree of fragmentation. The student population concentrated in Bayswater, Kensington and North London diverged sharply from both the new workers who were beginning to make their homes in Brixton and Ladbroke Grove and the older seafaring community centred in the East End. The patterns of leisure generated by each relatively discrete group did not always overlap. Each in its own way combined black cultures from a variety of sources with those of the different white communities into which blacks were being drawn as a replacement population. Dancing was for many a primary leisure activity and, being couple centred, a sequence of conflicts based on whether blacks and whites could fraternize and touch in public began to develop.

Enrico Stennett, a young Jamaican political activist who had moved to Britain during 1947, achieved such notoriety for his prowess in the dance-halls of London that, after first being banned from the Lyceum, the Astoria, the Locarno and the Hammersmith and Wimbledon Palais, he was eventually hired by the management to perform exhibitions of jiving and jitterbugging to the delight of the white working-class crowds. This employment took him to ballrooms throughout the south of England and earned him £25 per week for three nights work. Unable to find a black woman to be his partner, Stennett discovered that dancing with white women provoked intense hostility from the management and sometimes violence. He and his white partner were contracted to leave immediately their exemplary performances ended lest other white women asked him to dance. Operating under the name 'Sugar', he and other young black dancers congregated at the Paramount ballroom in London's Tottenham Court Road. The Paramount rapidly became known as the dance-hall for black teenagers. 'Sugar' and other dance-floor hustlers working under names like 'The Magic Boots' and 'The

Gladiator' equally quickly achieved a monopoly of the dance competitions organized by the ballroom owners.

It was ironic to see, in an area of white people, you could not find one white
male dancing. At the Paramount the atmosphere was always electric as the
big bands jostled to play for us. . . . At these moments they could really
enjoy their playing and by seeing the black people enjoying themselves to
the full, it gave them more room for improvisation. . . . Alas there were no
black women, but the Paramount was packed with young ladies coming in
from the stockbroker belt of Surrey, Essex and Hampshire and other small
villages and towns within a 60 mile radius of London.[7]

Stennett's account of the ballroom scene of the early 1950s is particularly valuable if read in conjunction with the autobiography of Leslie
Thompson,[8] a black musician who worked in many of the biggest
dance-bands during this period. Both testify to the ambiguous
penetration of blacks into mainstream working-class leisure space.
The contradictory nature of the black presence in those institutions
is exemplified by Stennett's tale of the ways in which 'racial' hostility
was tempered by the high status that derived from black pre-
eminence on the dance-floor.

The different responses of whites along gender lines are also highly
significant not only because they fracture the continuity of 'race' but
also because of the centrality of miscegenation to the racist ideologies
of the time. Stennett describes some of the conflicts which developed
when white women were drawn into the unfolding antagonism
between their black boyfriends and the police, who were particularly
angered by the sight of black and white together. According to his
account, both the police and the organized racist groups of the time
felt that the association of white women with black men which was
a marked feature of the Paramount sub-culture and actively discour-
aged by its management, degraded Britain as a whole. Hostile police
patrols and groups of racists would wait outside at closing time to
assault and intimidate any black man they could find with a white
woman.

On one occasion I had left the Paramount dancehall alone and walked to
the no. 1 bus stop in Warren Street. As I stood in a long queue of mostly
women, I saw three African men with five English women enter a small
café. They were not in the café more than five minutes when a gang of white
men entered the café, pulled them outside and set about attacking them.
The Africans were badly beaten so I rushed to the telephone to call the
police. It was not long before they arrived in their cars and meat wagons.
But the arrival of the police did not help the Africans. The leading police car
blew his horn repeatedly giving the white men the chance to escape. They
then proceeded to arrest the Africans. This did not go down well with the
women in the queue. They set about the police attacking them physically
with their stilletto heels as weapons. This resulted in many women being

162

arrested along with the three Africans and taken to the police station off the Marylebone Road.[9]

Writing of the relationship between black men and white women at the time Ras Makonnen (George Griffith) has suggested that a form of proto-feminism was to be found at the roots of women's support for the work of black political activists working in London.

We recognised that the dedication of some of the girls to our cause was an expression of equal rights for women. One way of rejecting the oppression of men was to associate with blacks. To walk with a negro into a posh club like the Atheneum was to make this point. But many of them were vigorously attacked for this (Makonnen, 1973, p. 147).

It would appear that long before the advent of 'rock n'roll', the rise of soul, disco and reggae, the cultural institutions of the white working class were hosting an historic encounter between young black and white people. This meeting precipitated not only fear of the degeneration of the white 'race' in general and defilement of its womanhood in particular, but also the creation of a youth sub-culture in which black style and expertise were absolutely central. Indeed black supremacy within this sub-culture inverted in the most striking manner the relationships of domination and subordination assigned outside the dance-halls on racial lines. Of course, away from the shared spaces in which blacks and whites could interact and overlap, a further layer of exclusively black cultural institutions, clubs and dives was being created. Hiro estimates that during this period there were up to fifty black-owned and managed basement clubs in South London alone (1971). In the centre of London, the 59 Club, the Flamingo, the 77 Club and the Sunset, all in Soho, and the Contemporanean in Mayfair all catered to the needs of black workers. Dances organized by the British Council in its hostel at Hans Crescent in Knightsbridge kept the students occupied.

Sebastian Clarke (1980), has pointed out that 'Melodisc', a specialist label on which 'race' records from various sources could be issued, was operating successfully in this country from 1946 onwards (Cowley, 1985). Early releases on this label included material from the American Savoy catalogue. Melodisc first released calypso records here in 1951, having signed the celebrated troubadour, Lord Kitchener, who had been living in England since 1948.

Daddy Peckings, the proprietor of Peckings's Studio One record shop in West London, was the first person to sell reggae and its antecedents – bluebeat, ska and rocksteady – in this country. He has described the gradual transformation of American musical forms, particularly jazz and jump blues, and their junction with traditional Jamaican musics. This cross-fertilization would eventually lead to modern reggae, the evolution of which can be traced through the development of 'sound systems' (Bradshaw, 1981) – large mobile discos – and their surrounding culture in Jamaica and Britain. According to Peckings, the sound systems playing in the dance-halls of Kingston in the late 1940s and early 1950s – Waldron, Tom 'The Great' Sebastian and Nick – offered a mixture of bebop and swing. The big-band sounds of Duke Ellington and Count Basie were reworked by local musicians: Milton McPherson, Redva Cooke, Steve Dick and Jack Brown. Travelling to England in May 1960, Peckings set up a UK outlet for the product of legendary Jamaican producer and entrepreneur Coxsone Dodd, boss of the legendary Studio One label and the man credited not only with the discovery of modern Jamaica's greatest musical talents – The Heptones, Freddie McGregor, Jackie Mittoo, The Wailers – but with the creation of reggae itself.[10] The fledgling sound system culture of urban Jamaica was transplanted into Britain during the 1950s and on his arrival, Peckings began to supply records to Duke Vin of Ladbroke Grove, the first sound system in this country.

The basic description of a sound system as a large mobile hi-fi or disco does little justice to the specificities of the form. They are, of course, many thousands of times more powerful than a domestic record player but are significantly different from the amplified discos through which other styles of music have been circulated and consumed. The sound that they generate has its own characteristics, particularly an emphasis on the reproduction of bass frequencies, its own aesthetics and a unique mode of consumption. The form of sound systems and the patterns of consumption with which they have become associated will be discussed in detail below. The mark of African elements can be identified on different aspects of sound system culture.

Regardless of their forms and characteristic content, it is necessary to comprehend the importance of the sound systems for both the Jamaican reggae music industry which grew directly out of their activities and for the expressive culture of black Britain in which they remain a core institution. Perhaps the most important effect of the sound systems on the contemporary musical culture of black Britain is revealed in the way that it is centred not on live performances by musicians and singers, though these are certainly appreciated, but on records. Public performance of recorded music is primary in both reggae and soul variants of the culture. In both, records become raw material for spontaneous performances of cultural creation in which the DJ and the MC or toaster who introduces each disc or sequence of discs, emerge as the principal agents in dialogic rituals of active and celebratory consumption. It is above all in these performances that black Britain has expressed the improvization, spontaneity and intimacy which are key characteristics of all new world black musics, providing a living bridge between them and African traditions of music-making which dissolve the distinctions between art and life,

164

artefact and expression which typify the contrasting traditions of Europe (Hoare, 1975; Keil, 1972; Sithole, 1972). As Keil points out, 'outside the west, musical traditions are almost exclusively performance traditions' (1972, p. 85). Sound system culture redefines the meaning of the term performance by separating the input of the artists who originally made the recording from the equally important work of those who adapt and rework it so that it directly expresses the moment in which it is being consumed, however remote this may be from the original context of production. The key to this process is the orality of the artistic forms involved.

The shifting, specialized vocabularies of sound system culture have changed and developed within contradictions generated by wider political and cultural processes – changing patterns of 'race' and class formation in the Caribbean, the US and Britain. The reliance on recorded music takes on even greater significance when it is appreciated that for much of the post-war period, Britain, unlike the US and the Caribbean, lacked both a domestic capacity to produce black musics and any independent means for their distribution. At this stage, the BBC was not interested in including African and Caribbean music in their programmes. When 'pop' charts began to be compiled, black shops and products were structurally excluded from the operations which generated them. This situation contrasts sharply with the position in the US where a well-developed market for 'race records' had grown up (Gillett, 1972), with its own distributors, charts and above all radio stations as a crucial means to spread and reproduce the culture.

Black Britain prized records as the primary resource for its emergent culture and the discs were overwhelmingly imported or licensed from abroad. The dependency of the British music scene on musics produced elsewhere has progressed through several phases. But even as self-consciously British black forms have been constructed, the basic fact of dependency has remained constant. The cultural syncretism that has taken place across the national boundaries that divide the African diaspora has involved relations of unequal exchange in which Britain, for demographic and historical reasons has until recently had a strictly subordinate place. The importing of music, often in small quantities, encouraged the underground aspects of a scene in which outlets into the dominant culture were already rare. Competition between sound system operators had been an early feature of the Jamaican dance-halls, and was entrenched over here as sound systems jostled for the most up-to-date and exclusive tunes imported from the US as well as the Caribbean. In a major survey of London's black music scene of the early 1970s, Carl Gayle explored the appeal of imported 'pre-release' records on the dance-hall circuit:

The youngsters today spend more than they can afford on records, but they want the best and the rarest. . . . 'We import our records three times a week from Jamaica' said a young guy called Michael. . . . 'Pre-release music to me and many people like Sound System men and their followers, is like underground music. As soon as it's released it's commercial music. So you find the youth of today, the ghetto youth like myself, pre-release music is like medicine. They'll go anywhere to hear it.'[11]

The identification of imported music as free from the commercialization which characterized the British music industry is an important expression of the politics which infused the roots music scene. The supposedly non-commercial status of imported records added directly to their appeal and demonstrated the difference between black culture and the pop-world against which it was defined.

The rivalry between 'sounds' over records was paralleled on the dance-floors by intense competition between their followers. The ritual expressions of both were dance competitions and the occasional fight. In the early 1970s reggae and soul scenes, the formal competitions centred on 'shuffling' and the rivalry between different sound systems was particularly intense where operators from north and south of the river clashed, each operator and toaster striving to match the other tune for tune, rhythm for rhythm, until the system with the best tunes and the weightiest sound emerged as the victor. Carl Gayle identified the level of violence in these encounters as one factor in the decomposition of the scene into sharply differentiated soul and reggae sub-scenes during the 1970s.

The rivalry which developed between North and South . . . was the foundation for much of the violence of the Ram Jam and other clubs and was perpetrated by the supporters of the Sound Systems – Coxon and Duke Reid in the South and Count Shelly in the North especially. This rivalry, which often erupted into violence was responsible for the division of the black music scene as a whole. . . . The clubs lost their respectability. Consequently many black youngsters dropped out of the once peaceful reggae-oriented sub-culture, opting for the more tranquil soul scene. Soul had always been popular with West Indians anyway and a lot of people just got scared of the hooliganism.

Gayle tentatively suggests that this violence was something which made reggae attractive to white youth and that it was a significant element in the forging of links between reggae and the skinheads around common conceptions of masculinity and machismo.

At its height, the late 1960s and early 1970s club scene involved alcohol-free daytime sessions completely dominated by dance at some of the best venues. For example, the Sunday afternoon 2–6 p.m. sessions at the Ram Jam in Brixton provided an antecedent for the equally drinkless Saturday lunch time events organized by DJ Tim Westwood, which were instrumental in the spread of hip-hop in London during the 1980s. Like the hip-hop mixers of the later era, the sound system DJs often removed the labels from the records which they used. This gesture combined the obvious desire to keep the information contained on the labels secret, with a comment on the distance which these sub-cultures had travelled from their commercialized, overground equivalents. The removal of labels subverted the emphasis on acquisition and individual ownership which the makers of black music cultures identified as an unacceptable feature of pop culture. This simple act suggested alternative collective modes of consumption in which the information essential to purchase was separated from the pleasure which the music created. The record could be enjoyed without knowing who it was by or where it was in a chart. Its origins were rendered secondary to the use made of it in the creative rituals of the dance-hall.

Deprived of access to the official charts, the black record sellers began to produce their own alternative indices of roots popularity in specialist publications devoted to black music and in the community's own news and political weeklies. The specialist monthly *Black Music* was launched in December 1973, at exactly the same time as minority programming of black musics was beginning to be introduced into the newly expanded local radio network. The size and distribution of Britain's black populations imposed severe limits on the amount of money which could be made from catering to their leisure needs. The communities remained diverse, small and scattered. These characteristics were important factors in the expansion of black leisure institutions and their partial adaptation to the demands of white Britons. The involvement of whites, particularly young people, in the consumption of black cultures was noted by commentators in the early 1960s. It has been discussed by other authors and by myself elsewhere (Patterson, 1966; Hebdige, 1979; Gilroy and Lawrence, 1982). The centrality of distinctively black forms to white youth cultures was observed by Hamblett and Deverson in 1964:

The Blue Beat is here to stay. . . . Around the dancehalls and discotheques the Blue Beat has been added to the youngsters' already overstepping dance crazes. . . . Many mods that I have spoken to say that the Mersey Sound is out and this new sound is the big thing at the moment. As one youngster put it to me 'The Beatles have been well and truly squashed and we don't dig their sound anymore'.[12]

This mod's use of black American slang, 'dig', and the Beatles' early reliance on cover versions of material from rhythm and blues artists like Barrett Strong and Larry Williams are probably as significant as the blue beat itself in the history of how popular culture has formed spaces in which the politics of 'race' could be lived out and transcended in the name of youth.

The development of Jamaican popular music in the encounter between folk forms and American R and B picked up from radio stations transmitting in the southern states is well known (Clarke, 1980; Kimberley, 1982). At each stage of its progress through blue beat, ska, rocksteady and reggae it is possible to indicate shifting patterns in the involvement of young whites. For example, a white reggae band 'Inner Mind' was formed in London during 1967 and was considered good enough to back such vintage Jamaican performers as Laurel Aitken, Alton Ellis and Owen Grey.[13] The band played at all the leading black venues of the period – Mr B's, the Q and Colombo's in London, the Santa Rosa in Birmingham and Wolverhampton's Club '67. In *The Empire Strikes Back* (1982) I have indicated some of the elements by means of which this substantial history of white involvement can be periodized. The mass marketing of Caribbean music as a pop form can be traced from Millie Small's 'My Boy Lollipop' through the reggae festival at Wembley Stadium in 1969 and into the selling of Bob Marley as a 'rebel superstar'. Simon Jones (1986) has pointed out that there were seventeen top twenty hits based on Jamaican music during the period 1969–72. The attempts of white companies to sell the music to whites also relied on the growth of minority programming within the newly established local radio network. The local stations which proliferated between 1970 and 1972 were concentrated in urban areas and each of them featured two or three hours of black music per week. This development was more significant in the history of Caribbean forms, because the pirate radio stations and the American Forces station in Europe already carried a certain amount of soul music to British fans. Radio Luxembourg, a leading pirate, broadcast Dave Christian's 'Soul Bag' early (1.30.a.m.) on Monday mornings. The new local stations made black music available to anyone who was interested enough to tune in to the unpopular slots – usually Sunday lunchtime – in which the minority shows were programmed. In the south-east, Steve Barnard's 'Reggae Time' on Radio London became particularly influential. Having experimented with several presenters for their reggae programme, Capital Radio launched David Rodigan's 'Roots Rockers' in October 1979. This show became the most important in reggae broadcasting, extending its running time from one and a half to three hours. The power of the show and the extent to which the reggae industry depended on it were revealed in 1985 when Rodigan announced that he had been threatened and intimidated by a small minority of record producers who sought to use the show to push their own product and ensure its commercial success regardless of artistic considerations. Rodigan did not name the producers responsible for his harassment, but told his listeners over the air:

I've reached the point of no return with these hustlers. I'm tired of the threats and I'm standing up to them from now on. I'm going to entertain the public, not the reggae producers. I'm not going to bow down any more. All they can do is kill me now – that's all they can do.[14]

The gradual involvement of large corporations with a broad base in the leisure industries in the selling of reggae stimulated important changes reflecting a conscious attempt to separate the product from its producers and from its roots in black life. Whatever the effect of the reggae film *The Harder They Come* in the Caribbean (Brathwaite, 1984), in Britain, it marked the beginning of a new strategy for white consumption. The film was presented as little more than visual support for the sound-track recording made available by Island Records, an Anglo-Jamaican company. Cinemas showing the film became artificially insulated spaces in which images of black life, in this case as backward, violent, sexist and fratricidal could be consumed without having to face the difficulties associated with sharing leisure space with real live black people. Island Records, the company who pioneered this ploy, elaborated it further in subsequent films of reggae artists in live performance and in the 'adventure fantasy', *Countryman* in 1982. This last film, a tale of Obeah and adventure, was based on a simple inversion of the Robinson Crusoe myth. 'Friday', recast in the form of a Rasta hermit-fisherman endowed with magical powers that originated in his total harmony with the natural world, saves and protects two young white Americans who fall into his Eden as the result of a plane crash. They are unwittingly involved in the drug business but with his help are reunited with their families and sent back to the US once the villains, the military wing of Michael Manley's socialist government, have been put in their place. This plot is less significant than the fact that the film was billed as 'A tribute to Bob Marley'. This time, the sound-track recording featured his songs.[15]

Island Records was also at the forefront of moves to sign black performers and, having adjusted their music and image to the expectations of white rock audiences, sell them as pop stars. The example of Bob Marley, an Island artist from 1972 until his death in 1981, provides the most acute illustration of a marketing process which was repeated by the company on a smaller, less successful scale with other lesser known (in rock terms) artists like the Heptones and Burning Spear. It was a strategy which was less productive for other rival British companies which lacked Island's roots in the Caribbean. Foremost among these was Virgin, who signed many leading Jamaican performers – the Gladiators, U Roy and the Mighty Diamonds – in the early 1970s. Marley's rise was also significant in that it facilitated the popularization of Rastafari ideology in Britain and throughout the world. The years between 1972 and 1981 saw him rise to outernational prominence and take reggae music forever into the lexicon of pop. There are good reasons to support the view

169

that his foray into pop stardom was a calculated development in which he was intimately involved, having realized that the solidification of communicative networks across the African diaspora was a worthwhile prize. The minor adjustments in presentation and form that rendered his reggae assimilable across the cultural borders of the overdeveloped countries were thus a small price to pay. His incorporation of bluesy guitar playing and 'disco' rhythms can be interpreted not as obvious concessions to the demands of a white rock audience (Walls and Malm, 1984), but as attempts to utilize the very elements most likely to appeal to the black audiences of North America.

Marley died at the very moment when he had steered reggae to the brink of an organic and overdue encounter with rhythm and blues. His work found considerable support in the new pop markets of Latin America and Africa, where he had performed at the independence ceremonies for Zimbabwe, symbolizing the recovery of Africa for the black peoples of the new world and the recovery of the new world diaspora for Africa. Whatever the ambiguities in Marley's music and mode of presentation, he provided a heroic personality around which the international mass-marketing of reggae could pivot. His 'Exodus' album remained on the British pop chart for fifty-six consecutive weeks in the period 1977–8. Marley acknowledged his newfound white listeners with the release of 'Punky Reggae Party' also in 1977. It signified not so much the confluence of two oppositional impulses – Rasta and punk – as the durability of pop and its capacity to absorb diverse and contradictory elements. The Caribbean was becoming an increasingly important sub-cultural resource once white British youth began to break free of their own dependency on American images and meanings (Hebdige, 1983). By consolidating reggae's position on the charts outside novelty categories and becoming a star, Marley created a new space in pop. In the period leading up to his death, it was a space filled primarily by the 'two-tone' cult. In this movement, earlier Caribbean forms, particularly ska, which had been exposed by the serious reggae fans' search for musical authenticity behind Marley's obvious compromises, were captured and rearticulated into distinctively British styles and concerns. This fusion took several contrasting paths. The assertively 'white' reggae of London bands like Madness and Bad Manners attracted the support of young racists, whose patriotic nativism had been reborn in the revival of the skinhead style. It contrasted sharply with the work of racially mixed groups from the Midlands. Where Madness simply hijacked ska and declared it white, the Beat, the Specials and other similar outfits sought to display the contradictory politics of 'race' openly in their work. Their best efforts acknowledged the destructive power of racism and simultaneously invited their audience to share in its overcoming, a possibility that was made concrete in the co-operation of blacks and whites in producing the music.

170

If Marley's excursions into pop had seeded the ground for this two-tone harvest, this era suggests that the lasting significance of his rise to prominence lies not at the flamboyant extremities of youth sub-culture where punks had reworked the themes and preoccupations of Rastafari around their dissent from and critique of Britishness, but in the youth–cultural mainstream. Here, the posters of Bob, locks flying, which had been inserted into his crossover product by Island, became icons in the bedroom shrines of thousands of young whites. In his egalitarianism, Ethiopianism and anti-imperialism, his critique of law and of the types of work which were on offer, these young people found meanings with which to make sense of their lives in post-imperial Britain. The two-tone bands appreciated this and isolated the elements in Marley's appeal that were most appropriate to the experiences of young, urban Britons on the threshold of the 1980s. They pushed the inner logic of his project to its conclusion by fusing pop forms rooted in the Caribbean with a populist politics. Marley's populism had been focused by the imperatives of black liberation and overdetermined by the language of Rastafarian escha-tology. Theirs was centred instead on pointing to the possibility that black and white young people might discover common or parallel meanings in their blighted, post-industrial predicament. The experi-ence of living side by side in a 'ghost town' had begun to raise this question. The Specials' song, which topped the chart as the rioting of 1981 was at its peak, asked, 'Why must the youth fight against themselves?' and cleverly entangled its pleas against both racism and youth–cultural sectarianism. The two-tone operation depended on being seen to transcend the various prescriptive definitions of 'race' which faced each other across the hinterland of youth culture. With Marley's death equilibrium was lost. One pole of the cultural field in which two-tone had formed ceased functioning. Marley's position was usurped eagerly not by the next generation of Jamaican and British artists who had been groomed by their record companies to succeed him, but by a new wave of post-punk white reggae musicians. The best known of these inverted the preconceptions of Rasta by calling themselves The Police and armed with 'Aryan' good looks and dedication to 'Reggatta de Blanc' served, within pop culture at least, to detach reggae from its historic association with the Africans of the Caribbean and their British descendants.

'Get up, get into it and get involved' – soul, Civil Rights and Black Power

This section turns away from the relationship between Britain and the Caribbean to focus on Afro-America, a second source of cultural and political raw-material for UK blacks in the post-war period.

The coming together of black and white young people explored above did not take place in pure and ideologically neutral settings. The black forms in which Britain's young people took pleasure during the 1950s and 1960s were not innocent. They were already articulated by political language, symbols and meanings given by the struggle of social movements for emancipation and equality. Like the cultural forms themselves, this political inheritance had to be dealt with and adapted to British circumstances. Looking at these complex processes of adaptation and transformation provides additional evidence of the syncretic qualities of diaspora culture in general and black British culture in particular. It also suggests that the European distinction between politics and culture cannot be easily and straightforwardly introduced into analysis of distinctly non-European traditions of radicalism (Benjamin, 1984).

Bob Marley's reggae was, like all reggae, a hybrid marked as much by its ties to American rhythm and blues as by its roots in Mento and calypso. One of the best known songs of Marley's middle period, 'Three O'Clock Road Block' is for example, extrapolated from Cole Porter's 'Don't Fence Me In'.

The cultural relationships between Jamaica and the US and between Jamaica and the UK have been explored much more fully than the third side of the diasporic triangle: the connection between black America and Britain which runs through the same post-war years. That relationship is considered in depth in this section.

Concluding his study of black music in the US, Ben Sidran (1971) argues that the major trend feature of black musical cultures in the post-war period 'has been its acceptance by major segments of white America – an acceptance on several levels of experience'. This insight is not restricted to the US. Analysing the same period, David Morse (1976) has pointed to the growth of black musical forms which anticipated white audiences and addressed the white world directly, breaking taboos about its overt representation which were among the defining characteristics of the blues as a genre. Gospel music on the other hand, the least outward of black musical forms had always addressed itself to the oppressor, through a complex of dense codes and rich biblical symbolism (Southern, 1983; Heilbut, 1985). The gradual secularization of that style which gave rise to soul coincided precisely with the formation of a social movement for racial justice and equality which became the 'largest mass movement for racial justice and civil rights in the twentieth century' (Marable, 1984). Black America was constituting itself into organizations and patterns of struggle which would finally bring down the Jim Crow system in what Manning Marable has called the 'Second Reconstruction'. Knowledge of these struggles was transmitted into black ghettoes and communities all over the world by Afro-American music. We have already seen how the British police reacted to the growth of Black Power.

The turbulent years between the 'Brown vs. The Board of Education' case and the march on Washington in 1963 were the period in which racial terror was displaced from its position as the primary mode of political administration in the southern states (Piven and Cloward, 1977; Harding, 1980; Marable, 1984; Baldwin, 1986).

This change in American society saw 20,000 people arrested between the autumn 1961 and the spring of 1963. As Manning Marable again points out: 'In 1963 alone another 15,000 were imprisoned [and] 1,000 desegregation protests occurred in more than 100 cities' (1984).

This movement will be remembered for the novelty of its tactics: mass 'jail-ins' which clogged the legal institutions of the South, its mass non-violent actions, its boycotts and the Freedom Rides (Farmer, 1985; Jordan, 1985), which realized the desegregation of interstate buses and trains. Emphasis on these forms of protest – unified by their strategy of mass mobilization rather than mass membership – can obscure the importance of culture to this movement. The Congress of Racial Equality (CORE) and the Student Non-Violent Co-ordinating Committee (SNCC), the leading organizations in the civil rights' struggle, were able to synthesize black culture and politics into a singular dynamic force which drew whites as well as blacks into mass action (Evans, 1980). Charting the rise of the movement for civil rights among southern students, Vincent Harding has described how, from its earliest moments, this force for change was infused with cultural energy and a sense of style:

Part of it was just being in style, but it was a great style to be in; better than anything they'd ever found. . . . The Black students were filled with vitality and passion, with belief and with cascading hope. They overflowed with songs and sermons from all the deep well springs of their people's long struggle. . . . Non-violence, love, reconciliation and justice were the major themes in their search for ideology. . . . There was an indescribable hope, idealism, courage and determination in those early months of organizing, marching, singing and going to jail. . . . They were believers. When they sang in jail, in mass-meetings, in front of policemen and state troopers, 'We Shall Overcome', they meant it . . . overcoming meant 'freedom' and 'rights' and 'dignity' and 'justice' and black and white together and many other things that people in a movement feel more than they define (1980, pp. 158–9)

Political culture was the principal means of contagion by means of which these beliefs and spirit spread, not just to northern blacks, but to whites as well. SNCC had its 'Freedom Singers' and cadres of cultural activists who translated that organization's belief in the efficacy of civil disobedience into music and song (Piven and Cloward, 1977). The cultural output of these organizations was not an accompaniment to their politics but a central part of them, lending

173

real strength and cohesion to the exemplary, symbolic protests with which they sought to draw attention to and dramatize the power relations of the Jim Crow system (Clark, 1966).

A fifth of the quarter of a million people who marched on Washington in August 1963 were whites. The rally which ended that march involved performances by Mahalia Jackson, Bernice Reagon, Josh White, Bob Dylan and others as well as Martin Luther King's famous 'I Have a Dream' speech. The appearance of gospel music in the seemingly secular context of the struggle for racial justice, compounded the steady secularization of the music which had been a feature of its transformation into soul. The protesters and demonstrators of the Civil Rights movement sang the Impression's 1963 arrangement of 'Amen' and later that year the Chicagoan group recorded 'People Get Ready', another civil rights anthem based in the gospel idiom which would later be covered by Bob Marley as part of a medley with his own 'One Love'. The Impressions' 'Keep On Pushing' addressed the movement again directly the following year:

> Keep on pushin'
> Keep on pushin'
> I've got to keep on pushin'
> I can't stop now
> Move up a little higher some way or somehow
> 'cause I got my strength
> And it don't make no sense
> not to keep on pushin'[16]

This song and Nina Simone's 'Mississippi Goddam' are two of the best known illustrations of the broad and general politicization of soul which preceded the displacement of the Civil Rights movement by demands for Black Power from the mid 1960s onwards.[17] 'Mississippi Goddam' perceived the gap between formal equality and the substantive inequality which was likely to remain after the passage of the 1964 Civil Rights bill. It highlighted the frustration on which the movement for Black Power would later grow and develop.

> Oh, this country's full of lies
> Y'all gonna die and die like flies
> I don't trust you anymore
> When you keep sayin' 'Go Slow Go Slow'
> But that's just the trouble
> Desegregation, mass participation, unification
> Do things gradually and bring more tragedy
> Why don't you see it?
> Why don't you feel it?
> I don't know I don't know
> You don't have to live next to me

Just give me my equality
'cause everybody knows about Mississippi
everybody knows about Alabama
everybody knows about Mississippi goddam.[18]

The gradual decomposition of the Civil Rights movement and the simultaneous growth of Black Power present historians with a series of problems which are beyond the scope of this chapter. These include the rise of the Nation of Islam as a political force (Essien-Udom, 1966), and a variety of schisms in the radical forces centring on issues like the war in Vietnam and black perception of the Johnson administration as well as tactical differences introduced by the contrasting experiences of blacks in the different regions of the USA. These political contraditions were compounded by tension between the leaders of the movement and by the effects of its institutionalization and bureaucratization. King's reputation had, for example, been severely damaged by his handling of the Selma to Montgomery march in 1965 (Marable, 1984; Harding, 1980). He had been absent from the initial protest which was attacked by state troopers under the direction of Governor George Wallace at Selma's Pettus Bridge. When leading a second march to the same spot two days later, King advised his fellow marchers to retreat before they reached the trooper's barricade, apparently as a result of a secret deal struck with President Johnson's Attorney General, Nicholas Katzenbach. The march was commemorated on the Staples Singers' album 'Freedom Highway'.

The passage of civil and voting rights legislation during the mid 1960s had resulted in the partial dismantling of the official system of segregation, but its informal, traditional structures remained and began to operate with renewed viciousness as a result of being threatened. There was a sharp increase in the use of violence and terror in the South and six blacks were killed in the voter registration drive of summer 1965. Organized racist groups, particularly the White Citizens Council adopted a high profile, and Lester Maddox, leader of Georgians Unwilling To Surrender (GUTS), was elected governor of that state. If the situation in the South appeared bleak, Wallace's campaign against Johnson in the Democratic primary elections of 1964 also showed that the white working class of the northern cities was ripe for the appeal of a white nativist politics. Malcolm X had meanwhile broken with the Nation of Islam. He criticized other Civil Rights leaders for endorsing Johnson's electoral campaign and for becoming too embroiled in the workings of a political system which could not operate in the interests of blacks. However, as Harding (1980) notes, immediately prior to his death in February 1965, Malcolm had 'decided to seek for ways to stand in solidarity with King and the troubled southern movement'. In death, Malcolm was

175

to become the focal point of a resurgent black nationalism more popular, vocal and visible than at any time since the days of Garvey.

The tactics of mass non-violence and civil disobedience which had been created in the southern struggle against Jim Crow could not be applied in the ghettoes of the northern cities where racial subordination assumed quite different institutional forms. The differences between areas were underlined by the massive black rebellions which erupted in almost every major city in the North, Mid-west and California during the mid 1960s. It is essential to grasp the scale of these uprisings:

The Watts rebellion left $40 million in private property damage and 34 persons killed. Federal authorities ordered 15,000 state police and National Guardsmen into Detroit to qwell the city's uprising of 1967. In Detroit 43 were killed and almost 2,000 injured; 2,700 white-owned ghetto businesses were broken into, and 50% of these were gutted by fire or completely destroyed (Marable, 1984).

The summer time revolts of 1964, 1965, 1966, 1967 and 1968 commemorated in several classic soul releases of the period, saw the older chants of 'Freedom' replaced by a new one – 'Black Power'. In the attempt to connect the northern, urban struggle with the southern situation, activists began to focus on the violence of the state which presented itself to them as a common denominator wherever they turned in pursuit of an elusive freedom. Harding's (1980) quote from Stokely Carmichael captures this clearly:

I've had so much law and order, I can swear to God I want some chaos! I want some chaos so bad I can taste it on my lips, from Canton, Mississippi to Watts, Los Angeles, to Harlem to Chicago – nothing but law and order.

Strengthened by the brutality which was meted out in response to black protest and by the emerging anti-war movement, Black Power developed into a potent, if not always coherent ideological force with a plurality of meanings covering the whole range of political sentiment. Endorsed even by Richard Nixon as a form of black capitalism (Allen, 1969) Black Power was a malleable idea appropriated by a variety of contrasting and sometimes directly opposed concerns. The various positions around which the different definitions of Black Power were constituted are less important for our concerns here than the fact that the idea was exported not just to Britain (Abdul Malik, 1968; Hiro, 1971; Knox, 1967) as we saw in the previous chapter, but to the Caribbean and even to Africa which had been visited by SNCC representatives as early as December 1963 (Marable, 1984).

The Black Power movement grew directly out of the work of CORE and SNCC in the rural South but spread rapidly to a new constituency in the urban ghettoes where soul[19] took pride of place amidst a burgeoning cultural nationalism. The maxims of that nationalism were to 'Think Black, Talk Black, Act Black, Create Black, Buy Black,

176

Vote Black and Live Black'. Maulana Ron Karenga whose (1968) commandments these were, carefully elided electoral politics and black capitalism into the philosophical and aesthetic assertions on which the movement was based. In this ideological climate the expressive culture of black America was to play an important role in establishing exactly what these injunctions were to mean. New styles of communication were developed and labelled black, Karenga even described the blues as 'counter-revolutionary' by virtue of its apparent endorsement of passivity, quiescence and suffering (Nicholas, 1971).

Frank Kofsky (1970) has explored the relationship between this cultural nationalism and the 'New Jazz' of the 1960s but the equivalent association of black radicalism with modern soul and rhythm and blues remains largely unexplored (Haralambos, 1974; Jones, 1967). This is far more important in the understanding of black British and Caribbean forms because these styles were the popular music of ghetto communities outside America which the new jazz never reached. In contrast to the more esoteric sounds of the latter, soul and rhythm and blues were primarily but not exclusively dance styles and their take up throughout the black diaspora reflects that aspect of their appeal.

James Brown's 'Say It Loud I'm Black and I'm Proud', the Chi-Lites 'Power To The People' and various versions of Weldon Irvine jnr's 'Young Gifted and Black' were all taken to the heart of black communities many miles from those in which they were created. These recordings are only the most obvious illustrations of the character of a period in which soul was revered as the principal criterion for affiliation to the Black Power movement. *Ebony* pronounced 1967 the year of ''Retha, Rap and Revolt' and during this time, singers, typified by James Brown 'Soul Brother no. 1' and Aretha Franklin 'The First Lady', were identified as the spiritual and moral guardians of the inner meanings not merely of black music but of black American culture as a whole. They were a priestly caste guarding the spirit in the dark which represented a political community's sense of its history (Jones, 1967). These singers did not simply provide a sound-track for the political actions of their soul sisters and brothers. They were mandated to speak on behalf of the community in elaborate, celebratory, ritual performances. The privileged position which flowed from enjoying a public voice was used by artists to blend the contradictory elements of the Black Power movement into an uneasy unity and to create an anti-racist current among whites particularly the young. Song after song from this era urges the oppressors to 'think' while simultaneously warning them of the dire consequences which would develop if freedom did not follow.[20] The most powerful songs from these years provide a musical counterpart to the urgent definitions of Black Power which were

177

being advanced as 'the last reasonable opportunity' for American society to work out its racial problems (Carmichael and Hamilton, 1967). The Impressions were, like many others, swept along by the tide of black pride and articulated these aspirations in their late 1960s hits 'We're Rolling On' and 'We're a Winner': 'No more tears do we cry, We have finally dried our eyes and We're moving on up'.

The reformist strategies of the Civil Rights period had developed hand in hand with the movement's espousal of non-violence, creating, indeed requiring, a musical culture which pointed to the patience, dignity and determination of blacks in the furtherance of racial justice. With Black Power, both the tone and the tactics changed. The political focus shifted towards the idea that civil disobedience had to be supplemented by a capacity for defensive violence which was symbolized by Huey Newton's armed Panthers on patrol in Oakland (Newton, 1974).

The defensive militarization of elements within the Black Power movement may have started as a simple response to police harassment and repressive use of the legal system. However, once blacks were speaking the contending revolutionary languages of Marxism–Leninism and cultural–nationalism, in public and seen to be armed, bold and confident, the full weight of state violence descended upon them. The FBI's Counter-Intelligence Programme (Cointelpro) spearheaded the governmental response but other less overt forms of harassment were employed ranging from assassination to petty persecution, surveillance and dis-information or 'smearing'. In 1969 alone, twenty-seven members of the Black Panther party were killed by the police and another 749 arrested. The effects of these repressive operations can be judged from the relative decline of the more overt expressions of commitment to revolutionary black struggle in either of its principal forms. Clear open statements were replaced, in musical culture at least, by more oblique forms of signification often more stylized and satirical in their stance. The iconography of soul shifted away from the pseudo-military macho imagery of clenched fists in black leather towards the dress and cultural emblems of ancient Africa. The forthright photographs of Aretha Franklin as a militant African queen which appeared on the cover of her 1972 album 'Young Gifted and Black' were replaced on her next set 'Hey Now Hey The Other Side Of The Sky' by drawings depicting her as a winged Egyptian deity, her microphone plugged into the roots of an African tree in a red, green and black pot. These and other more elliptical statements like Roy Ayers memorable 1973 album, 'Red, Black and Green', spoke to blacks directly and repeatedly on the subject of their African heritage but withdrew from direct communication with a white audience. Sly Stone whose Family had been the first multi-racial band to achieve any kind of prominence, commented on the transition from Black Power to mystical Pan-Africanism by seguing the track 'Africa Talks To You (The Ashphalt Jungle)' into a non-existent cut entitled 'There's A Riot Going On'. Griel Marcus (1977, p. 97) has pointed out that Sly's album of the same name

represented . . . the attempt to create a new music appropriate to new realities. It was music that had as much to do with the Marin shootout and the death of George Jackson as [Sly's] earlier sound had to do with the pride of the riot the title track of this album said was no longer going on. 'frightened faces to the wall' Sly moans. 'Can't you hear your Mama call? The Brave and Strong – Survive! Survive!' I think those faces up against the wall belonged to Black Panthers, forced to strip naked on the streets of Philadelphia so Frank Rizzo and his cops could gawk and laugh and make jokes about big limp cocks while Panther women, lined up with the men, were psychologically raped.

There were still, particularly at election time, records which like James Brown's 'Payback' and 'Funky President' addressed themselves to the political conjuncture and correctly recognized its significance as a 'second reconstruction':

It all started with 40 acres and a mule. . . . But nothing good is simple. . . . As yesterday's windmills turned to today's skyscrapers and farms to parking lots . . . anger and revenge increased. As time ran out, putting politicians and hustlers in the same bag. . . . Backstabbin' scrappin but never rappin' the message cried to live and let live. . . . [21]

Political and cultural activists who were not primarily known as musicians had also been drawn towards popular black music as a result of its interventionist potential. Amiri Baraka (Leroi Jones), chairman of the Congress of African People in Newark, enlisted members of The Commodores, Kool and The Gang, and Parliament to support his own bands The Advanced Workers and The Revolutionary Singers. Together they issued 'You Was Dancin' Need To Be Marchin' So You Can Dance Later On' on the People's War label.[22] These assertive statements would reappear in the wake of Reagan's 1980 election victory, but they declined steadily after 1972. Instead, as the war in Vietnam developed, Uncle Sam's imperial adventures were satirized by references to 'Uncle Jam's Army' and tales of 'specially trained Afronauts capable of funketizing galaxies'. The vision of a black homeland whether in Africa or in an independent republic inside the southern borders of the USA was secularized and modernized. The dream of life beyond the reach of racism acquired an otherworldly, utopian quality and then manifested itself in a flash hi-tech form deliberately remote from the everyday realities of the ghetto lifeworld.[23] If the repressive and destructive forces unleashed by a 'maggot brained' and infanticidal America were rapidly acquiring a global character, the answer to them was presented as flight, not back to the African motherland, for that too was tainted by Americanism but into space. The cover of Funkadelic's 1978 set 'One

179

Nation Under a Groove', for example, showed a squad of 'Afro-nauts' raising the red, black and green standard of Africa as they stepped off the planet earth. The celestial and interplanetary themes in the soul and funk of this period provided a means to satirize American imperialism and to advance utopian visions of a recon-structed society in which the black nation, united under a groove, would thrive in peace. The destructive capacity of America's techno-logical rationality would be held in check by mystic, natural forces contained within the pyramids of ancient Egypt, a durable symbol of black pride and creativity most powerfully evoked by the Jones Girls' 'Nights Over Egypt'.[24] The futuristic emphasis in these images served to underline the impossibility of strategic political calculation. The means by which black America was to get from where it was to its reconstituted future was as inconceivable as time travel itself. The political repertoire which stretched between mass non-violent direct action to open militarization appeared to have been exhausted.

This period also witnessed the re-emergence of jazz as a truly popular music (Palmer, 1974; Siggerson, 1977), a development which had been foreseen by Leroi Jones (1967). This shift, spearheaded by Pharoah Sanders and Albert Ayler in the late 1960s and developed to its logical conclusion by Miles Davis, Herbie Hancock, John Handy and others during the 1970s, connected the most innovative players directly to the dance-floors and gave an added impetus to the work of popular funk musicians who had few pretensions to jazz-based respectability. The most important exponents of this fusion of jazz, nationalism, satire and dance-orientation were also two of the most popular black bands of the 1970s: Earth Wind and Fire and Parliament/Funkadelic. In 1975, the latter, a loose aggregate of musicians led by refugees from James Brown's backing band, the JBs, cut what is arguably the greatest of all black nationalist dance records, 'Chocolate City'. This was a ruminative piece of funk set to a relentless drum machine beat and decorated freely with Bernie Worrell's piano, Bootsy Collins's, bass and some free, meandering saxophone solos. The rap vocal from George Clinton, which gave the record its title, explored the post-Black Power situation by speculating about the effects of black inner-city residents electing black local governments and looked at the implications of the move from open protest to electoral politics. 'You don't need the bullet when you've got the ballot', argued Clinton, suggesting that the latter had become a more appropriate tactical vehicle for black liberation than the former in the aftermath of Cointelpro. The Chocolate City referred to was not simply Washington DC, the national capital in which 'vanilla suburbs' surrounded an inner core populated by impoverished blacks, but rather all cities in which blacks had been able to capture control of municipal government:

180

There's a lot of Chocolate Cities around
We got Newark
We got Gary
Somebody told me we got LA
And we' working on Atlanta

The record climaxes in some frenetic interplay between saxophone and bass. This instrumental passage is introduced by the idea that the transformation of American Democracy is itself within the grasp of blacks. The proposition is made concrete by Clinton's nominations for a new set of leaders: Mohammed Ali for President, Reverend Ike (a well known evangelist noted for his ability to extract money from his ghetto flock) as secretary of the Treasury, Richard Pryor as Minister of Education, Stevie Wonder as Secretary of Fine Arts, and Aretha Franklin, as ever, the First Lady. This record was still being played on London's pirate black music radio stations (Mosco and Hind, 1985) in 1985. To the further delight of black audiences on both sides of the Atlantic, the band which made it signified their political contempt for the music business in which they were forced to operate by signing to competing record conglomerates under a variety of different names.

Earth Wind and Fire's political development covers the same ground as Parliament/Funkadelic but their movement was in precisely the opposite direction. They began in the early 1970s with mystical, veiled statements of Pan-African themes. These were presented in arrangements which were heavily reliant on the sound of the African thumb piano or Kalimba which was to become the group's trademark. The group's unique sound also drew on the jazz tradition. Their arrangers, particularly the Chicagoan Tom Washington, attempted to adapt the big-band sounds of Ellington and Basie to a dance funk context. Later on, the mystical material gave way to open political commentary on songs like 'Stand Tall (Let Me Talk)' which harked back to 'Stand' by Sly and the Family Stone and 'Freedom Of Choice' a forthright attack on monetarism which was banned by several radio stations. The band's early work was dominated by a desire to represent *in their music* the continuity between black American and African cultural creation. This project was fully realized later on by other artists, particularly Ralph MacDonald who created a musical equivalent to Alex Haley's *Roots* with his 1978 set 'The Path'. Earth Wind and Fire took Jesse Jackson's Black Litany, 'I am Somebody' (which would have been known to their audience from the film 'Wattstax' and the JBs' dance classic 'Same Beat' if not from any immediate political experience), and pared it down to its essential content – a potent affirmation of black humanity and dignity. It became simply 'I am' the title of their 1979 album.

Jackson was a central figure in the relationship between Afro-

American music and politics long before a legion of rappers, singers, producers and musicians lent their talents to support his presidential candidacy in 1984. An ex-CORE student leader and aide to Martin Luther King, Jackson had worked in Chicago during the 1960s creating 'Operation Breadbasket', a programme for boycotting ghetto supermarkets which refused to hire local black staff or lodge their profits in ghetto banks. The idea had spread to seven other cities by 1970 and claimed to have created 5000 new jobs for ghetto dwellers.[25] In 1967, the Operation Breadbasket activists under Jackson's direction in Cleveland had become involved in the campaign to elect the city's first black mayor, Carl Stokes. It was the power of soul music which helped to secure the articulation of the mass movement of blacks with this comparatively narrow electoral aim. Breadbasket's own band toured the ghetto early on election day instructing registered voters to get up early and vote for Stokes (Preston *et al.*, 1982). Jackson was again prominent in the campaign to elect a black mayor in Newark. This time, the candidate, Kenneth Gibson, enjoyed the support of James Brown and Stevie Wonder who both performed on his behalf. By 1970 black mayors had been installed in Washington and Gary as well. Jackson's combination of black capitalism and militant self-held rhetoric, 'we do not want a welfare state. We have potential. We can produce. We can feed ourselves' (Haralambos, 1974) was appealing. However, the cultural dimension to his political interventions was an important element in their success which has been overlooked by some commentators (Marable, 1985).

The extraordinary level of support for Jackson which was expressed by musicians, artists and performers in 1984 had been triggered by the election of Reagan and the subsequent erosion of black living standards which followed it. In 1981, Gil Scott-Heron's commentary on the Reagan victory, 'B Movie', had been a surprise hit, demonstrating that as far as the soul charts were concerned, it was possible to be simultaneously radical and successful. The Fatback Band, the Valentine Brothers and Syl Johnson, whose early classic, 'Is It Because I'm Black?' had been sung over in reggae style by Ken Boothe, were some of the artists who came forward with denunciations of Reaganomics.[26] Their statements were all underground hits on the British soul scene and significantly drew additional strength from a re-examination of the black militancy of the 1960s. This was an early product of the explosion in New York which created rap, electro and hip-hop in the context of a street culture centred on dance, graffiti and new forms of music-making which will be discussed in detail below.

The rappers and breakdancers who once again established America as the primary source of material for the cultural syncretisms of black Britain, articulated a clear political line which was well received here. 'Rappers' Delight', the Sugar Hill Gang's version of Chic's hit 'Good

Times' reached Britain in the summer of 1979. There were better rap records to follow. In late 1980, Brother D, a maths teacher and community activist from Brooklyn, issued 'How We Gonna Make The Black Nation Rise?' with his group Collective Effort on the radical reggae label 'Clappers'. Taking their cues as much from the success of Rappers' Delight as from the rap genre's emergent tradition of signovers and cover versions, the group used the backing track from an established dance-floor favourite, Cheryl Lynn's 'To Be Real'. The original chanted chorus – the phrase 'to be real' – was left intact between the rapped segments, giving the didactic and pedagogic elements in the second version authenticity and urgency, as well as emphasizing their organic relationship to the underground culture which had made 'To Be Real' into a classic. The rap was a strident and provocative call for solidarity and organization in the Reagan era. It denounced the drug abuse and passivity which Brother D discerned in ghetto life and sought to warn his listeners of the danger they were in.

> As you're moving to the beat till the early light
> The country's moving too, moving to the right
> Prepare now, or get high and wait
> 'cause there ain't no party in a police state

The lyric went beyond a nationalist stance. It noted the rise of the Klan and the possibility of 'racial' genocide but made a clear statement on the ecological crisis, suggesting rather as Bahro (1984;1982) has done, that the crisis in the biosphere could achieve the unification of political forces across the conflictual lines of 'race':

> Cancer in the water, pollution in the air
> But you're partying hearty like you just don't care
> Wake up y'all you know it ain't right
> That hurts everybody black and white

Though stylistically a fast soul piece aimed at the very discos it denounced, the record made conspicuous attempts to open a dialogue with the reggae world in which 'Clappers' was established: 'there's a message in our music for I n I'. Picked up for British release in a licensing deal by Island Records, the disc was a dance-floor hit in the soul and hip-hop clubs twice between 1982 and 1985. It also picked up substantial sales in the rock market.

As the smoke from the uprisings of 1981 hung in the inner-city air, young Britons were absorbing the 'Don't push me, 'cause I'm close to the edge' message transmitted by Grandmaster Flash and the Furious Five, and pondering the relevance of Afrika Bambaataa's 'Zulu Nation' to their own experience of structural unemployment,

183

police harassment, drug abuse and racial disadvantage. In both America and Britain, a rediscovery of the black politics of the 1960s has been a consistent feature of hip-hop culture. It has been expressed in a variety of ways including, most obviously, an enthusiasm for politically articulate dance music of the period. James Brown's 'Get Up Get Into It and Get Involved' was a favourite and the same trend may explain the British popularity of many political waxings on the Philadelphia International label. Of these, 'Let's Clean Up The Ghetto' was so sought after that it was eventually re-released in 1985. Originally produced in 1977 by label bosses Gamble, a Muslim, and Huff, the record used the combined talents of Teddy Pendergrass, Billy Paul, Lou Rawls and others to comment on the need for self-reliance and political autonomy in the context of the municipal strikes in New York City. More significantly, records in this vein exported to Europe the idea that black communities in the inner city, particularly the young, could define themselves politically and philosophically as an oppressed 'nation' bound together in the framework of the diaspora by language and history.

The Pan-African desire to reconstitute and unify new world blacks into a single self-conscious people was given a further musical boost in the summer of 1983 by the release of 'The Crown', a rap on the themes of black history and pride which had been produced by Gary Byrd, an early rapper, lyricist and radio DJ, and Stevie Wonder, the soul musician who had pioneered the adaptation of reggae to black American tastes. The record passed largely unnoticed in the US but was a major hit in Britain, a remarkable development because it was over ten minutes long and its creators refused to issue it in an edited format thus denying the record any airplay on the legal radio stations. This was a wholly underground success popularized by the clubs and the pirate broadcasters. It remains significant because it demonstrated that the Ethiopianist and Pan-African ideas associated with reggae could be perfectly integrated into a soul setting and that the results could be popular.

> I do recall so very well
> when I was just a little boy
> I used to hurry home from school
> I used to always feel so blue
> because there was no mention in the books
> we read about our heritage
> So therefore any information that I got was education
> Bums, hobos at depot stations
> I would listen with much patience
> Or to relatives who told the tales
> that they were told to pass ahead
> And then one day from someone old
> I heard a story never told

of all the kingdoms of my people
And how they fought for freedom
All about the many things we have unto the world contributed
You wear the crown. . . .
Its not Star Wars, its not Superman
Its not the story of the Ku Klux Klan. . . .

Stevie Wonder's involvement in the campaign to secure a US public holiday for Martin Luther King's birthday provided a further opportunity for black music to become politically engaged and, of course, drew attention to the political legacy of the 1960s which was being commemorated. In support of this campaign, a number of records including Wonder's own 'Happy Birthday' (issued with selections of King's speeches on the b-side) addressed themselves to both King's death and the continuing relevance of his political achievements. In both rap and more conventional soul styles, some of these tunes even used tapes of King's own voice to develop their arguments. The most interesting of these were Bobby Womack's 'American Dream' and 'Martin Luther' by Hurt 'em Bad and the SC Band. Both featured extracts from the 'I Have A Dream' speech, the latter setting the scene with a rap about the struggle for desegregation.

King's was not the only black radical voice which was retrieved and woven into rap and electro records. The general revival of interest in the struggles of the 1960s was conveyed in particular by 'No Sellout' a record issued by Tommy Boy, a leading rap and electro label and credited to Malcolm X. Keith Le Blanc, the white drummer with the house band at Sugar Hill records, the company which had spearheaded the commercial exploitation of radical raps, edited together a number of Malcolm's aphorisms and observations into a political commentary which was set to a fragmented electronic rhythm track and punctuated by the spoken chorus 'Malcolm X, no sellout'. The record was an underground hit in Britain during 1984 and received the support of Malcolm's widow, Dr Betty Shabazz. She told the British paper *Black Music:* 'This recording documents Malcolm's voice at a time and space in history some 19 years ago. Its meaning is just as relevant today as it was then.'[27]

The 1983 election provided the first opportunity for Britain's soul and electro sub-culture to implement the political tactics which had been transmitted across the Atlantic with these new forms. One London rapper, calling himself Newtrament after the milky drink popular with the Afro-Caribbean community, recorded 'London Bridge Is Falling Down' a rap based on the nursery rhyme previously adapted for radical purposes by the reggae group Culture. His version chronicled police malpractice and inner-city decay while suggesting that electoral politics were a sham. Whoever won the contest, he argued, the political processes of significance would take

185

place far from parliament and the plight of the dispossessed and the poor would be essentially unaffected:

> Election Fever on all four channels
> . . . Red or Blue. . . .
> Win or lose, lose or win
> jobs will still be getting thin

A speech by Labour Party leader Michael Foot could be heard faintly in the background while a voice chanted 'vote vote vote, there ain't no hope'. A second more orthodox soul record which appeared at this time was 'Thatcher Rap' by the Phantom, an anonymous artist who had cut an anti-NF reggae 45 at the time of the first ANL carnival. Here again, snippets of a politician's speeches were assembled so that they became the vocal in a funky dance piece. Mrs Thatcher's lines were interspersed with the chorus – 'they tell me there's a crisis going on'.

Reagan's decision to seek a second presidential term and Jesse Jackson's tactical campaign for the democratic party nomination both generated a number of overtly political soul, rap and funk records during 1983–4. Tunes denounced Reagan and praised Jackson in almost equal measure.[28] Some of used Reagan's voice, either mimicked or recorded, and even rearranged his words to emphasize the unpleasant features concealed behind his avuncular exterior. Several took Reagan's well-publicized *faux pas*, 'we begin bombing in five minutes', and transformed it into the centrepiece of satirical synthesized dance music. The best of these records, significantly perhaps the furthest away from a distorted but none the less realist presentation of his opinions, was Air Force One's 'See The Light Feel the Heat'. This gave the president some surreal lines: 'We still have a lot further to tango' and cut them into a chilling invocation of the nuclear holocaust and a mumbling discourse on the defence budget.

Once again the detail of these records is less significant than the fact that they were enthusiastically received by the inhabitants of Britain's black music sub-cultures. Those who could not afford to pay inflated prices for imported discs could look forward to hearing them on and taping them from the pirate radio stations which had begun to transmit regularly in the autumn of 1981. These outlets were important sites in which the black cultures of the US and the Caribbean were diverted into the working-class mainstream of southeast England. Their illegal status carried over into the soul scene through a close relationship between the radio DJs and the clubs where they worked when they were not on the air. A mood of opposition was cultivated by the stations who were frequently shut down by the Department of Trade inspectors. Their resistance of the government's attempts to regulate their broadcasting added substantially to the underground connotations attached to the music itself.

The forward march of Rastafari halted

The study of black cultures within a diaspora demands some consideration of Rastafari. The growth of the movement, particularly during the 1970s, would appear to confirm the potency of culture as a conductor of political idealogies between the Caribbean and the overdeveloped world. The movement's influence increased steadily in Britain between 1970 and 1981 and its Pan-African, Ethiopianist ideology can be considered to have formed the core of a mass movement in this country during the mid 1970s.

The conception of Rastafari which underpins this account of the movement's recent history in Britain challenges both the dominant sociological views (Miles, 1978; Cashmore, 1979; Kitzinger, 1969) and some of the definitions of the movement which have emerged from the black community (Jah Bones, 1982; Lee, 1982). These positions are not as divergent as they might at first appear. All, to varying degrees, rely on the belief that the movement's political and cultural complexities can be grasped adequately through terms like cult and sect which emphasize its religious dimensions. This approach carries with it a number of problems rooted in attempts to analyse the movement as a religion or as a 'sub-culture' rather than as a popular phenomenon. The naïve Eurocentric elements in the religious approach have been criticized by Yawney (1979; 1985a; 1985b). The sub-cultural approach shares with them fundamental and persistent difficulties in establishing core tenets and ideas and using them to specify exactly who is legitimately entitled to belong to the group. The repeated differentiation of false and true Rastafari on the basis of theological, doctrinal and dogmatic criteria which are inevitably arbitrary is an obvious symptom of these conceptual tensions. Instead, by looking at the broad and diverse use to which the language and symbols of Rastafari have been put, it is possible to conceive it as a movement in which the lines dividing different levels of commitment are necessarily flexible. From this perspective, Ethiopianist and Pan-African ideas, images, language and style have brought historical and philosophical meaning to individual and collective action. They have created in Edward Said's (1985) phrase 'an interpretive community'. It extends beyond Afro-Caribbean young people who wear locks, colours and wraps, or smoke God's herb, to old people, soul boys and girls, some whites and Asians. The effect of the movement has been detected in the politics of resistance to racism (CCCS, 1982) but remains to be studied in the more evasive and more significant realm of everyday life in which

187

overt resistance is tied to strategic negotiation and other more subtle and refined forms of political antagonism.

The political forces which had created Reagan's presidency were not confined within the borders of the USA and have had visible roles in southern Africa (WMACAS, 1978) and the Caribbean (Jagan, 1984), two areas which are essential in the formation of political consciousness and diaspora identity among black Britons. In Jamaica, Michael Manley's socialist government was ousted by Edward Seaga's American-backed regime in 1980. This change had cataclysmic effects on the relationship between music and politics there, transforming both the content of the music and the structure of the music business. The largely Rasta-inspired singers, songwriters and dub poets who had guided the music to its place as a vibrant populist force for change in the society were brushed aside and their place was taken by a legion of DJs or toasters. Manley's own path to a populist socialist politics had been guided by the semantics and vision of Rasta reggae, a fact he acknowledged in a discussion (1983) of Bob Marley's art, 'the greater part' of which he recognized as 'the language of revolution'. Under Seaga, the singers' and songwriters' influence faded and they retreated from the revolution which their Rasta language had demanded. The DJs took centre stage.

The different musical practices of the sound system and the live performers had been held together, cemented by the cultural hegemony of Rastafari. This alliance also split apart. The singers were denied opportunities as much by the rise of 'white reggae' in the international market as by the immediate dangers in daring to chant down Seaga's Babylon at home.

Jamaica's DJs steered the dance-hall side of roots culture away from political and historical themes and towards 'slackness': crude and often insulting wordplay pronouncing on sexuality and sexual antagonism. I am not suggesting a simple polarity in which all toasters were agents of reaction and all singers troubadours of revolution. The Jamaican DJ tradition had been as involved in the spread of Rastafari during the late 1960s and early 1970s as recorded *song*. The two aspects of reggae culture interacted and combined in complex fashion. Even as slackness achieved ascendancy there remained popular toasters like Peter Metro and Brigadier Jerry who fought to maintain rhymes with a social content in the dances. However, the role and content of reggae changed markedly after 1980. This shift related to the consolidation of Seaga's regime and the consequent militarization of ghetto life. Both were also expressed in roots music and in the social relations of sound system sub-culture where guns became an increasingly important aspect of the rituals through which the crowd communicated its pleasure to the DJs (Jones, 1985).

The decline of radical reggae can be illustrated by reference to the career of Winston 'Yellowman' Foster, the most popular toaster of the early 1980s whose work took both Britain and Jamaica by storm during 1982. After two explicitly political sides chronicling the rise of authoritarian statism in Jamaica – 'Soldier Take Over' and 'Operation Eradication' (the latter a particularly effective version of The Itals' heavy 'Ina Disya Time' rhythm), he opted for the safety of nursery rhymes, animal noises and anti-woman jive talk.

The British scene's dependency on musical styles produced abroad meant that these changes further eroded the support which reggae had won in the 1970s when sophisticated and politically engaged forms were in the ascendant. The degeneration of Jamaican music and its recomposition around a new and less oppositional stance was one of several factors which provoked a series of exciting and innovatory developments. Britain's black music was transformed so that indigenous local styles of reggae and soul emerged not simply as a minority taste but, for the first time, as the dominant voices, exports and authentic pop voices rather than mere copies of Caribbean and American materials. The Jamaican scene stagnated under the heavy manners enforced by Seaga's Eradication Squad. Black America recharged its political batteries, re-examined its legacy of 1960s activism and forged the Rainbow Coalition under the leadership of Jesse Jackson (Marable, 1985), a politician who, as we have seen, cut his teeth on the use of music and ghetto culture to bind the fragmented Black Power movement into the system of electoral politics.

The British scene was rebuilt in the contradiction between these developments. Locally based reggae singers and musicians were, as I have already suggested, at a disadvantage when compared to the popularity and influence of the DJs. None the less, a small number of artists had been able to survive provided they were able to negotiate and cultivate audiences outside the black communities. For example, Aswad, one of the oldest British reggae bands, solved these problems by adapting their performances to the expectations of rock audiences and juggling them against the contrasting needs and aesthetics of black roots culture. The band led, in effect, a double life and conducted two quite separate careers in reggae and pop. Other established bands like Misty and Steel Pulse, the most disciplined and politically consistent of all the British outfits, developed a strategy which relied on their performing abroad for much of the time. In the Lovers' Rock style (Futrell, 1980; Garratt, 1985), a more melodic form of the music dominated by female singers and songwriters and produced for couples to dance to *together*, a close relationship developed with soul sub-culture which served the same purpose. This style of reggae had been inaugurated by Louisa Mark's cover version of Robert Parker's rhythm and blues hit 'Caught You In a Lie'. Soft, romantic soul records like Betty Wright's 'Pain' and Patrice Rushen's 'You Remind Me' were frequently translated into the reggae idiom. They crossed over into the soul scene, generating extra income and interest that subsidized the work of singers and writers like Carol Thompson, Jean Adebambo and Janet Kay.

Britain's DJs and toasters had no comparable difficulties. Though they made records, their primary sources of income and popularity lay in the sound system sessions from which live singers were excluded. The creation of a popular indigenous reggae culture reflects the hierachy which placed them at the top and the singers and songwriters at the bottom. With a secure base in the dance-halls which acted as a barometer for their experiments and innovations, the DJs responded directly to musical developments in the Caribbean and the US. They took the confidence of the Jamaican slackness toasters but from the rap MCs they took a refined fascination with the power of language, with the potency of words rather than rhymes. In the oral style of the South Bronx, they found a language which allowed them to speak directly about the social and political contradictions generated in the urban crises of the overdeveloped world. 'The Message' had hit home. Its imagery of urban entropy, its resolute modernity and the targets of its criticism all contrasted sharply with the language and style of Rastafari which were grounded in antiquity. Rastafari culture of the Marley/Manley era had sought to align black Britain with the underdeveloped world and to focus perception on a different Babylon which was becoming increasingly remote. In the Caribbean, people were actually starving. Their sun, sea and sensemilla was overlaid by unspeakable squalor and mind-boggling repression. In Britain, things were different.

The riots of 1981 coincided with the death of Bob Marley, the entrenchment of political reaction in the Caribbean and the simultaneous revitalization of soul boosted by its political opposition to Reagan, the Jackson candidacy and the stylistic energy of rap, hip-hop, breakdancing and graffiti, modern urban cultures born in the coming together of Afro-Caribbean, Hispanic and American black cultures in New York. The interpretive community formed around Rasta language and symbols, presided over and tutored in dread ethics by Marley and other outernational reggae artists, simply could not withstand these changes. Its cultural and political hegemony began to dissolve. A more pluralist relationship between the various constituent groupings which composed the urban social movement of black Britain began to take its place. One significant index of these changes is provided by the appearance of non-Rasta black Christianity in the community's popular music. In the United States, the ascent of Jackson and the revival of interest in Martin Luther King had been fed by the work of soul artists who set out to reconstruct their relationship to traditions of spiritual music making from which soul had originally been a secular offshoot. Phillip Bailey, former lead singer with Earth Wind and Fire, was in the vanguard of this move with the release of 'The Wonders Of His Love' a gospel/dance funk set. After Reagan's victory, the Rainbow Coalition turned its energies towards a critique of American foreign policy in Central America and Southern Africa (Jordon, 1985). Gospel/funk artists like the Followers of Christ and the Winans took up these issues in their records, which matched appeal to the dancers of the soul underground with a deeper project: the forging of links between the US black churches and the theologies of liberation in South Africa and Latin America (Cone, 1985). In the autumn of 1985, the Winans had a major hit with 'Let My People Go' a modern dance gospel cut pronouncing on the moral and political evils of apartheid. A similarly spiritual Pan-African theme was articulated by the Isley Brothers' 'Caravan of Love' which topped the soul chart at about the same time. British gospel choirs were more wary of entering into political controversy but February 1984 had seen the Reverend Basil Meade, minister of the Latter Reign Outpouring Revival Pentecostal Church touring soul clubs and discos in London, Manchester and Liverpool to promote 'Fill My Cup' the first release by the London Community Gospel Choir (LCGC).[29] Reverend Meade told the *Guardian* 'The time has come to take the music out of church buildings', one younger member of his choir added 'watch out for the charts to get prayed up'. The LCGC's success was the most prominent feature of a process which had begun taking place long before 'Fill My Cup' was released. A growing number of gospel/funk bands – Clarity, the Trumpets of Zion and most notably Paradise who had crossed over into the pop world briefly with 'One Mind Two Hearts' in 1983 – signalled that Rastafari no longer monopolized the association of spiritual language and dance music in black popular culture. Behind their spiritual commentary on the state of the capitalist world lay a moral superiority and a commitment to non-violent direct action which were the political bequest of Martin Luther King's teachings. Britain's own street riots served merely as a sign of the correctness of King's non-violent populism.

Rastafari did not disappear but its ethical dominance was broken. Pan-African feeling had not become an incongruous feature of black culture increasingly rooted in British cultural conditions but it was articulated in different forms by the revitalized Church and from within soul and hip-hop styles. Compared to these dynamic developments, the style and vision of Rastafari began to appear limited. The shortcomings of its response to contemporary British conditions became particularly apparent in the aftermath of the 1981 riots. The political flux following these street disorders saw the instigation of the Scarman Inquiry and an extensive public debate about the extent and meaning of 'race' in Britain. Yet the organized sections of the movement could not translate the popularity of their language, style and vision into a single social or political initiative. The officially

191

recognized and sponsored leadership drawn preponderantly from theologians and dogmatists rather than artists and musicians, was ill-equipped to meet the historic challenge posed by negotiation with rather than (mental or physical) escape from Britain's Babylon.

The spiritual concepts and oppositional sentiments associated with the movement had retained their appeal in part because they were able to articulate an intensity of aspiration for which there was no secular alternative available. They were now forced to compete against an equally utopian and spiritually-charged alternative rooted elsewhere in popular culture and with its own distinct political connotation drawn from the US and Africa rather than the Caribbean. The community's cultural and political centre of gravity shifted. New sources of 'good sense' were being located and the effects were immediate. In London, the polarization of black culture into discrete soul and reggae scenes had begun to break down. An East London band, Light of the World, expressed this in 1980 by recording two important attempts to take over the political philosophy of Rasta reggae and work it into soul. These were a funk version of Bob Marley's 'I Shot the Sheriff' and an anti-police disco cut 'The Boys in Blue'.

The pirate radio stations, though primarily soul oriented,[30] worked hard to create an integrated black music format which catered to the full diversity of tastes in the community and in so doing, pulled the rival audiences together. All day dances (all dayers) which featured both soul and reggae under one roof, emerged as a growing part of the black music scene and several bands who had operated in reggae, particularly in the Lovers Rock style, transferred their effort to making a distinctively British soul-based pop music. An illustration of this is provided by the career of the Cool Notes, a racially mixed band from South London who had scored a major hit on the Lovers Rock scene with 'My Tune' in 1979. They switched from reggae in 1981 and made a new, highly successful career as soul artists.[31]

The purely stylistic antipathy between reggae and soul sub-cultures was also significantly eroded. A British soul band, Loose Ends, and Cashmere, an American one, took dreadlocks, the central symbol of Rastafari, into the discos. The biggest reggae hit of 1984, Shinehead's 'Billie Jean/Mama Used to Say' was a Jamaican medley of two soul songs, one American, the other British. When licensed for a British release by Virgin Records it was a hit in both reggae and soul clubs.

Renegades of funk and the Cockney Translation

Hip-hop culture had its origins in the adaptation of Jamaican sound system techniques and styles to the dance sub-culture of the South Bronx (Hager, 1982; 1985) which had been pioneered by Kool DJ

Herc, a Jamaican who had moved to New York in 1967. It is not surprising then to find that it took root readily in Britain and, once expanded to include the full panoply of interlocking practices – scratch-mixing, breakdancing, rapping, and graffiti – made significant inroads into the reggae and soul scenes. London's leading crew of hip-hop DJs, the Mastermind Road Show, grew out of a reggae sound system and retained its structure and division of labour (Dick, 1984). If funk–gospel challenged reggae's monopoly of the spiritual, the close correspondence between the structures of reggae and hip-hop sub-culture ensured that the latter would be able to usurp the themes of fraternity and solidarity. They were recreated in an alternative language which drew on Black Power and emphasized a view of hip-hop culture's affiliates as a Pan-African national group along the lines of the Bronx's original Zulu Nation. Afrika Bambaataa, an original member of the Zulus, described them as 'a youth organization that's into all different things, rappers, DJs, dancers, people who just down to be down, people who are working, people who are into music, people into Hip Hop'.[32] This definition provided a warrant for loose, pluralistic and diverse relationships. Rastafari became one vital element among many within a coalition of forces in which the loudest voices were often the youngest.

Nowhere were these changes more apparent than in the work of Britain's reggae DJs and toasters. Not only were they falling under the influence of rap as a distinct form, but the content of their rhymes was also changing to reflect the post-1981 situation. They began to create a black British substitute for the politically engaged content which had evaporated from reggae as slackness had taken over.

The definitive conventions of sound system culture layed great emphasis on its communicative functions. News and underground information was transmitted and alternative analytical statements aired, recording the community's views of historical and political events in ritual processes which also served to establish the limits of the community itself.

Street protests and riots had been the subject of recordings by British-based reggae artists as early as 1976 when the Pioneers' 'Riot Ina Notting Hill' and Tapper Zukie's 'Ten Against One' celebrated and commented on the carnival disorders. As we saw in Chapter 3, the New Cross Massacre protests led into the April riots of 1981. This sequence of events prompted a host of recordings which mark the beginning of a whole new style of reggae immediately identifiable as a British product. Two South London DJs calling themselves Laurel and Hardy issued a 45, 'You're Nicked', on the independent reggae label Fashion in summer 1982. The record had in a typically derivative style adapted two of Yellowman's popular trademark devices. His chant of 'left right left right' from 'Soldier Take Over' which had conveyed the onward march of Seaga's military to the dance-halls of

Jamaica became, with the addition of the phrase 'Evening all, what have we here?', the sound of British police preparing to make an arrest. A fragment of Yellowman's dialogue with the feared Eradication Squad from 'Operation Eradication': 'Him look pon mi shirt, him see seh it a red. Him seh mi ave a good mind fe lick off yuh head' was similarly transposed so that it appeared as a conversation between a youth from South London's black ghetto and his local bobby: 'Him look pon mi neck, him see Rasta scarf. Him seh "Do you know about the fire down at New Cross?".' The originality and appeal of the tune lay not simply in these exchanges, but in the toasters' ability to switch between the different speech idioms which characterized the policeman (South London respectable working class) and his black prisoners (black London patois, the language which marked the boundaries of the Rasta community even when other signs and symbols were not used). These ideas were developed further by another reggae DJ also signed to the Fashion label: Culture Smiley. So named because of his refusal to chat 'slackness' in his rhymes, but renamed Smiley Culture by his management, David Emmanuel was a popular DJ with the Deptford based Saxon sound system run by Lloyd 'Musclehead' Francis and Dennis Rowe. His 1984 hit 'Cockney Translation' addressed itself directly to the contradictions which 'You're Nicked' had only hinted at.

The aesthetics of sound system culture had from its inception been built around the pleasures of using exclusive or specialized language in cryptic coded ways which amused and entertained as well as informed the dancing audience. For example, highly ritualized exchanges between the DJs and the crowd that conveyed appreciation of a particular rhythm (record) or style (sequence of rhymes) frequently involved the systematic corruption of ordinary innocent English words into new forms of public speech. 'Massive', 'Safe', 'Settle' and 'Worries' are all words which were playfully endowed with meanings unrelated to those invested in them within the dominant discourse. In this context, the subversive potential in the ability to switch between the languages of oppressor and oppressed was already appreciated.

At one level, 'Cockney Translation' offered a satirical commentary on the basic strategy of linguistic exclusion with which the community had protected itself from the encroachment of unwanted white listeners. The languages it introduced – Cockney rhyming slang and London's black patois – connote fixed positions of class and 'race'. Both were illegitimate and unofficial, and each marks out a minority cultural and political community with an historically-grounded collective identity. London's urban blacks were constantly in motion between the identities these languages symbolize and consolidate. The implicit joke beneath the surface of the record was that though many of London's working-class blacks were Cockney by birth and experience (technical Cockneys), their 'race' denied them access to the social category established by the language which real (i.e. white) Cockneys spoke. 'Cockney Translation' transcended the 'schizophrenic' elements which composed the contradictory unity that provided the basic framework for a potential black Britishness. The record suggested that these elements could be reconciled without jeopardizing affiliation to the history of the black diaspora. It initiated a new response to the fundamental contradictions of being both British and black, political categories which, as we have seen, are presented in the language of both popular and official racisms as mutually exclusive.

The record started from the idea that for many inner-city blacks an ability to speak perfect formal English represented nothing more than the failure of equality, ubiquitously denied by the experience of urban crisis. However, the subordination and poverty of inner-city urban life are not understood as simple effects of racism and racialization. Their very urban context suggests that white friends, neighbours and peers, represented by the Cockney alternative but equally applicable in other cities where distinct local identities and languages exist, must experience something similar. The patois into which the record translates white working-class dialect is shown to be more than a merely defensive argot, more even than a vehicle for the collective identity and solidarity of the blacks who have created it. It is the oppositional core of a black culture based no longer in a wholehearted rejection of Englishness that answered the exclusionary effects of racism, but on an idea of its overcoming and redefinition in the association of black and white urban sub-cultures and their characteristically encoded communications which the toast makes mutually intelligible. 'Cockney Translation' conveys a view of these languages as genuinely interchangeable alternatives disrupting the racial hierarchy in which they are usually arranged. It presents them as equivalent 'nation languages' facing each other across the desperate terrain of the inner city. To be black and to express that political identification in the use of black language is, it says, nothing more nor less than what it means to be a Cockney in this city. A sub-text refers listeners to the popular television representations of Cockney life. They are then invited to consider whether their knowledge of blacks is any more accurate or reliable than the stereotypical images of the cheeky Cockney villains presented in series like 'Minder' and 'Eastenders'. How is it that one group is labelled a 'race' and the other escapes definition even as an 'ethnic group'? The record expands this point by playing with the association of rhyming slang with East End gangsterdom and using this connotation to make a statement on the racist image of blacks as a disproportionately criminal group. It says that if both groups are to be seen as criminal, then this too must be done on an equivalent basis, particularly as

195

the economic relationships created by the institutionalization of certain forms of criminality have become an interface between the two groups and a means by which mutual respect and trust have been negotiated.

> Say Cockney fire shooter. We bus' gun
> Cockney say tea leaf. We just say sticks man
> You know dem have a wedge while we have corn
> Say Cockney say 'Be first my son' we just say Gwaan!
> Cockney say grass. We say outformer man . . .
> Cockney say Old Bill we say dutty babylon. . . .
>
> Cockney say scarper we scatter
> Cockney say rabbit we chatter
> We say bleach Cockney knackered
> Cockney say triffic we say wackaard
> Cockney say blokes we say guys
> Cockney say alright we say Ites!
> We say pants Cockney say strides
> Sweet as a nut . . . just level vibes. Seen.

Neither of the two languages available to black Londoners appears adequate for the expression of their complex cultural experience by itself. Both are needed and the partial and inadequate versions of inner-city culture for which each sets a boundary are shown to be residues from the syncretic processes which have created both the song and the social movement for which Culture Smiley is an organic intellectual (Gramsci, 1971). The ease with which he moves from one idiom to the other is counterposed to the barrier which racism has erected between the two language groups and which is signified in the separate, parallel positions occupied by these two inner-city voices. The record contains a veiled but none the less visible statement that the rising generation of blacks, gathering in the darkened dance-halls, were gradually finding a means to acknowledge their relationship to England and Englishness. They were beginning to discover a means to position themselves relative to this society and to create a sense of belonging which could transcend 'racial', ethnic, local and class-based particularities and redefine England/Britain as a truly plural community. They were able to express their reluctant affiliation to it in the same breath as their ties to the African diaspora. This possibility had been blocked by the language and politics of Rastafari.

'Cockney Translation's' innovations were rapidly imitated and extended by a number of records which featured various DJs imitating the speech of their parents, doctors, police and even white neighbours irate at the level of noise emanating from the party in which the record was being played.[33] The contradictions surrounding national membership, ethnicity, 'race' and inner-city culture were given a further airing by Asher Senator, another ex-Saxon DJ, on his 1985 hit 'The Big Match' – a toast telling of victory over Germany in the world cup by an England football team composed entirely of black players. Sergion and Herbtree's 'East Enders', a 1986 hit exploring the appeal of the TV soap opera of the same name in the black community, refined the particular language games which Culture Smiley had evolved in 'Cockney Translation'.

Smiley himself consolidated the success of 'Translation' by taking a similar follow-up record to number twelve in the national pop chart during February 1985. This disc, 'Police Officer' described a street confrontation between Smiley and police who stopped and searched him. The song's chorus referred to the pattern of petty harassment in which officers carrying out a stop would arrange for black drivers to have to produce their driving documents at a police station even if nothing appeared to be amiss with their vehicle. Smiley narrates being released by the officers, despite the fact that he was in possession of ganja, because they and their relatives had enjoyed listening to 'Cockney Translation' and wanted his autograph. This record was significant not only for the ways in which it extended the serious points at the heart of its predecessor and took them to a huge national audience, but for the distance it appeared to have travelled from Rastafari. The police were still an object of criticism, but the level at which their malpractice was being analysed and the language in which the analysis was presented were new. Both exemplified a shift away from an abstract, diachronic, macro perspective rooted in the experience of Jamaica's peasants and urban poor and towards a synchronic, every-day, micro focus capable of addressing the problem of British police harassment where it reached directly, even trivially, into people's lives.

Dread culture, wild style and the critique of capitalism

I have shown how the interpretive community which had been consolidated around the language and politics of Rastafari in Britain between 1972 and 1981 was dispersed. At the turn of the decade, profound political changes in the politics of black Britain were wrought by developments in the Caribbean and in the US black movement, as well as by the effects of Bob Marley's death and the growth of violent street protests in inner urban areas.

In stressing the loss of Rastafarian hegemony, I have tried to emphasize that the radical, critical and militant aspects of Rastafari livity and culture did not simply evaporate, or degenerate into redundant, anachronistic forms. I shall now demonstrate that these qualities of dread culture were in fact conserved and refined and that they constitute an important seam of continuity beneath the general drift

197

away from reggae and Rasta which defines the post-1981 period. Furthermore, they comprise a radical politics capable of universalizing the issue of emancipation beyond the primary question of racial or ethnic particularity.

Many of the oppositional themes associated with Rasta (Campbell, 1985) can be shown to be common to other modes of cultural expression which have contributed to the formation of British black culture and to the politics of the social movement described in and reproduced by that culture. These themes include a critique of various forms of racial subordination and a general analysis of key features of the capitalist mode of production. It is the critique of capitalism which helps to locate the continuity which exists in spite of the important stylistic and political changes discussed so far.

This connection reveals the dimensions of a social movement. It exists beneath the varying surface manifestations of black British expressive culture and can be examined in two distinct but related fields of communication. The first centres on the overtly political content of these expressive cultures, conveyed in particular by critical and analytical lyricism in songs, raps, and toasts. The second involves consideration of inferred and immanent political positions, specifically of the *musical* forms involved and the social relations in which they are produced and consumed. In view of the divergence of surface expression and intrinsic position which characterizes black meta-communication, this second level necessitates a form of analysis capable of moving beyond words and speech.

Both levels of communication display their anti-capitalist character in different ways. It centres on the denunciation of capitalist social relations for which the memory of slavery serves as an enduring metaphor, and on a critique of the commodity form to which black humanity was reduced during the slave period.

The Pan-Africanist, Ethiopianist and diaspora-conscious content of both soul and reggae has been referred to above and has been transmitted as much by records which crossed over into pop culture like Keni Burke's 'Rising To The Top' and Deniece Williams's 'Black Butterfly' as by the sounds of the black underground. The political import of black expressive cultures does not rest exclusively on the effect of calls to solidarity and collective identity which, in the context of British pop, become sub-cultural appeals to the soul fraternity, black and white for the transcendence of 'race'. The struggles for civil rights, black power, racial equality or freedom from police harassment which are celebrated and transmitted by these musics generate demands which cannot be contained within the structures of the contemporary British political system as it stands. But the cultural expressions which articulate the social movement for black rights and justice, giving it a sense of its collective power and shape, internationally as well as within national borders, involve more than

198

a descriptive commentary on the conjunctural features of national capitalist development. They address, within their own epistemology and standards of analytical rigour its abstract, structural features. Distinct and explicit anti-capitalist themes, some utopian, some pragmatic and immediate, recur repeatedly in Britain's ghetto culture and provide a source of affinity with black cultures elsewhere.

It is not being suggested that black expressive cultures consist of anti-capitalism alone, or that their anti-capitalist ethics and politics are privileged or uniquely significant. These musical cultures have plenty of other features which make them pleasurable and which are equally if not more important in bringing white audiences into the scope of black influences and styles. The most obvious feature of this type which is not examined in this chapter is second only to the espousal of black freedom as a central defining attribute of these cultural forms, namely their openness to addressing issues of gender conflict, sexuality and eroticism. Both soul and reggae give these issues a prominent place and the fact that they have not been explored here should not be read as a denial of their significance nor of the autonomous field of political action which they map out.

Similarly, in a closed cultural world characterized by synthetic, predictable and interchangeable musical products (Attali, 1985), the spontaneity of black forms, their performance orientation (Vansina, 1985) and commitment to improvization (Rockwell, 1985) have all become attractive features which contribute to the appeal of soul, rap, reggae, African and Latin American forms to white audiences (Gilroy, 1984). These are primary attributes common to all the new world black musics (Storm-Roberts, 1972) and mark their inheritance from Africa (Chernoff, 1979; Nketia, 1982; Bebey, 1975; Hoare, 1975). Beside them, the political content to which the rest of this chapter is devoted reveals secondary but none the less important characteristics which have become more significant by virtue of their complete exclusion from the bulk of critical writing on the subject (Toop, 1984; Chambers, 1985; Clarke, 1979).[34]

There are three core themes around which the anti-capitalist aspects of black expressive culture have been articulated:

1 A critique of productivism: work, the labour process and the division of labour under capitalism.
2 A critique of the state revolving around a plea for the disassociation of law from domination, which denounces state brutality, militarism and exterminism.
3 A passionate belief in the importance of history and the historical process. This is presented as an antidote to the suppression of historical and temporal perception under late capitalism.

The critique of productivism is obviously reinforced by the structural location of black labour power in the overdeveloped countries. It incorporates an analysis of the implications of the micro-processor revolution for blacks and for working people as a whole:

> I spent years perfecting my craft
> Now my boss is giving me the shaft
> Is this the future?[35]

It can also be seen to connect with the active rejection of certain kinds of work by young blacks in his country. Its effects are visible not just in this tendency to reject opportunities to do menial and poorly paid work, but in the related antipathy towards registration for unemployment benefits (Roberts, Duggan and Noble, 1981).

The experience of labour has, since slavery, been a central topic in black expressive cultures. Their origins in slavery have meant that the relationship between unfree labour and the subtler imperatives of wage slavery has been long debated by blacks in their music making and non-work activity. It is a fundamental issue in both rural and urban blues traditions and can be found thoughtfully displayed in the beginnings of modern soul, where Lee Dorsey's 'Coal Mine' and Sam Cooke's 'Chain Gang' were offered as early metaphors for the exploitation of black labour. In the Caribbean where the gruelling cultivation of sugar cane[36] occupies the central metaphorical space devoted to cotton in the musical culture of the southern US, these concerns also manifested themselves in a popular critique of the alienating effects of work. This has been most powerfully articulated by singers and writers inspired by Rastafari.

> Since man has become the worshippers
> of doings of their own hands
> then we have stopped living naturally
> just existing by outventions
> As far as I can see
> We are all living mechanically
> In a worldly mechanism
> All from the beginning a Babylon system
> pure ism and schism in Babylon system.[37]

Prince Lincoln's words recall the Marx of the 1844 manuscripts in a striking manner. A few lines condense an understanding of the fetishism of commodities, a distinction between necessary objectification and capitalist alienation, and a commitment to some sort of base and superstructure model in which social production articulates with ideological relations.

Bob Marley's connection between the remoteness of the boss and the liberatory rationality of burning and looting has been repeated and expanded by many artists in the different genres which together make up reggae. It also resonates directly with black America's recent

'Street Symphonies', telling of lay offs, shut downs, strikes and money too tight to mention.[38] Explicit American commentaries on Reaganomics and recession have been well received by Britain's soul underground.

These songs share a premise, whether they have been aimed, like Zapp's 'We Need The Buck', at the growth in unemployment – 'There's a million factory workers with no place left to toil' – or like Fatback's 'Is This The Future?', at the fundamental irrationality of the economic system and its inability to manage crises – 'We've got people working 9 to 5 while over 10% are trying to stay alive'. All of them, economistic or revolutionary in their rhetoric, acknowledge the dispiriting effects of work and the particular forms in which it is both made available to and withheld from blacks in the metropolitan centres of the overdeveloped world. This sensitivity draws, in the case of black America, on older themes associated with the blues which suggest that work, though it may be an 'historically necessary evil', is also destructive of physical and spiritual health (Garon, 1975).

The historical memory of slavery has left similar traces in the expressive arts of the Caribbean and their British offshoots. The slave experience remains a central metaphor for the processes of work in general. They are frequently counterposed to the realm of autonomous desire and collective self-realization in an equation typified by the threat in Gregory Isaac's classic 'Slave Master': 'But if I don't get what I desire, Then I set the plantations on fire.'

As the predicament of blacks in the Caribbean and Britain has come to involve what appears to be permanent mass unemployment, this too has become an object of criticism. For example, Dillinger's 'Tamarind Season' described the relationship between unemployment and crime in Jamaica, while Lion Youth's 1982 '3 Million on The Dole' registered protest at similar developments as they are experienced in this country:

> . . . It is a posse of 3 million on the dole
> See some from high school, some from college
> some from university
> They're still waiting for the chance
> but there's no opportunity
> School leavers in job centres searching with no surety
> What a situation on the nation, what a policy
> A zugi zugi zugi zu.[39]

The state which plans exploitation and orchestrates this waste of human potential, raising taxes to finance irrational initiatives that symbolize futility and hopelessness to the black poor, is also criticized directly. Space flights have been identified as expressive of these problems by both reggae and soul performers. Kenny Gamble's

201

sleeve note on Dexter Wansel's 1976 album 'Life On Mars' makes this clear.

On July 4, 1976, 'the viking probe' – a man made vessel – will send back pictures to earth to let man see if life is on Mars. For what reason? Man has not mastered his existence here on earth. He cannot live in harmony with his natural environment yet. . . . Man is the only creation that is out of order with The Universal Order of Things.

Similar sentiments are expressed by Prince Lincoln Thompson on his 1980 reggae song 'Spaceship':

> . . . Little earthling, what are you doing?
> I don't need a space trip
> I and I ain't coming along with it
> If you cannot manage on earth,
> How you gonna do in outer space?
> The aliens gonna whip you
> and put you in your rightful place
> with your spaceship.

Zapp's work is again definitive:

> They want to camp in space, experiment
> and make the people pay the rent
> all the money I make that the bills don't take
> I've got to give to the government
> I can't use it no no. . . .

These statements typify a direct, realist approach to political criticism. The kind of commentary they involve is widespread but it is entirely overshadowed by the volume of hedonistic themes which celebrate non-work activity and the suspension of the time and discipline associated with wage labour. These themes are omnipresent in both soul and reggae and are shared by artists whose styles and musical genres appear at first sight to be antithetical. Soul singer Luther Vandross sweetly asks 'Who wants to go to work to hustle for another dollar?' and his question is echoed by the Sugar Hill Gang's rapped plan for overcoming the nine to five mentality as well as by Bob Marley's sardonic contrast between spiritual work and the more remunerative variety.[40]

In these cultural traditions, work is sharply counterposed not merely to leisure in general but to a glorification of autonomous desire which is presented as inherent in sexual activity. The black body is reclaimed from the world of work and, in Marcuse's (1972) phrase, celebrated as an 'instrument of pleasure rather than labour'. Sexuality stands therefore not only as an area of conflict in its own right, but as a symbol of freedom from the constraints of the discipline of the wage.

202

What may be loosely termed the Saturday night or 'Thank God its Friday' syndrome is fundamental to both reggae and soul. The inversion of work values and priorities in the celebration of desire is articulated by both male and female performers on an equal basis and provides the primary context for statements about love and gender-based antagonism. Cissy Houston's 'Morning's Much Better', for example, represents the views of a woman who is too tired to 'get it on' when she returns home from work at night. Marlena Shaw's 'Go Away Little Boy' berates a man who gives up his job to become self-employed under the influence of Black Power ideology. She relents, even though this means going out to work full time, once her partner starts licking her earlobes. Much of the work of Rick James and other male artists like Bobby Nunn who have followed in his wake, similarly sets out to entangle the imagery of different kinds of non-work pleasure. Sex and other types of hedonistic recreation are blurred together in a dense discourse which 'carnivalizes' (Bakhtin, 1984) the residues of work, transposing them into a source of collective pleasure, a funky party for which sexual 'private parties' between 'freaks' and 'party animals' are either a prelude or a lingering coda. The party also signifies the context in which it is anticipated the music will be heard, the social relations which support its textuality.

These tropes are supported by the multi-accentuality and polysemy of black languages. For example, in black American ghetto speech the word work can mean dancing, labour, sexual activity or any nuanced combination of all three. This adds considerable depth and irony to the chant of 'We want to work let us work' which fades in and out of Zapp's 'We Need The Buck' discussed above. The ambiguities surrounding this word have been explored at length by Michael Jackson on his 'Working Day and Night'.

Criticism of various governments around the themes of work, production and labour tends to stop short of any extended commentary on the state. This is, however, powerfully expressed in the parallel commentaries on policing, law, imprisonment and criminal justice which have a well-established presence in both Afro-Caribbean and Afro-American cultures, as well as in the critiques of militarism and exterminism which have developed more recently as the anti-nuclear movements have grown.[41]

Law has been a focus of political antagonism since the days when, as slaves, blacks first felt the effects of judicial systems which were not just incapable of realizing the promise of their own democratic rhetoric, but also an important component in the mechanisms that ensured exclusion from the constitutional categories in which authentic humanity was validated (Higginbotham, 1978).

Soul and reggae still reveal the primary ethical and semantic influence of the Bible on new world black cultures. This legacy is particularly visible where both traditions highlight a perceived disjuncture between the standards of human and heavenly justice. The manifest injustice which characterizes the operation of earthly courts has been the target of critical commentary in black folk arts for a considerable period of time. It is, for example, central to images of a just and righteous heaven which emerge in the songs of slaves (Cone, 1972). In the post-war period, records like the Coasters' 'Framed' and Shorty Long and Pigmeat Markham's different versions of 'Here Comes the Judge' are only the best known examples of black satire on judicial procedures conveyed by humorous inversion and exaggeration of courtroom practice:

> I denied the charges of robbing the liquor store
> I denied the charges of carrying a .44
> I denied the charges of vagrancy too
> but when the judge came down, poured whisky on my head
> turned to the jury and said 'convict this man he is drunk'
> what could I do?[42]

The same device occurs in the rocksteady records which portrayed Judge Dread's management of his court and the gross punishments which Rude Boys who appeared before him could expect.

A similar concern appeared in a different sub-cultural setting, when as part of the 1985 London Rap Championships, the eventual winner Junior Gee, delivered a rap entitled 'The Truth'. It began with him holding up the bible and saying 'I swear by almighty God that the Rap I shall give will be the truth, the whole truth and nothing but the truth.'[43]

The language of equal rights and justice connects these views of the law to a series of critical observations about the political nature of policing and the likely results of being arrested. The failure of police to provide protection and assistance to the poor is also a recurrent theme.[44] In reggae culture, the oppressive edifice of Babylon is unified by its reliance on the coercive violence of the police and the military which, though legally legitimate, is often presented as an extension of the slave judicature. Police are called the Babylon not only as a way of emphasizing the dubious moral basis of their authority, but also because the social and economic relations of capitalist society are seen to depend ultimately on the brutality which they supply. The absence of justice and its distortion in capitalism's debased, pseudo-legality are weighed against an authentic morality formed in the association of truths and rights. The word right acquires here a greater force than it has in formal English. It means more than a legal claim and its archaic resonances are amplified so that it connotes emphatically 'not wrong'. For example, in the toast 'Trouble In Africa' Phillip Levi refers to Steve Biko as a

'Truth and Rights leader'. Bob Marley's 'I Shot the Sheriff' is the best known statement of these themes, but the dominance of truth, rights, equality and justice in reggae discourse should not be allowed to obscure the enunciation of similar sentiments in soul and blues, as well as jazz, where the naming of instrumental music often affords opportunities to convey the same aspirations.

Bobby Womack's 'American Dream', mentioned above as one record which uses Martin Luther King's recorded voice,[45] belongs in a distinct genre of soul which creates pleasures in the interplay of personal and public histories. The specificity of each realm is invoked so as to demonstrate their articulation and, in bringing them together, generate both truth and freedom. Aretha's 1968 hit, 'Think', provides an earlier example of similarly complex interpenetration of social and political fields. She addressed white America and a troublesome lover interchangeably. Each passionate appeal added new layers of meaning to the other:

> Oh Freedom! Freedom! Oh Freedom! Yeah Freedom!
> Right now, Freedom! Oh Freedom! Gimme some Freedom!
> Oh! Freedom, right now!
> Hey! Think about it! You! Think about! . . .
> You need me and I need you
> Without each other there ain't nothing either can do
> Think, Think, about what you're trying to do
> Think about it, baby, Think about it.[46]

King's voice introduces 'American Dream' with these words while Womack is heard singing wordlessly in the background. 'America is essentially a dream. It is a dream of a land where men of all races, of all nationalities, of all creeds can live together as brothers. . . .' Womack's sung vocal enters as this phrase dies away. He sings:

> I wish I could live in a fantasy world
> where everything is just make believe
> where nothing is wrong in the words of my song
> and your love is all that I ever need.

King's dream establishes a public political context for the personal pain which is expressed by the combination of words and wordless singing that makes up Womack's vocal. According to the song, the American state which, after all, is believed by many blacks to have been directly responsible for King's death, creates a specific form of *unfreedom*. Though this oppression emanates from political and social structures and relationships it is felt most acutely in private, personal experience. Its consequences are lived out in the intimate emotional environment of black Americans. They can be protected from its

205

destructive effects initially by love and then by the soul which provides a bridge between personal tragedies and the sense of community which has carried new world blacks successfully through the experience of slavery. The song's chorus begins with Womack reminding his partner/confidant of 'the time when my heart wasn't mine', a condition perhaps akin to slavery, and then describing their love as a balm for the fact that he feels 'not that free' even now. The next verse follows a brief glimpse of the pastoral American idyll 'where children run free in the home of the brave' and from which he feels blacks have so far been excluded. It is delivered with all the evangelical fervour that he can muster:

> I wish I could fly, like an arrow through time
> to the arms that my destiny holds
> when war is all done, and my father comes home
> and our love will never grow old.

Though many of his audience would know that Womack's father had in fact died recently, the returning father image resonates with the recovery of King himself and through him, the memory of the 1960s civil rights struggles. The second chorus states more directly the conclusion of the first: 'Can't you see that I'm not *that* free.' The record ends with further extracts from King's speech:

I have a dream this afternoon that the brotherhood of man will become a reality, in this day with this faith I will go out of a tunnel of hope, through the mountains of despair and transform dull yesterdays into a bright tomorrow. With this faith we will be able to achieve this new day.

This closing statement establishes firmly the redemptive capacity of the pursuit of freedom and the truth which is inseparable from it. Though no open references to the legal and constitutional structures of American society are made, the song summons an alternative moral order with its own standards of liberatory truth. It brings to mind DuBois's observation that

Through all the sorrow of the sorrow songs, there breathes a hope – a faith in the ultimate justice of things. The minor cadences of despair change often to triumph and calm confidence. Sometimes it is a faith in life, sometimes a faith in death, sometimes assurance of boundless justice in some fair world beyond. But whichever it is, the meaning is always clear: that sometime, somewhere, men will judge men by their souls and not by their skins (DuBois, 1969, p. 274).

American Dream's 'naturally veiled and half-articulate' message is authenticated by the quality of Womack's witness, his testimony; by an appeal to the political authority of King who shares the record with him; and above all, by active participation in the struggle for civil rights which has been reborn in the campaign to make King's birthday a national holiday in the US. Womack was the most popular soul performer in Britain the year that this record was released.

Both soul and reggae traditions associate freedom and justice with truth and have identified the pathological truthlessness of capitalism's inauthentic democracies as a key element in the continued subordination of blacks. For example, Cameo's 'Talking Out the Side of Your Neck' echoes Bob Marley's assertion that you can't fool all the people all of the time in the context of a violent attack on the mendacity of America's political leaders. 'American Dream' illustrates the equation of personal freedom with the enhancement of democracy which has been a feature of numerous Reggae records. Reggae voices its own critique of the legal apparatuses used by successive Jamaican governments to gain control of the mass of the urban poor. But even the most interventionist and 'realist' tunes telling of the 'Gun Courts', 'Indefinite Detention' or life in Kingston's 'General Penetentiary' are exported. Thus dislocated from their original context, they become in British parties, dances and shebeens, abstract, metaphysical statements about the nature of oppression, constraint, liberty and punishment.[47]

The final core theme which binds together the different black expressive cultures is the premium they place on history itself. All these musics announce themselves as 'roots', a complex term which combines the obvious organic similies of Garveyism – 'A nation without its past history is like a tree without roots' – with a belief in philosophical and political archaeology for which Alex Haley's book stands as both an example and a paradigm: 'I was drifting away from reality, so far away from the roots in me.'[48] A grounding in history is seen as an essential precondition for the realization of both individual and collective freedom. For example, in the song 'Rat Race' Bob Marley instructs his listeners 'Don't forget your history. Know your destiny.' The recovery of historical knowledge is felt to be particularly important for blacks because of the nature of their oppression is such that they have been denied any historical being. Their banishment from historicity is presented as originating in the slave experience approximating what Orlando Patterson has called the state of 'social death' in which slaves exist (Patterson, 1980). It has been described significantly as a state of namelessness by London DJ Phillip Levi on his seminal toast 'Mi God Mi King'. He relates the introduction of the word 'negro' to the same moment:

Dem tek wi fram de wonderful lan of afrika
tuh slave fe de plantation ownah
dem tek whe wi name and call wi niggah
de onli word we know is 'Ise commin massa'

The repression of the memory of slavery is felt to be a central achievement of the colonial regimes which followed emancipation and of contemporary racism. Burning Spear asks the question 'Do You Remember the Days of Slavery?' because confronting that historical memory, grounding the contemporary experience of racial oppression in the past is recognized as a first step in progress towards emancipation from the mental slavery which has remained intact even as the physical bonds have been untied. Spear's performances combine an actual history lesson with a dramatic re-enactment of slavery made all the more vivid by his struggle to find a language sufficient to convey its horrors. Apart from the institutions of slave society itself, he covers the pre-Colombian history of the Caribbean and indicts Colombus as a liar for claiming that he discovered Jamaica. Though Spear is more open about his educational mission than other artists, his Rasta pedagogy is far from unique. For example, 'Slave Trade' by the Jewels, one of the greatest songs in the vocal trio style, explores multiple ironies surrounding the fact that the first English ship to carry slaves across the Atlantic was called the Jesus of Lubeck. This type of detail plays a vital role in establishing the epistemological and historical superiority of roots knowledge and culture over the partial and unstable knowledge(ism) which guides the practice of the oppressors. The oppressed stand firm, girt about with truth and steadfast in the protection afforded them by more profound and substantial knowledge (overstanding). As the Ethiopians put it: 'Hacking at the roots with the truth the whole truth and nothing but the truth.'

When compared to the dominance of historically minded Ethiopianism in reggae, soul culture invokes the slave experience with relative infrequency. The Temptations 'Slave', the O Jays 'Ship Ahoy' and Melle Mel's 'Jesse', with its chorus of 'Land of the free, home of the brave but it might as well be the land of the slave', being obvious exceptions. However, the historical focus can still be found. It simply assumes different forms laying less emphasis on slavery itself, more on the category of citizen and in particular on the revision of history which is integral to Americanism. The revision of black history required by orthodox accounts of the post-bellum period is, for example, attacked with the same vehemence that Afro-Caribbeans and black Britons have used to challenge the repression and dilution of slavery. Jazz trumpeter Wynton Marsalis called his 1985 album 'Black Codes from the Underground' in an attempt to link the contemporary effects of racism with the legal order of the South during Reconstruction. During the same year, rapper Kurtis Blow set out to convey an alternative history of America in an epic nine-minute cut which combined rap, singing, scratching, dub, recorded snippets of historical dialogue and the words of presidents past and present, in a collage of electronic dance music which topped London's hip-hop chart. The record, simply titled 'America', begins with the words 'Four score and seven years ago, our fathers brought forth on the continent a new nation.' They are followed by an extract from the oath of allegiance. Slavery and the genocide of native Americans are noted as parts of the same process which lead to the formation of modern America. As the line 'Don't You Love America? My Favourite Country' is sung sweetly by a choir, the flow of the piece is interrupted by Reagan, Nixon, Kennedy, Luther King and General MacArthur and the repeated statement 'The Issues Are Global'. This is followed by a controversial rap dealing with the threat of nuclear war precipitated by the incompetence and malevolence of Reagan himself.

Both soul and reggae consciously reconstruct and celebrate their own histories through complex sequences of answer records in which different artists criticize and comment on each other's work or extend a narrative over several discs by putting different points of view.[49] In reggae, the same idea has been refined to a point where an alternative sense of time and the historical process is one of the most important effects of the constant repetition (versioning) of particular pieces of music. For example, in the nine months following the release of Wayne Smith's 'Under Mi Sleng Teng' in 1985, an estimated 239 versions of the rhythm were produced by different artists.[50] Very often the repetition of a certain piece is a calculated invitation to embark on an archaeological operation, tracing it back to its original version. This impulse lay behind the explosion of interest in reggae from Coxsone Dodd's Studio One label in the early 1980s. Many of the classic rhythms of reggae were cut there by his various session musicians.

The limits of language

Frederick Douglass's warning that analysis of words is insufficient must now be taken on board. This section moves away from consideration of the overt politics of black expressive cultures and looks instead at the political positions immanent within the very forms which those cultures have created. The premium placed on history has been carried over into the form of jazz by an aesthetic valuation of quotes and references to preceding styles and players. This makes the past literally audible in the present. In reggae the same result is achieved by the repetition of certain key pieces of music rather than individual instrumental innovations and technical trademarks. Both these strategies are present in soul where they are often supplemented by words which, in the best tradition of the blues, tell the history of a particular style or artist that has contributed to a disc or genre. For example, Zapp's 1986 hit, ironically titled 'It Doesn't Really Matter', tells the whole history of R and B from the 1950s to the

1980s. Similarly, Asher Senator's record 'Fast Style Origination' chronicles and validates the history of the 'fast style chat', an innovatory rap-influenced form of toasting developed by British DJs and used to establish the specific formal characteristics of their unique style of reggae.

A full account of the political aspects of these musical traditions must be able to comprehend the forms in which the music appears and the distinctive social relations of consumption with which these forms are matched. Here too correspondences can be found which link the different styles in a common anti-capitalism.

The critique of capitalist reification which was expressed in lyrics above, is reinforced by a powerful antipathy towards the commodity form which is actually practised in these cultures.

Consumption takes place at times and locations which are expressive of this deeper struggle. The town halls and municipal buildings of the inner city in which dances are sometimes held are transformed by the power of these musics to disperse and suspend the temporal and spatial order of the dominant culture. As the sound system wires are strung up and the lights go down, dancers could be transported anywhere in the diaspora without altering the quality of their pleasures.

The oppositional implications of a culture which, as we have seen, rejects the legal subjectivity on which policing rests are compounded as these locations become the object of hostile surveillance by the police. However, more significant than the rejection of capitalism's legal system is the critique of the economy of time and space which is identified with the world of work and wages from which blacks are excluded and from which they, as a result, announce and celebrate their exclusion. In these patterns of consumption, the night time is the right time. The period allocated for recovery and reproduction is assertively and provocatively occupied instead by the pursuit of leisure and pleasure. The producers of the musics anticipate a certain type of audience and a preferred setting in which their work will be experienced. They orient their art towards it, using the languages of their ghetto constituency and, as where a voiceless dub version is left on the 'B' side of the disc, anticipate and invite the supplementation of their original artistic effort by further complementary input from toasters, MCs and DJs. The dialogic aspects of the culture are incorporated into its unfinished, participatory forms.

These cultures have developed an approach in which records are not simply played and heard. In reggae, the immediate power of the DJs works on the raw material provided by dub cuts and voiceless versions. Consumption is turned outwards; no longer a private, passive or individual process it becomes a procedure of collective affirmation and protest in which a new authentic public sphere is brought into being. The same features are shared by all the black

210

cultures we have looked at. This can be illustrated by a brief examination of the hip-hop scene formed as the Jamaican sound system culture was adapted to the experiences of urban New York. This expressive sub-culture has in turn been imported into Britain as a style in its own right. Hip-hop revels in the reduction of music to its essential African components of rhythm and voice. Created in urban poverty where real instruments are an expensive luxury but where record players are commonplace, the everyday technology of consumption has been redefined and become an instrument with which music can be produced (Gilroy, 1984). Records are deprived of the authority and reverential treatment appropriate to a fixed and final artistic statement. They become little more than a basic tool in complex processes of creative improvization. Percussive sounds are made by pulling the stylus back and forth across a disc and they become as important as the real vocal phrases and passages of instrumental music which are allowed to pass unmolested. Fragments of an existing record or records are combined with scratching sounds and other percussive beats obtained either from cheap and wieldy digital electronic drum machines (beat boxes) or from human impersonations of the sound these computers make. A patchwork or collage of melody, voice and rhythm is created when these sounds come together with rapped vocal commentary and chants which draw on Afro-America's older traditions of communication. As with sound system culture, consumption becomes an active, celebratory process. The original records become a vehicle for the imagination of the DJ or scratcher who, together with rapper(s), interacts with the audience. A favourite or relevant phrase may be repeated, snippets of different records may be juxtaposed to create an entirely new meaning and the recorded voices of political figures – heroes or villains – may be introduced into the performance and treated accordingly. Complete reorganization of a particular record can be performed by using two or more copies of the disc and several synchronized turntables. Britain's premier hip-hop crew, the Mastermind Roadshow, use six turntables simultaneously.

In the preferred and anticipated setting of consumption, these forms and devices articulate particular conceptions of space and time, what Bakhtin (1981) has usefully called chronotopes. They combine with specific invocations of truth and causality: 'we are here because you were there', to facilitate the dispersal and carnivalization of the dominant order. The past and the conceptions of truth which derive from meditating on it, not only provide an answer to the mystifications which are integral to racial subordination – its laws and its division of labour. They become central to the regulation of collective memory, perception and experience in the present, to the construction of community by symbolic and ritual means in dances, clubs, parties and discos.

211

This reveals a more profound and complex struggle against the political, ideological and economic structures of capitalism than that powerfully spoken in the poetics of the songs involved. The whole cultural package assumes differing but essentially similar forms in the various overlapping black sub-cultures. There is a deep structure beneath the superficial diversity of styles which is manifest on their contradictory surfaces. It constitutes the hub of a makeshift answer, part intuitive, part calculated, to the problems which the commodification of art has set for radical, committed artists and their audiences. It is the solution arrived at by black artists working amidst an 'abundance of real suffering which tolerates no forgetting' for whom 'it is now virtually in art alone that [their] suffering can still find its own voice, consolation, without immediately being betrayed by it' (Adorno, 1977).

This deeper antagonism can be glimpsed in the ways that language is itself used in these patterns of cultural struggle. It is possible, for example, to interpret the screams, wails, grunts, scatting and wordless singing that appears in all these black cultures as both indicative of a struggle to extend communication beyond words and as a commentary on the inadequacy of language as a means for expressing certain truths. There are here meanings and feelings so potent, so dread that they cannot be spoken without diminution and trivialization.

The association of music and dance in black cultures may itself betray a sense of the limitations of spoken and written languages as well as an enthusiasm for total forms which, be combining different media, communicate more than each can convey on its own. Rather as Culture Smiley required two languages to convey the peculiarity of his experiences as a black Londoner, records which combine singing with toasting or rap became commonplace after the introduction of the 12 inch single in the late 1970s. Both types of communication involving different kinds of language were required if meanings were to be conveyed in their full complexity. The 12 inch was seized and transformed to the special requirements of the black underground cultures. The extended playing time made possible by this format enabled further innovations. For example, in reggae one side of the disc could be given over to a vocal cut, a toasting version and a dub of the same tune while the 'B' side could still carry an instrumental or a second dub that could be used as the backdrop to dance-hall toasting.

However, long before the 12 inch and the hip-hop culture which formalized and rationalized the assault on the privileges of recorded music, both soul and reggae were evolving forms which relied on multiple coded appeals to their dancing listeners. James Brown's first hit record 'Please, Please, Please' has been recognized as perhaps the paradigm case for analysis of language use in soul performances:

'. . . at one point he wails the word "I" nine times in succession before moving on to the next part of the sentence . . . as if the pressure of emotion is causing a breakdown of coherence' (Hoare *et al.*, 1975). This is not incoherence but rather a highly stylized alternative coherence. Like the scatted vocals, animal noises and nonsensical sounds found elsewhere which are further legacies of Africanism in black expressive cultures, Brown's 'breakdown' provides another pointer to the power of what cannot be spoken. A later record by Brown, the single version of his 'The Payback' provides a second interesting example of the need to use more than one type of language to adequately convey a soulful meaning. It involves, at the vocal level alone, three quite different types of communication which operate through contrasting modes of address.

The first is a sung vocal centring on a call and response relationship between James and the chorus which reinforces his verbal points. When he tells his listeners 'I don't know Karate but I know Ka-razor' the chorus answers 'Yes We Do'. The second involves his wordless singing, screams, whoops and yells. This type of communication objectifies soul for the listener and makes palpable what cannot be put into mere words. The third element is made up of the interventions of a narrator figure who interjects into the other speech and singing, aiming the musical and verbal salvoes and commenting on the overall meaning as it unfolds, telling the audience in their own coded language exactly how to listen to the performance they can hear:

This is *some* funk . . . this record is stone . . . this is for Atlanta . . . this is for Los Angeles . . . this record is too much . . . this record is for the people . . . this record is for everybody.

The meaning of the piece – revenge, the big payback; i.e. reparation for black America – emerges only in the association of these different appeals, instructions and comments with the music.

Other variants of this subversive strategy of communication are visible in forms which still bear the marks of slavery. Religion is particularly important here as a site of oppositional meaning and collective strength. The tradition of singing in which Brown operates has retained much of the style and rhetoric of the black church. These are still apparent beneath the secular sheen generated by soul ideology. Bobby Womack also operates in this genre, in his performances the rhetoric of spiritual catharsis is retained and used to alert audiences to movement from one mode of address to another, it marks the different types of discourse specified by each. Sung or spoken asides and questions which appear to reverse the power relations of performance by seemingly submitting the artist to the authority of the audience by soliciting their assent – 'Would you mind if I just talked to you a little bit?' 'Can I preach a little while?'

– become shifters. They illuminate the transition from one kind of commentary or testimony to another, demonstrating in doing so the relationship between different orders of experience, between public and private spheres.

Live shows by reggae artists like Burning Spear, Freddie McGregor or Dennis Brown involve the same type of dramaturgy. However, as the music is based on sound systems rather than live concerts, the same complexity is mirrored in the relationship between the words or noises of the DJ or toaster and the original vocal which remains as an absent textual presence in the instrumental version of the tune which forms the basis of a toast. Where a dubbed version is used, fragments of key words or phrases from the original vocal cut may be left in the mix. These can become the focus of comment and acquire new meanings in the processes which transform the piece. This irreverent treatment of language relates directly to another important characteristic of black musical cultures which has been mentioned above but not explored. This is their orientation towards improvization, spontaneity and performance, 'part of a wider pattern in black music whereby the act of expression took precedence over the artefact as the final goal' (Hoare, 1975). I have described these qualities as an African legacy. They pivot on an attempt to dissolve the distinction between art and life which is a feature of consumption of European culture in general and concert music in particular. Black performers aim to overcome rather than exploit the structures which separate them from their audiences. The relationship between the performer and the crowd is transformed in dialogic rituals so that spectators acquire the active role of participants in collective processes which are sometimes cathartic and which may symbolize or even create community.

This orientation is an unbroken thread that links the most apparently disparate forms. It has itself been celebrated recently on 'The Show' by Doug E Fresh, a hip-hop record which crossed over into Britain's pop market in late 1985. Fresh was one of the first artists from the Bronx to specialize in vocal imitations of the percussive sounds of a drum kit as they emerge from being stored on the digital memory of a drum computer. Calling himself 'The Original Human Beat Box' he made several records featuring this ability. 'The Show' combined this skill with rap, scratching, fragments of song, synthesizers and a 'real' drum computer to produce a performance which asserts the value of intimacy and immediacy. It is ironic that a piece that strives to be as live and spontaneous as possible, which is animated by the desire to demonstrate the power of performance over artefact, can be captured on vinyl and mass marketed as just another recorded item. This is an illustration of the chronic conflict between black musics and the forms in which the leisure industries have sought to commodify and sell them. Improvizations have been

214

curtailed and constrained by the limited playing time available on discs, performances refined and reconstructed so that they cease to be dramatic performances in the sense outlined above.

The conflict between these traditions in black music and the constraining forms demanded by the political economy of the music business is an extensive one. Live recordings were issued as a way of remaining true to the traditional aesthetics of spontaneity. James Brown, who had been in the forefront of these developments, also cut tracks which occupied all of one LP side. The 7 inch, 45 rpm singles, which became the standard format of pop consumption, were subverted by continuing the same piece on both sides. By using two copies of a record, a DJ could then reconstruct its original form, pleasing dancers and changing the quality of their experience by significantly lengthening the music.

We have already seen that the arrival of the 12 inch single with a longer playing time created new artistic possibilities. There is a subtle dialectic between technological developments and the outcome of struggles between the priorities of black consumers and those of the record companies on which they were forced to depend. There is no reason for example, why rather than making 12 inch singles which played at 45 rpm, the industry could not have popularized 7 inch singles which played at 33 rpm and offered the same extended playing time. This would have used less vinyl and would have been cheaper to buy. There were Jamaican experiments with this format during the 1970s.

These struggles over the form in which the music appeared were encouraged by social relations of consumption which de-prioritize the use of music by isolated, individual consumers. We have also seen that reggae, soul and hip-hop share a cultural pattern in which listening to music, inseparable from dancing to it, becomes an active social process. The received sounds imprisoned in vinyl from which the commercial labels have been removed are moulded and reworked by the DJ's commentary and sound effects. In the case of scratch mixing, they may be completely reassembled. The deconstructive aspects of dub (CCCS, 1982) are paralleled precisely in the work of hip-hop DJs who, like their reggae counterparts, lay bare the anatomy of a piece and transform it by reorganizing it in a new order.

The liberatory rationality which is spelled out in the lyrics, if there are lyrics, is thus manifest in the consumption of the musical culture. The whole dialogic process that unites performers and crowds is imported into the culture's forms. It becomes the basis of an authentic public sphere which is counterposed to the dominant alternative, from which, in any case, blacks have been excluded. The arts which, as slaves, blacks were allowed instead of freedom, have become a means to make their formal freedom tangible.

The extent of this alternative public sphere can be gauged from the stress which soul and reggae cultures lay on names. Performers and those who support them in the division of labour which makes their art available, take new names which are specific to their under-ground cultural networks. James Brown thus calls himself 'The Godfather' and 'The Minister of the New Super Heavy Funk', Culture Smiley, Brother D, Papa Levi, Afrika Bambaataa, Junior Gee, Doug E Fresh and Asher Senator have all been mentioned above. In rap and go-go (Cosgrove, 1985) performances, naming is at the centre of elaborate rituals in which MCs and rappers establish their right to speak before doing so and connect collective identity to community territory.[51]

The impulse to cement a critique of the world by unnaming and renaming it also shapes the reggae undergound profoundly. It is revealed in the handbills and posters on which forthcoming events are advertised and circulated to their inner-city constituencies. One poster announcing a three-way sound system competition between Leeds, London and Birmingham provides a characteristic example of collective self re-creation and affirmation of cultural and political autonomy:

Maverick Internash from Chapeltown Leeds the King of The North . . . at the control Selector Scully Roots along with MCs KO Ranko, Sampson Dread, Daddy Stylo, Pablo Dee, Little Ritchie, Lady Sharon and Champion Singjays Sugar Merchant and Fluid Irie. . . . From London Sir Coxsone Outernational World Champion Sound, Blacker Dread operator, Gappy Selector, MCs Jah Screechy, General Singjay Levi Roots. . . . From B'ham Radicks Hi Powa, controlla and operator Dalphus aided and abetted by Fitzy, Patto, General Freddie, Stickman and the rest of the sodam posse . . . Level Vibes.

Another less prestigious gathering in East London brought together the Saxon Sound originators of the fast style, with Trojan, a local sound. The handbill advertising the dance conveyed the same sense of an exclusive yet public world with its own detailed genealogies:

In response to public demand Harmony productions and HYC bring you a big Ram Jam charity session for the Ethiopia Famine Relief appeal . . . star-ring the South East London answer to Sound perfection, King Saxon Studio . . . co-staring the debut performance of East London sound represen-tatives Trojan B.I. Boom system . . . featuring the Trojan VIPs System keeper and manager Deadlie Eddie, lyricologist and lyrics poet Joe 90 ridimologist and system technician Hi Fi . . . love and unity in the community.

Sometimes the proliferation of aliases and chosen names becomes so dense that artists use two or even three to signify their public self-designated identity: 'Knockie otherwise the Mighty Jah Shaka', 'The man called Blacker Dread the Dub Organiser', 'MC Boob aka Steady B'. As I shall show in the next chapter, it is highly significant that this language of public association is strongly associated with locality and neighbourhood (Kohl and Hinton, 1972; Castleman, 1982). These

216

too become important sources of effect. They contribute to the ability of the group to define itself and symbolize its collective identity in cultural expression

'Race' ethnicity, syncretism and modernity

The black cultures which form the basis of this chapter all originate in the experiences and histories of the African diaspora. Given that these constitute only some of the forces which contribute to the emergence of a black Britishness and a British blackness, my argument may appear to be incomplete. However, such a view involves a misreading of the discussion of cultural syncretism which began this chapter. Culture is not a fixed and impermeable feature of social relations. Its forms change, develop, combine and are dispersed in historical processes. The syncretic cultures of black Britain exemplify this. They have been able to detach cultural practices from their origins and use them to found and extend the new patterns of metacommunication which give their community substance and collective identity. Milo (the Bassmonger), a hip-hop DJ from Bristol, where local toasters perform their own 'Bristol Translation' in blues dances and parties, has become known for scratching break beats into reggae rhythms.[52] The defensive walls around each sub-culture gradually crumble and new forms with even more complex genealogies are created in the synthesis and transcendence of previous styles. The effects of this can be seen not only where the cultural resources of the Afro-Caribbean communities provide a space in which whites are able to discover meaning in black histories, style and language, but also where a shared culture, overdetermined by its context of the urban crisis, mediates the relationship between the different ethnic groups that together comprise black Britain. The explosion of interest in hip-hop culture which occurred in West London's Asian areas during 1985 is an important example of this creativity. For these young people, the language, symbols and artistic repertoires produced in the confluence of Afro-American, Hispanic and Caribbean cultures in the Bronx have yielded powerful sources of solidarity and pleasure as well as a means to organize themselves. In August 1985, the *Blues and Soul* hip-hop columnist, Tim Westwood, captioned pictures of 'Wild Style' graffiti in West London with the words:

The Southall scene and the Homeboys from Haze. A tough underground Hip Hop scene is busting loose with the Asian brothers on the West Side. Graffiti by the boss crew TDA-defane (Total Dynamic Art) who are Crush, Sizzle, Bizerk, Skandle and Kaoz. And watch out for the rather treacherous DJ crew Polar Bear . . . plus lethal scratchers Aprish and Jager. . . . Put them together with rappers Spyrock and Jakal and you touch down on a def jam – Southall style.[53]

In October, Westwood announced the formation of the Westside Organization (WSD) a new 'Nation' of hip-hoppers which 'has developed in West London (from Shepherds Bush out to Southall/Uxbridge/Hounslow) under the guidance of MC Spyrock'. He added

They have regular meetings *fighting to keep hip hop alive as a life style and defend it as a culture.* [My emphasis] Any credible Westside crew or individual can register with the organization. The Asian Brothers are doing it right![54]

The relationship between these cultural forms which assert the need for peace, love and unity in the distinctive language of Afro-America's 1960s black nationalism and the growth of gang culture and conflict in the same Asian communities is a complex question which cannot be gone into here.[55] The fact that West London's Asian hip-hop scene may represent a critique of, or an answer to the activities of gangs does not in any case invalidate the point I am seeking to make. A political relationship between Afro-Caribbeans and Asians on which the future of black Britain may depend is being created in these cultural encounters.

Black British cultures have been created from diverse and contradictory elements apprehended through discontinuous histories. They have been formed in a field of force between the poles of under- and overdevelopment, periphery and centre. Their bi-lingual character expresses these origins and dislocates the languages of sometimes antagonistic political formations – black and white, slave and slaveholder, class, people, nation and locality into new meanings. This illustrates the process which Bauman (1982, p. 3) has described as

constant negotiation between learned proclivities and new dependencies marked by the resistance of the traditional language to resign its authority over perception of reality and the normative regulation of group behaviour.

The outcomes of this cultural and political interaction reconstruct and rework tradition as they pursue their particular utopia. A vision of a world in which 'race' will no longer be a meaningful device for the categorization of human beings, where work will no longer be servitude and law will be disassociated from domination.

We have seen that contemporary black British culture has important qualities that give substance to the basic oppositional frameworks which derive from tradition, and historical memories of slavery. Today in soul, reggae and their various offshoots, affection and intimacy are created in collective rituals, and a view of society is articulated which stresses its 'ontological depth' (Bhaskar, 1979; 1980) demanding specific standards of truth from the forms of knowledge which will guide the community towards authentic freedom in the future. This combination of historical, temporal awareness, affect,

218

and a perspective which asserts that the phenomena visible on the surfaces of capitalist society can only be understood be reference to another realm, unseen yet somehow determining, mark the distance between these black cultures and current aesthetic analysis premised on the identification of 'post-modern' forms from which all these qualities are argued to be increasingly absent (Jameson, 1984; Latimer, 1984; Hebdige, 1985). Yet the playful, utopian celebration of change and entropic city life coupled with the deconstructive, radical forms of signification (dubbing, scratching, breakdancing and the 'visual pollution' of graffiti) which have been developed, out of necessity, by the cultural communities examined in this chapter, suggest a different conclusion.

As Orlando Patterson has pointed out, the categories of modernity and ethnicity have a close and intimate association. Yet the relationship of blacks to modernity, born perhaps in the plantation institutions which required them to 'live together in a social relation far closer than any proleteriat of the time' (James, 1983) has remained substantially unexplored. For whites, the aesthetics of modernism may have centred on a 'detachment if not revulsion from the human' (Cook, 1984), captured in the image of Gregor Samsa as a beetle and made concrete in Adorno's reflection on the barbarity of writing lyric poetry after Auschwitz (1977). For the African diaspora, constituted for several centuries in a 'milieu of dispossession', modernity raised a different set of issues centring on the need to recover and validate black culture and reincarnate the sense of being and belonging which had been erased from it by slavery.

The completion of that project by literary and musical means underpins this chapter. The cultural and political practices with which it has been concerned indicate a more substantive 'post-modern' vision where they have stepped outside the confines of modernity's most impressive achievement – the nation state.

Notes

1 C. L. R. James's *Beyond A Boundary* (Hutchinson, London 1969), is an excellent example of the type of cultural history that I am suggesting. On the role of significance of cricket elsewhere in the British Empire see Amirah Inglis's *The White Woman's Protection Ordinance. Sexual Anxiety and Politics in Papua* (Sussex University Press, 1975; esp. pp. 92–3).

2 The information about this case was obtained from the sleeve note of the 1983 Steel Pulse album *Earth Crisis* (Wiseman Doctrine 002).

3 A detailed account of how Douglass's freedom was secured is provided by Ida B. Wells's autobiography *Crusade For Justice* (University of Chicago Press, 1970).

4 The story of the settlement of Sierra Leone in the late 1780s is covered

by several authors. Kenneth Little's *Negroes in Britain* (RKP, London, 1948) suggests that the white women who went to Africa with their black partners were prostitutes who were decoyed or lured on board the ships. Fryer's (1984) *Staying Power* supplies an interesting corrective to this view. Geiss (1974) examines the connection between the settlement project and the English abolitionist movement.

5 This quote comes from the O Jays 'Letter To My Friends' from the Philadelphia International (1983) album 'When Will I See You Again?'

6 Hiro (1971) periodizes the early settlement and argues that skilled and semi-skilled settlers were in the majority between 1948 and 1955. In the later period between 1955 and 1962 'the "typical" migrant was unskilled or semi-skilled with a rural or semi-rural background' (p. 10).

Peach (1968, pp. 41–2) has figures on the gender difference among the black settler population. According to his tables, women were only an overall majority of immigrants in 1958 and 1959 though the percentages of men and women varied quite widely between the different West Indian territories. In 1958 for example, 60.6 per cent of Guyanese and 48.3 per cent of Jamaican emigrants were male.

7 *Caribbean Times*, 241, 25.10.85. I spoke to Mr Stennett in October 1985.

8 See Leslie Thompson's autobiography (1985).

9 *Caribbean Times*, 242, 1.11.85.

10 The Cables 'Baby Why' (Studio One) is one of the first discernably 'reggae' recordings, and typifies the Coxsone approach of the period.

11 *Black Music*, 1, no.8, July 1974.

12 Charles Hamblett and Jane Deverson, *Generation X* (Tandem Books, London 1964).

13 *Black Music*, March 1976.

14 *Time Out*, 16–22 May 1985.

15 The growth of reggae as a form of pop or rock music during the 1970s resulted in a proliferation of pictorial 'coffee table' books about Rastafari, reggae and Jamaica. Soft core porn photographs of black bodies, male and female, were interspersed by journalistic commentary about the brutishness and the hedonism of this Caribbean idyll. Typical manifestations of this genre include Michael Thomas and Adrian Boot's *Jah Revenge* (Eel Pie/Hutchinson, 1982) and Adrian Boot and Vivien Goldman's *Bob Marley Soul Rebel-Natural Mystic* (Eel Pie/Hutchinson 1981).

16 'Keep On Pushing' and most of the other Impressions hits of this period can be found on the ABC double album 'originals' (ABSD 303).

17 Little Milton's 'We're Gonna Make It' (Checker 1105), Syl Johnson's 'Is It because I'm Black?' (Twinight LPS 1002) and Sam Cooke's 'A Change Is Gonna Come' are some of the discs I have in mind here.

18 Nina Simone 'Mississippi Goddam' is available on 'The Best of Nina Simone' (RCA LSP 4374).

19 The discussion of what constitutes soul in Chapter 7 of Charles Keil's *Urban Blues* is particularly interesting. 'Reviewing the elements in the soul ideology, the full range of lyrics, blues performances in toto and the

party line at WVON, however, I think it is possible to interpret the soul and solidarity syndrome as a key phase in an incipient movement or perhaps as a complex response to the civil rights movement' (p. 185).

20 The lyrics from Aretha Franklin's 'Think' which are reproduced below typify this mood.

21 These words come from the sleeve note to James Brown's double album 'The Payback' (Polydor 2679 025, 1973).

22 *Rolling Stone*, 10.2.77.

23 The sleeve illustrations to any of the Parliament releases after 'Chocolate City' bear this out. The best examples apart from their 'Mothership Connection' are two Dexter Wansell album sleeves 'Life On Mars' and 'Voyager' which depicts him in a space suit preparing to leave earth.

24 The Jones Girls 'Get As Much Love As You Can' (Philadelphia International 85347, 1981).

25 *Time*, 6.4.70.

26 The Valentine Brothers 'Money's Too Tight To Mention', Syl Johnson's 'Keep On Loving Me' (Epic 25300) are two songs which make overt reference to Reaganomics.

27 *Black Music*, February 1984, p. 10.

28 Face 2000 'Run Jesse Run' (RSP 1001); Melle Mel 'Jesse' (Sugar Hill 32016); Reathel Bean and the Doonesbury Break Crew 'Rap Master Ronnie' (Silver Screen SSR115); Gil Scott Heron 'Rerun' (Arista AD1–9216); Bonzo Goes To Washington 'Bombing In Five Minutes' (Sleeping Bag SLX13); Uncle Sham and The Politicians 'Vote For me' (Easy Street EZS 7509); and Captain Rapp 'Bad Times (I Can't Stand It)' (Becket KSL 10) are some of the better politically articulate discs of the 1984 election period.

29 *Guardian*, 11.2.84. 'Fill My Cup' is on Island 12IS 124.

30 Out of twenty-six stations listed as transmitting in the fifth (March 1986) edition of the illegal broadcasters magazine *TX*, ten described themselves as black music stations. These were Emperor Radio, Fame FM, Radio Funk, Inner City Radio, JBC Radio, London Weekend Radio, TKO, Trax FM, Radio Tree and Twilight Radio. *TX* is available from P.O. Box 539, Blackpool, Lancashire FY1 4RE.

31 The band were interviewed by Dave Collins on another pirate station – Solar Radio, 14.4.85.

32 *Black Music*, March 1983, p. 15.

33 Tippa Irie's 'Complain Neighbour' and Patto Banton's 'Allo Tosh' and 'Gwan' are the best examples here.

34 These works are all dismissive or gestural in their treatment of the political ideologies of these black forms. Toop reduces the political aspects of hip-hop culture to the distinction between what he disapprovingly calls 'Message Raps' and the rest. Chambers is particularly offensive in his treatment of blacks as feeling but not thinking beings. For him, soul is all body and no mind. Blacks have 'stretched' and expanded the body, whereas in my approach it is Europeans who have

221

shrunk its domain. Chambers dismisses soul brothers James Brown, Wilson Pickett and Joe Tex as 'black proud and . . . sexist' (p. 148). He interprets James Brown's screams as evidence that he is 'trying to mouth the inarticulate'.

35 The Fatback Band 'Is This The Future' (Polydor).

36 Two good examples of reggae on the theme of work are 'Hallelujah Time' by the Wailers and Jnr Murvin's Upsetter–produced masterpiece 'Working In a Cornfield'.

37 These words come from Prince Lincoln's song 'Mechanical Devices' on the Rasses album 'Natural Wild' (United Artists).

38 People's Choice 'Strikin' (Mercury); Rich Cason and The Galactic Orchestra 'Street Symphony' (Private Eye).

39 Lion Youth '3 Million on The Dole' (Virgo Stomach).

40 The Sugar Hill Gang's 'Hit It Live From 9–5' is on the double sampler set 'Rapped Up Tight' (PRT). The Bob Marley track referred to is 'Work' from the album 'Uprising' (ILPS 9596).

41 Trouble Funk's 'Drop The Bomb' (SugarHill) and the Gap Band's 'You Dropped a Bomb on Me' (Total Experience) are the best examples here.

42 The Coasters' 'Framed' (Atlantic).

43 *Blues and Soul*, 425, 5.2.85.

44 The Rake 'Street Justice' (Streetwave) is a good example of this.

45 Bobby Womack 'American Dream' is on his album 'The Poet 2' (Beverley Glen).

46 'Think' by Aretha Franklin is on 'Aretha Now' (Atlantic SD 8186).

47 The most moving songs in this genre are Dennis Brown's 'Three Meals a Day' (Joe Gibbs) and Bunny Wailer's 'Battering Down Sentence' (Solomonic). There are plenty of others: Gregory Isaacs's 'Out Deh' (Island); Black Uhuru's 'Conviction or Fine' (RAS); Barrington Levi's 'Prison Oval Rock' (Volcano).

48 Bobby Womack 'The Roots In Me' from the album 'The Roads of Life' (Arista).

49 The Roxanne Saga of 1985 is a good example here. The story of a street confrontation between a girl (Roxanne) and a boy who propositions her was expanded into a multiple disc saga in which the girl, the boy, her parents, doctor, and various other commentators gave their view of the incident. A sample of these would have to include Dr Fresh 'Roxanne's Doctor' (Zakia); Gigolo Tony and Lacey Lace 'The Parents of Roxanne' (4 Sight) and Roxanne 'The Real Roxanne' (Select).

50 *Blues and Soul*, 15 October 1985.

51 GoGo music with this feature can be heard on the Pump Blenders 'Funk The People Live' (CoolTempo) and the sampler album 'The Sound of Washington DC' (London).

52 *Blues and Soul*, no. 446, November/December 1985.

53 *Blues and Soul*, no. 438, 6–19 August 1985, p. 34.

54 *Blues and Soul*, no. 442, 1–14 October 1985, p. 34.

55 *Observer*, 15.12.85.

6 Conclusion: urban social movements, 'race' and community

It is directly at the level of the production of social relations that capitalism is vulnerable and en route to perdition. Its fatal malady is not its incapacity to reproduce itself economically and politically, but its incapacity to reproduce itself *symbolically* (Jean Baudrillard).

As an analysis of the mode of capitalist production, Marxism defines the conditions under which the system enters a state of crisis. As a theory of revolution, it lacks the analytic instruments required for defining the actors and political forms of socio-economic transformation (Alberto Melucci).

The expressive culture examined in the previous chapter has been loosely described as the voice of social movement. It provides an opportunity to gauge the character, scope and orientation of a movement among British blacks and their inner-city associates which is encouraged and enabled by the patterns of cultural creation discussed above. However, the collective action which that culture marks out, and the interpretive and participative community which is produced in the process of consuming it, is not confined to the dance-halls, parties and clubs which constitute an alternative public sphere beyond the colour line.

The counter-cultures and sub-cultures of black Britain may have held the movement together at certain crucial moments. They provide, among other things, important rituals which allow its affiliates to recognize each other and celebrate their coming together. But culture, though integral to the social movement, is not its totality. It is therefore necessary, having moved through the content and form of the movement's cultural aspects, to explore its social and political position. Analysis of black Britain must be able to address the synchronic, structural aspects of the movement as well as its diachronic, historical dimension.

The first chapter of this book raised the question of historical agency and, as part of its critique of class theory, argued that class analysis of contemporary Britain could be reconceptualized in the light of an extended exploration of 'race'. This concluding chapter suggests that social movement theory can provide a valuable starting

223

point from which this analytical and political transformation might be accomplished. The problem of agency is addressed again, this time in the context of a study of disorderly protest. We focus directly on the kind of collective political action which 'racial' subjectivities allow people to execute. Links between 'race' and the urban environment are discussed at length as are the language and politics of community which have been a notable feature of this relationship.

The term 'social movement' is used here in a way which derives from the theoretical elaboration which the concept has received in the works of Alain Touraine (1977; 1981; 1983a; 1983b), Manuel Castells (1983) and Alberto Melucci (1980; 1981a; 1981b). All have used it to examine new patterns of political action and organization, which have emerged in the overdeveloped countries as their old industrial order has begun to decompose and social and political collectivities based away from the workplace have become as vocal, militant and politically significant as the residues of the workers movement (Freeman, 1983). Touraine and his collaborators link the appearance of these new anti-industrial and anti-bureaucratic political forces – the women's movements, youth movements, anti-nuclear and peace movements, ecological movements, and various urban or citizen movements – with changes in the mode of production. In particular with the growth of large-scale structural unemployment, the expansion of nuclear power, the rise of new technologies, and new communicative networks.

. . . in a society where the largest investments no longer serve to transform the organisation of labour, as in industrial society, but to create new products, and beyond that, new sources of economic power through the control of complex systems of communication, then the central conflict has shifted. It no longer opposes manager and worker, subjected to the rationalising apparatuses which have acquired the power to impose patterns of behaviour on people according to their own interests (Touraine, 1983a, p. 4).

These new movements may challenge the mode of production and struggle for control of the ways in which a society appropriates scarce resources, but this is not their primary orientation. They are struggling not only for the reappropriation of the material structure of production, but also for collective control over socio-economic development as a whole. Their goals involve the transformation of new modes of subordination located outside the immediate processes of production and consequently require the reappropriation of space, time, and of relationships between individuals in their day to day lives. All these are perceived to be the results of social action. The struggle over production is broadened, and spreads into new areas: 'The defense of identity, continuity and predictability of personal experience is beginning to constitute the substance of new conflicts' (Melucci, 1980). Thus for Touraine and Melucci the new social movements are not phenomena of class politics in any simple sense. Both argue that society should be understood as a self-creating process rather than a finished edifice or structure. The distinctive feature of these movements, diverse as they are, rests on their potential for universalizing the issue of emancipation beyond the particularistic interests of industrial workers employed full time in work that produces surplus value. It is located in their common struggle for the social control of historicity: 'the symbolic capacity that enables [society] to construct a system of knowledge together with the technical tools which it can use to intervene in its own functioning' (Touraine, 1977).

We have seen in Chapters 2 and 3 that in contemporary Britain the symbols associated with 'race', nation, national culture, patriotism and belonging have acquired potent new meanings which are deeply implicated in the way in which national crisis is represented and mediated. In a sense, these symbols and the various meanings attached to them suggest that the painful experiences of crisis and decline can be reversed if not postponed.

Contrasting it with the political and cultural vitality of the new social movements, Touraine identifies the decline of the workers' movement in the overdeveloped countries as an important part of a 'far more general disintegration of the culture of industrial society' (1981). The decomposition of this culture has been articulated to the appearance of a 'modernising cultural critique' which emanates in part from the new social movements and in turn, encourages their development. These new movements are part of a new phase of class conflict so far removed from the class struggles of the industrial era that the vocabulary of class analysis created during that period must itself be dispensed with, or at least ruthlessly modernized. It must be replaced with or reformed into a theory capable of linking analysis of new social, economic and political structures with analysis of the new social actors who inhabit and create them (Bookchin, 1978).

The accumulation of capital is no longer fed by the mere exploitation of the labour force. It depends increasingly on manipulation of complex organizational and informational systems, 'on control over the processes and institutions of symbol formation, and by intervention in interpersonal relations' (Melucci, 1980). This change lends cultural politics an additional cutting edge, particularly where advanced capitalism has developed a

capacity for intervention and transformation which extends beyond the natural environment and exerts an influence on social systems, on interpersonal relations and on the very structure of the individual (personality, the unconscious, biological identity) (Melucci, 1980, p. 218).

Melucci expands on Touraine's view that Marxism has wrongly separated the analysis of social systems from the analysis of social actors, individual and collective. He goes further than Touraine in suggesting several core characteristics which connect the disparate social movements and allow analysts to perceive their novelty and common identity. He begins by comparing their modes of collective action with those of class politics and observes that the new movements tend to refuse mediation of their demands by the political system against which they have defined themselves. The sociology of these social movements cannot therefore centre, as class analysis has done, on the study of the articulation of class behaviours in the political system. The first characteristic which unites the new movements is the resolutely non-negotiable nature of their demands. This relates directly to a second characteristic feature visible in the extent to which the new movements are not primarily oriented towards instrumental objectives, such as the conquest of political power or state apparatuses, but rather towards 'control of a field of autonomy or independance vis a vis the system' and the *immediate* satisfaction of collective desires. Acknowledging that this quality has been criticized as a weakness, particularly by Marxian writers, Melucci instead interprets it as an indication of the movements' potential strength. He argues that it manifests the specificity of the new forms of collective action they have developed. The very refusal to accept mediation be the existing frameworks and institutions of the political system or to allow strategy to be dominated by the task of winning power within it, provides these movements with an important focus of group identity.

The creation of solidarity from a sense of particularity is an objective for these groups and their political behaviour is not exclusively directed towards the outside. Their characteristic rejection of a politics of representative delegation and their enthusiasm for direct participation and direct action also distinguishes these new social movements from the ossified practices of corporatist class politics (Bauman, 1982; Panitch, 1981).

Melucci identifies two further issues which play a fundamental, definitive role in the new movements. The first is the central place they give to the body, and through it to an understanding of human beings as part of the natural world. Blacks who live 'in the castle of their skin' and have struggled to escape the biologization of their socially and politically constructed subordination are already sensitive to this issue. The attempt to articulate blackness as an historical rather than as a natural category confronts it directly. The escape from bestial status into a recognized humanity has been a source of both ethics and politics since the slave system was first instituted and there is an extensive literature which surrounds the absurdities of racial biology and the difficulties associated with its overcoming (Larsen, 1929; Weldon Johnson, 1965). Black artists have thus identified the body as a seat of desires and as a nexus of interpersonal relationships in a special way which expresses the aspiration that skin colour will one day be no more significant than eye pigment and, in the meantime, announces that black is beautiful. Whether it is anti-racist universality or spurious racial classification which is being invoked, the black body bears some potent meanings. However, a similar concern and fascination with the body has been expressed by the women's movement, the gay movement and sections of the peace movement where the body has become, in various different ways, a cultural locus of resistances and desires. A sense of the body's place in the natural world can provide, for example, a social ecology and an alternative rationality that articulate a cultural and moral challenge to the exploitation and domination of 'the nature within us and without us' (Ben-Habib, 1981; Daly, 1979). A homology has also been identified between care of the body and care of the planet and its biosphere. In black cultures, the themes of bodily control and care emerge most strongly in relation to dance and martial arts. George *et al.* (1985) support this view by pointing persuasively to the similarity between breakdancing and Capoeira, the martial art of Brazilian slaves. However, the same themes are present in the eschatological notion of reconciliation with nature which is central to Rastafari ideology. They have been refined into a holistic concern with ital (natural) eating and physical fitness[1] which has remained in the 'good sense' of the community even where some of the movement's more antiquated or theological concepts have been de-emphasized.

A religious or spiritual component is the second fundamental element which Melucci identifies as connecting the diverse new social movements. Spirituality is more than just a consistent factor in the origins of these various movements. It has acquired powerful radical dimensions not only because religious language can express an intensity of aspirations for which no secular alternative is available but because the political order which these movements criticize and oppose is itself increasingly secular in its rationalizations. In these circumstances, religion may become detached from the institutional life of the official church. Its moral authority increases where the instrumental, secular rationality which informs the operations of the dominant order can be shown to be pragmatic rather than principled. Where the new movements have kept their distance from the institutions of the political system, the moral and metaphysical attributes of religious language can provide a legitimacy which significantly appears to be above politics. The distinction between authentic human emancipation and the formal freedoms guaranteed by politics is constantly underlined.

Britain's social movement around 'race' exhibits all the characteristics suggested by Touraine and Melucci. Its demands around work, law and racism are non-negotiable and where they are not openly hostile to the institutions of the political system, its organizational forms fit only loosely and partially into it. There is, as we saw in the previous chapter, a degree of hostility to these institutions and the types of politics they promote. This feeling – 'A terrifying sense of powerlessness which is easily mistaken for apathy' (Bookchin, 1978) – has been identified as a problem and as an object of state intervention by inner-city local governments. The anti-racist programmes examined in Chapter 4 are aimed directly at alleviating it. The campaign for 'black sections' in the Labour Party is similarly designed to show that the discredited political institutions of the working class retain an importance for blacks (Howe, 1985). Both campaigns have had only limited success in countering the idea that being political now requires complete disassociation from the corporate structures of formal politics which are in need of drastic re-politicization. Authentic politics is thought to recommence with this act of withdrawal.[2]

The importance of local factors and local state initiatives as well as the intersection of territoriality and identity in urban black cultures provide a further clue to the character of contemporary 'race' politics. It demands that the role of distinctively urban processes and experiences are recognized. Chapters 2 and 3 showed that Britain's 'race' politics are quite inconceivable away from the context of the inner city which provides such firm foundations for the imagery of black criminality and lawlessness. We must therefore confront the extent to which the cultural politics of 'race' reveals conflict over the production of urban meanings and situate the meanings which have already been identified as constitutive of 'race' in their proper place as contending definitions of what city life is about.

We have already seen that the image of black and white neighbours living side by side yet estranged from each other is a recurrent theme in the discourse of contemporary racism. Chapter 3 argued that there is a sense in which Powell's 'wide grinning piccaninnies' tormenting the aged white woman, have metamorphosed into a riotous mob energized by the deviant impulses of their pathological alien culture. The *Daily Express* version of the Tottenham riot of October 1985 reveals the enduring potency of these images in its account of 'Old folk left helpless as looters strip their homes. . . . Elderly couples told how they were pulled from their flats and had to stand and watch as youths looted their homes.'[3] These and similar images derive their power partly from what they convey about the incompatibility of black and white people and their respective 'ethnic' cultures conceived along absolutely separate lines. They are also highly significant for what they communicate about the city in which blacks and whites encounter each other with such negative results.

The idea of the city as a jungle where bestial, predatory values prevail preceded the large-scale settlement of Britain by blacks in the post-war period (Langer, 1984). It has contributed significantly to contemporary definitions of 'race', particularly those which highlight the supposed primitivism and violence of black residents in inner-city areas. This is the context in which 'race' and racism come to connote the urban crisis as a whole and that crisis to embody racial problems even where they are not overtly acknowledged or defined.

'Race' has become a marker for the activity of urban social movements and their conflict with urban political systems and state institutions. This connection between contemporary British racism and the city is an important reminder that 'race' is a relational concept which does not have fixed referents. The naturalization of social phenomena and the suppression of the historical process which are introduced by its appeal to the biological realm can articulate a variety of different political antagonisms. They change, and bear with them no intrinsic or constant political effects.

We have seen in Chapter 4 that the local state has been especially prominent in recent 'race' politics as a key source of anti-racist activity. This prominence is a further sign of the importance of the urban context in shaping racial meanings. The municipal anti-racism discussed above has become an important issue in its own right, separate from the struggles of black city dwellers. The Labour councils who have set out to 'attack' racism and win active support from their black citizens by changing 'Britannia Walk' to 'Shaheed E Azam Bhagot Singh Avenue'[4] or by telling environmental health officers who monitor noise on their estates to be lenient with noisy parties which are the product of black ethnicity, while prosecuting white infringers whose anti-social behaviour lacks any comparable cultural explanation[5] have been severely criticized in the popular press. Their initiatives have been presented as the inevitably disastrous effect of a mistaken desire to secure racial equality by means of an active policy. The true tyranny revealed by the 'race' issue is thus no longer the oppression of blacks by whites that is institutionalized in Britain's social and political life. It is defined instead as the anti-racist autocracy which blacks and their socialist allies are able to practice on a tolerant population by means of their hold on the local state. This is demonstrated in the reporting of anti-racist policies which have been described as a 'sinister attempt to first curb and then destroy freedom of speech'.[6]

The popular opposition to municipal anti-racism also constructs a version of the national past which directly challenges the emphasis on slavery which we saw emerging in Chapter 5 from the expressive culture of Britain's blacks: 'British people are not and have never been, racist. This country has always involved a reputation as a tolerant, welcoming haven for refugees and immigrants' (*Sun*, 24.10.85). Racism has been redefined as the product of black and anti-racist zeal that is both destructive of democracy and subversive of order. The right to be prejudiced is claimed as the heritage of the freeborn Briton and articulated within the discourses of freedom, patriotism and democracy while despotic anti-racism is associated with authoritarianism, statism and censorship.

The power which this ideological package has acquired can lead to its municipal context being overlooked. However tokenistic, ill-considered and poorly presented to the public recent attempts to rename and unname streets, areas and public, facilities at least express something of the fundamental connection between 'race' and the city. They seek to make visible the consonance of social and physical space and this becomes all the more important because ethnic absolutism appears to have forsaken the distinctively urban dimensions of 'race' altogether. The supposed cultural essences of Britain's black populations have been accorded a determining role irrespective of their surroundings. Concern with the relationship between 'race' and the urban environment which was an important feature of the early sociology of 'race relations' has faded.[7]

Manuel Castells (1983) has developed a theory of the distinctively urban dimensions of the new social movements which can contribute to the theorization of contemporary 'race' politics in this country. He argues that urban social movements share some basic characteristics in spite of their obvious diversity. They consider themselves to be urban, citizen or related to the city in their self-denomination; they are locally based, territorially defined and they tend to mobilize around three central goals: 1 collective consumption; 2 cultural identity; 3 political self-management. Collective consumption refers to the goods and services directly or indirectly provided by the state; cultural identity becomes an issue where it is closely associated with a specific territory and is defended on that basis; and political self-management relates to the attempt by urban groups to win a degree of autonomy from the local governments which directly oversee their immediate environments providing use values, income and services.

Each of these features can be found in the recent history of Britain's black communities: struggles over the services provided by the state, particularly the quality of educational opportunities for black children have been intense;[8] the cultural dimensions to the struggle of black inner-city dwellers have already been examined; and the demands of community organizations have repeatedly focused on the need to gain a degree of control over the processes which shape day to day experience. Local campaigns for police accountability, prompted by concern about the organization and role of the force in inner-city areas, perfectly illustrate the type of issue which falls in Castells's last category (Scraton, 1985).

There are good grounds on which to argue that the language of community has displaced both the language of class and the language of 'race' in the political activity of black Britain. Though blacks identify themselves as an exploited and subordinated group, there

230

are marked and important differences between the political cultures and identities of the various black communities which together make up the social movement. Local factors, reflecting the class, ethnic and 'racial' composition of any particular area, its political traditions, the local economy and residential structure may all play a decisive part in shaping precisely what it means to be black. As we saw in Chapter 1, the relationship between Afro-Caribbean and Asian descended populations is the most obvious factor of this type. The forms of racism which develop in areas where the two groups are closely associated are quite different from those which obtain where there is a measure of antipathy or even conflict between them. Some inner-city whites, particularly the young, may find much in 'West Indian' culture which they can evaluate positively. If black culture appears in syncretized Afro-Caribbean forms which are relatively desirable and attractive when contrasted to the more obviously 'alien' Asian varieties, the white racist may be faced with considerable problems (Gilroy and Lawrence, 1982).

According to Castells, it is only when all three of these goals combine in the practice of an urban movement that social change can occur. The separation of any one goal from the others reduces the potential of the social movement and recasts it in the role of an interest group that may be 'moulded into the established institutions of society, so losing its impact' (Castells, 1983). He views these social movements as precarious, fragile collectivities which may be unable to fully accomplish all the projects promised by their organizational rhetoric. Their specific appeal and the popular power they represent cannot necessarily survive contact with the agencies of the state against which they struggle: 'they lose their identity when they become institutionalised, the inevitable outcome of bargaining for social reform within the political system'.

The theory of urban social movements correctly emphasizes that they are not ready-made agents for structural change but rather 'symptoms of resistance to domination'. They have their roots in a radical sense of powerlessness and though their resistances may have important effects on cities and societies, they are best understood as defensive organizations which are unlikely to be able to make the transition to more stable forms of politics. This lends these movements certain strengths as well as the obvious weaknesses. The utopian strands in their ideology, which demand the immediate satisfaction of needs, require totalizing, historically feasible plans for economic production, communication and government. The movements are unlikely to be unable to supply these without losing the very qualities which make them dynamic and distinct. Their orientation towards local governments and political institutions, on the immediate conditions in which exploitation and domination are experienced, is a result of the simple fact that those whose grievances

231

give the movements momentum have no other choice. They lack any sense of credible democracy other than the grassroots variety practised in their own organizations. As Castells puts it, 'When people find themselves unable to control the world, they simply shrink the world to the size of their community'. The 'politricks' of the system is replaced by an authentic, immediate politics.

Like Touraine, Castells lays great stress on the decline of the workers' movement which has been apparent in inverse proportion to the rise of the new social movements (Wallerstein, 1980). This decline has been hastened by the fact that the parties and organizations of Labour operate an obsolete analysis which privileges industrial work and depends ultimately on a mystical view of the proleteriat as a 'universal class' which, in liberating itself, is expected to liberate everybody. Further problems have arisen where the idea of socialism has itself been discredited by the barbarities practised in its name by the 'actually existing socialist' states. Castells sums up the situation thus:

. . . the philosophical rationalism of the political left and the one dimensional culture of the Labour movement lead the social movements of industrial capitalism to ignore sub-cultures, gender specificity, ethnic groups, religious beliefs, national identities and personal experiences. All human diversity was generally considered a remnant of the past, and class struggle and human progress would help to supercede it until a universal fraternity was arrived at that would provide, paradoxically, the ideal stage for both bourgeois enlightenment and proleterian marxism. Between times, people continued to speak their languages, pray to their saints, celebrate their traditions, enjoy their bodies and refuse just to be labour or consumers'.

Andre Gorz (1982) also discusses these issues. He points to several problems in Marxist theory which have a direct bearing on the relationship between the new social movements and industrial class politics. His central proposition is that the large-scale, structural unemployment produced by crisis and technological change combines with a related loss of ability to identify with work among those who remain employed. Together these patterns are bringing about a complete transformation of work in the overdeveloped countries.

Just as work has become a nondescript task carried out without any personal involvement, which one may quit for another equally contingent job, so too has class membership come to be lived as a contingent and meaningless fact (1982, p. 67).

By the same remorseless logic with which earlier forms of capitalism created the proleteriat, the crises of late capitalism are creating a 'non-class of non-workers' from the unemployed, part-timers, and those who work with no security – 'all the supernumeraries of present day social production'. This historical and structural problem
232

is compounded in Marxist theory by the idealist residues of Hegelianism which are concentrated in Marx's analysis of the proleteriat. Gorz argues that rather than being confined to Marx's early writings, metaphysical, ontological views of the origin and mission of the proleteriat pervade Marx's mature work.

This thesis has been stated in a more circumspect manner by other authors, particularly Murray Bookchin and Rudolph Bahro.[9] It rests on a contentious reading of Marx with which I have considerable sympathy even though it has been described by one critic as 'trivializing'.[10] It can supply an important corrective to Marxian theories of 'race' which have sought, as we saw in Chapter 1, to use outmoded criteria as a means to measure the activities of the new social movements and find them wanting. Gorz suggests that the Hegelian philosophy which constructs the proleteriat as a universal class has encouraged a 'mythologized proleterian ideal' which can never be matched by the composite, fractured and heterogeneous actions of the empirical working class.

The same Hegelian traces, described by Gorz as a 'theology translated as a theophany' also lead Marxists to deny the necessary space between individual autonomy, freedom and happiness and *social* being which is allocated pride of place in their theory. Individuals will not necessarily find their self-realization congruent with the socialization of their needs and Gorz insists that there are some aspects of life which are not in any case amenable to socialization. He argues forcefully that socialists have abandoned this area of individual autonomy to the right with disastrous results. Yet it is precisely this sphere of autonomous self-realization which is addressed by many of the new social movements.

We saw in the previous chapter how black expressive cultures which prize non-work time and space have articulated a political and philosophical critique of work and productivism – the ideology which sees the expansion of productive forces as an indispensable precondition of the attainment of freedom. The critique of work in general and the capitalist division of labour in particular described by these forms involves a more modest formulation of the project which Gorz describes as 'the abolition of work'. It can be more accurately summarized in his three points for a utopian political programme: work less; consume better; and reintegrate culture with everyday life.

There are considerable difficulties in Gorz's analysis. Not least of these are his inability to see beyond Europe and an unsatisfactory attempt to unify the disparate forces which share an ambiguous relationship to the world of work, in the non-class of non-workers category. However, his post-industrial utopia finds a resonance that cannot be overlooked in many of the themes and preoccupations which have emerged spontaneously from the political culture of black Britain.

Operating in a similar but less rhetorical vein to Gorz, Rudolph Bahro has also sketched the elements of a utopian vision which combines a critique of productivism with an ethical dimension and some explicit concern with the necessary realization of individual autonomy. Bahro's definition of Cultural Revolution is encapsulated in a single desire: 'to create that new organisation of labour and social life on which it will be possible to base a community that deserves the old name of a free association of individuals in solidarity' (1978). The overcoming of racial segmentation and ethnic absolutism is implicit in this formula, since for Bahro 'This is a society in which there is no longer any domination of man by man [sic].' He reduces this maximum programme to five essential demands which also find echoes in the expressive culture discussed in Chapter 5.

1   The goal of production as rich individuality.
2   A new determination of the need for material goods and the availability of living labour from the standpoint of the optimization of conditions of development for fully socialized individuals.
3   A more harmonious form of reproduction.
4   Accounting for a new economy of time.
5   Individual initiative and genuine communality.

Bahro recognizes that the emancipatory potential signalled in these demands is 'already in train spontaneously'. He argues that the insights they contain must be expanded and developed through an extensive educational process.

For the social movement of blacks in Britain, the context in which these and other similar demands have been spontaneously articulated has been supplied by a political language premised on notions of community. Though it reflects the concentration of black people, the term refers to far more than mere place or population. It has a moral dimension and its use evokes a rich complex of symbols surrounded by a wider cluster of meanings. The historical memory of progress from slave to citizen actively cultivated in the present from resources provided by the past, endows it with an aura of tradition. Community, therefore, signifies not just a distinctive political ideology but a particular set of values and norms in everyday life: mutuality, co-operation, identification and symbiosis. For black Britain, all these are centrally defined by the need to escape and transform the forms of subordination which bring 'races' into being. Yet they are not limited by that objective. The disabling effects of racial categorization are themselves seen as symbols of the other unacceptable attributes of 'racial capitalism'. The evident autonomy of racism from production relations demands that the reappropriation of production is not pursued independently of the transformation of capitalist social relations as a whole. The social bond implied by use of the term 'community' is created in the practice of collective resistance to the encroachments of reification, 'racial' or otherwise. It prefigures that transformation in the name of a radical, democratic, anti-racist populism. This is not so much

a distinct set of political opinions as a mobilisation of people who [share] a common understanding of how life ought to be. Not all of the people are mobilised at any one time but the mode of understanding [is] widespread (Calhoun, 1980; 1982, p. 98).

The generalization of this mode of understanding coincides with the formation of what has already been called an interpretive community. It has been spread through the distinctive communicative networks which were examined in the previous chapter.

The cultural focus of this book requires that attention be paid to the symbolic dimensions of community. It is necessary, therefore, to briefly discuss the means by which community is constructed symbolically as part of or in support of the collective actions of a social movement. As Anthony Cohen points out:

. . . community might not have the structure or direction which we associate with social movements, it may nevertheless serve a similar need. It is a largely mental construct, whose 'objective' manifestations in locality or ethnicity give it credibility. It is highly symbolized, with the consequence that its members can invest it with their selves. Its character is sufficiently malleable that it can accommodate all of its members' selves without them feeling their individuality to be overly compromised. Indeed, the gloss of commonality which it paints over its diverse components gives to each of them an additional referent for their identities (Cohen, 1985, p. 109).

This definition of community depends on the distinction between symbols and meanings. The former are flexible vehicles for a variety of potentially contradictory readings which may be held by a movement's adherents. The idea of a social movement as an interpretive community should not lead to an undifferentiated monadical view of the group from which it wins active support. The strength of symbols is their multi-accentuality and malleability. Sharing a common body of symbols created around notions of 'race', ethnicity or locality, common history or identity does not dictate the sharing of the plural meanings which may become attached to those symbols and cluster around them.

Community is as much about difference as it is about similarity and identity. It is a relational idea which suggests, for British blacks at least, the idea of antagonism – domination and subordination between one community and another. The word directs analysis to the boundary between these groups. It is a boundary which is presented primarily by symbolic means and therefore a broad range of meanings can co-exist around it reconciling individuality and commonality and competing definitions of what the movement is about. The political rhetoric of leaders is, after all, not a complete

235

guide to the motivations and aspirations of those who play a less prominent role. In Cohen's words again:

just as the common form of the symbol aggregates the various meanings assigned to it, so the symbolic repertoire of a community aggregates the individualities and other differences found within the community and provides the means for their expression, interpretation and containment. . . . It continuously transforms the reality of difference into the appearance of similarity with such efficacy that people can still invest [their] community with ideological integrity. It unites them in their opposition, both to each other and to those 'outside' (1985, p. 21).

In Chapters 2 and 5 we examined some of the points at which closures have been introduced into the symbolic repertoire of black Britain. These can be identified where particular definitions of 'race' and nation or of the meaning attributed to skin colour have been invested with special significance by a group which tries to fix their reading of these symbols as a universal one capable of binding the whole community together. It bears repetition that these tensions are part of a political struggle inside the black communities over what 'race' adds up to.

Such conflicts are possible because black Britain's repertoire of symbols is relatively unfixed and still evolving. It includes the languages of Ethiopianism and Pan-Africanism and the heritage of anti-colonial resistances as well as the inputs from contemporary urban conflicts. These diverse elements combine syncretically in struggles to reconstruct a collective historical presence from the discontinuous, fractured histories of the African and Asian diasporas. Multiple meanings have grouped around the central symbol of racial alterity – the colour black – and it is difficult to anticipate the outcome of the political struggle between the different tendencies they represent – ethnic absolutism on the one hand and a utopian, democratic populism on the other. Yet despite their differences, the 'black professional' in a local authority social services department, the Afro-Caribbean ancillary in a hospital and the hip-hopping Asian youth of West London may all discover within that colour a medium through which to articulate their own experiences and make sense of their common exclusion from Britain and Britishness. The actions of organizations of the urban social movement around 'race' may themselves assume symbolic significance. Particularly where people are mobilized to protest, innumerable political and ethical grievances, desires and aspirations may be condensed and unified in the symbolism which dissent provides.

Disruptive protest and the symbolism of community

Not every protest or collective action in which blacks take part expresses the character of the social forces I have described. The
236

recent riotous protests in Britain's inner cities may, for example, appear to be far from the values of mutuality and co-operation which I have argued are a feature of the political outlook of that community. The riots during the summer of 1981 and the autumn of 1985 were described by the left as 'barbarous acts of criminality'[11] and symptoms of the 'absence . . . of any viable tradition of ethnic politics'[12] while the right argued that they were a 'cry for loot rather than a cry for help'.[13] Yet, it is possible to find, even in the media representations of these events, evidence which does support a view of their origins in a social movement.

It is important not to exaggerate the uniformity of the riots and essential to look into the local factors which have shaped each eruption. There were many differences between them but there are also enough similarities to justify raising general analytical and political issues. I want to suggest that these forms of protest can be interpreted in a way which does not reduce them to either 'marginality' or 'deviance', terms which imply that they are nothing more than crude reactions to crisis, lacking cognitive, affective and normative dimensions.

Disorderly protests reflect the experiences of participants and by conveying antagonism against the world as it is, they can be shown to embody a view of how participants would like it to be. This relates directly to the concerns of the social movement around 'race' which have already been outlined. In order to appreciate the political character of these protests, it is however, essential to grasp the manner in which the symbolism of disorder has come to dominate its instrumental aspects. Even the portrait of Britain's inner-city rioters and their motivation which emerges from press coverage can be used to support this view.

S. D. Riecher's detailed study of the riots in Bristol's St Paul's area during April 1980 operates rather narrowly within the disciplinary confines of social psychology, but contains plenty of insights into the political philosophy of the people who participated actively and passively in the riot. He argues that members of the riotous crowd on that occasion took part in disorderly protest as 'social actors: that is to say as members of a social category rather than as private individuals' (1982).

In Reicher's research, this observation is supported by interviews with participants who describe their own involvement and that of others as the action of 'everybody, the whole community'. 'Just everybody came out of their houses, just everybody local.' Similar perception of the social character of riotous protest has been expressed by participants elsewhere. Frequently the social categories in which rioters place themselves relate directly to the categories in which racial subordination is imposed and consequently to a sense of themselves as an oppressed and disadvantaged group with a

237

particular history, a definite structural location and an intimate association with the local area. As we saw in Chapter 3, surveillance and control of these areas became a major issue during the 1970s and policing is often seen as an oppressive and therefore illegitimate intrusion into their lifeworld. The violence of the crowd can thus be presented by participants as a simple answer to the repressive practices of the police with an equivalent moral status: 'the police do what they want and we do what we want – its called democracy' (Murji, 1985). Young black men in Handsworth put a similar argument to a *Guardian* reporter:

There is close co-operation between black youths and we have discussed the issue of plastic bullets. We are prepared to tackle any such moves by the government and the police to suppress our grievances. *It's not just unemployment. We're regarded as third class citizens and we're not prepared to be treated like that any longer.*[14] [My emphasis]

These words are significant for the fact they define the origins of the riots in differential access to civil rights and national belonging – third-class citizenship which operates along 'racial' lines. A '31-year-old black electronics engineer' made essentially the same point to the *Observer*: 'There's a lot of love in Handsworth, black, white and Asian. But the Asians are second-class citizens, and we're the lowest of all. We're the third.'[15] In Brixton, a young, white nurse living in a squat near Coldharbour Lane described the 1985 riot as 'a real family night out'. His description points to the important gap between participants' perceptions of the events and the way the same events are constructed differently from the outside, by observers who perceive in them only mindless violence. Reicher's Bristol interviews also found participants describing the riots in terms of joy, freedom and pleasure: 'it was lovely, I felt free'; 'People were so warm: they said "glad to be with you, brother" and put their arm around you'; 'It was really joyful, that's what they [the media] all leave out, the "joy".' He includes one particularly interesting example of the discrepancy of meaning between participants and observers:

[A] BBC radio car . . . was seen reversing furiously with a look of terror on the face of the driver, alongside a large Rastafarian was running, banging on the roof. As the car passed by my informant heard what the Rastafarian was saying 'Play us a request, play us a request . . .'.

An atmosphere of carnival engendered by spontaneous feelings of joy has been noted by many observers in different riots. It has been presented in the popular press as further evidence of the inhuman, alien behaviour of Afro-Caribbean people:

Song of Joy By Rioters – Whooping West Indians sang Oh, What a Beautiful Morning as they surveyed the riot wreckage [in Handsworth] yesterday. They laughed and drank while one section of the community mourned the victims of the violence. And they jeered and booed the police and firemen dealing with the burnt out cars littering a stretch of road.[16]

The relationship between the Brixton and Tottenham riots and the shooting of Cherry Groce and the death of Cynthia Jarrett respectively provides important indications of the normative and moral aspects of the riotous protest which followed these tragedies. The Brixton riot was described in several papers as an act of revenge for the shooting.[17] It began after members of the Groce family, their supporters and sympathizers had marched to the local police station and 'a splinter group tried to storm the yard at the rear of the station shouting "Come out, come out we want to talk to you".'[18] Similarly, the Broadwater Farm Youth Association has consistently claimed that the riot there took place because 'youths were not allowed to leave the estate to protest outside Tottenham police station at the death of Mrs Jarrett'.[19] In Handsworth, too, the belief that the disorders had originated in conflict between police and a black woman was widespread (Ousley et al., 1986).

A further contradiction of the media definition of the disorders as anomic, irrational explosions by 'an unruly criminal element'[20] is provided by evidence that the rioters' behaviour was purposive. The targets of their violence, for example, appear to have been far from random. Everywhere in what appears to be a consistent pattern, the crowds were highly selective in what they attacked. In Tottenham's Broadwater Farm for example:

In the Tangmere shopping precinct, the supermarket and off license was looted and burnt, but not the laundrette, the fruit and veg shop or the hairdressers (all run by community co-ops); nor the welfare rights centre nor the neighbourhood office. The premises of The Broadwater Farm Youth Association, run by and for youth on the estate and visited by Princess Diana earlier this year, were damaged, but only when police broke in to carry out a search (Platt, 1985).

Reicher notes that in Bristol, participants who threw stones at targets which the norms of the crowd defined as illegitimate (buses and private cars) were strongly rebuked by other rioters. In Brixton 1985, two Afro-Caribbean men fighting with each other in the crowd were strongly censured by their disorderly peers. An Asian man told them 'We shouldn't fight among ourselves', and a woman added 'There's a principle involved. They've shot a woman and that's why we're here' (Murji, 1985). In Brixton, a group of young men outside a pub in Atlantic Road gave their names to one reporter as 'Jack the Dog', 'Turnip Head', 'Mr Bang Man' and 'The Jewel'. They told him: 'This will happen again. . . . As long as there is Thatcher's policemen doing this to our people, there will be burning.'[21] The human targets of crowd violence seem to have been almost exclusively police and media workers. Hostility to reporters and camera people had been reported in riots as early as 1980[22] but became a major issue in the 1985 disorders suggesting again the purposive aspects of the rioters' behaviour.[23] Some reporters were asked which papers they worked for:

Sun Man's Terror at Hands of the mob. . . . Colleague Hugh Whittow and I had watched cars overturned and set alight in Birmingham's riot-torn district. Suddenly we were surrounded by the menacing gang – many wearing masks – who had broken away from a horde being chased by the police. They demanded; 'What paper are you from, man? Don't write bad things about us.' When we said the *Sun* they began prodding and poking us and tried to snatch our notebooks.[24]

Another reporter, this time in Tottenham, was warned, 'Don't write any of that crap about unemployment' (Platt, 1985). In Brixton, an ITN camera crew had the windscreen of their car smashed and were told 'If you value your lives, get out.'[25] This hostility arose not because of any symbolic identification of the press with oppressive authority, but rather because the media, like the police, are recognized as violating the community's right to control its own existence.

Where community members saw their authority over their own history and experience being undermined, the right to control their streets and the representation of them in the media was forcefully demanded (see Appendices 1 and 2).

According to Reicher, a similar concept of popular local control was 'central to the response of all sections of the community' in St Paul's. The same idea of community autonomy has also been recognized by commentators on Liverpool's Toxteth district. There the emphasis fell both on the absence of community control and on illegitimate local government regulation of community affairs. David Shepherd, the Bishop of Liverpool, told the *Guardian* 'The black community has no representation in the town hall. People feel they are not listened to.'[26]

In accounts of the more recent riots, these issues emerged most strongly in coverage of a deal supposedly struck between police and the Rastas of Handsworth whereby the latter would ensure peace in the area in exchange for a police withdrawal. Though senior officers including the Chief Constable of the West Midlands, Geoffrey Dear, denied that this added up to the creation of a 'No Go Area'[27] and even that any agreement had been reached, papers reported that Rastas were patrolling the riot area in place of police, the *Daily Mail* was typical:

Rastafarians were last night patrolling the streets of riot-torn Handsworth after a special deal with police. Only a handful of police were in evidence and West Indians in dreadlock hairstyle, one carrying a police loudhailer, were out in force to keep the peace . . . even the limited police presence in the area in which two people died in Monday night's rioting, angered some local Rastafarians. 'We don't want them here' declared one. 'We want everyone off the streets – and that includes the police. Once they go everyone else will go and there will be no more trouble.'[28]

It is tempting to analyse this report in detail, pointing out that the words of the unnamed local Rasta anticipate the preferred response of *Mail* readers to this deal which also 'astonished local MPs'. I have pointed out elsewhere how the construction 'in dreadlock hairstyle' has been used to differentiate these disreputable disorderly Rastas from the authentic, religious variety from whom they are outwardly indistinguishable.[29] In the context of *riotous* protest, however, these details are less important than the competition between the police and the mob for control of the riot-torn area. The idea that these local people might gain control over their own neighbourhood was viewed by the *Mail* and the other papers as particularly horrible. It is a nightmare vision of what city life might be like if law and order broke down, yet it addresses fundamental issues. In particular the relationship between territory and identity in the urban context, and the strong connection between the disorders and a particular area which represents itself culturally in a distinct and visible way, i.e. 'Rastafarianism'.

In Chapter 3, we observed Rasta-inspired deviancy inflected with connotations of masculinity, even machismo in the case of 'Rasta Everton'. It is true that where 'Rastafarians' have become a visible, public problem they have been overwhelmingly constructed as male. However, the Brixton riot was one occasion on which deviant black women were identified as active participants in disorder. They too were found signifying their affiliation to the cultural core of 'West Indian' otherness. Under the headline 'Terror of Bomb Girl in Pink' the *News of The World* announced that a 'Rasta-haired girl dressed all in pink started the riot that rocked London's flashpoint Brixton district [sic], it was claimed last night.'[30] Its reporter had seen her 'Hurl the first petrol bomb at the police station. It was the first organised trouble.'

The *Mail*, perhaps less aware of the manner in which the 'weave on' extension hairstyle popular with young black women had adapted and transformed the dreadlock aesthetic in the direction of femininity, told its readers that there had been 'six teenage black girls . . . with Afro-style hair' who had chanted 'Burn it down burn it down they are murderers' as they lead the mob's assault on Brixton's police. This time the headline on the article was 'Girls lead Police Station Mob attack'.[31] These young women's collaboration with and leadership of the insurgent mob deprives them of one type of femininity and endows them with a second altogether more masculine variety appropriate to the 'West Indian' culture from which their hairstyles tell the reader they have come. There is here an additional reference to the pathology of black family life which articulates the discourses of family, nation and culture together to prove the presuppositions of ethnic absolutism.

The same ideological motifs were in play elsewhere in coverage of the riots. They were particularly pronounced in the portrayal of Dolly Kiffin, a leading community activist on the Broadwater Farm estate who had been prominent in the self-organization of estate residents and who, before the riot, had been credited with improving life there dramatically. The estate's Youth Association, which had been founded by Dolly and others in 1982, created its own centre and support facilities as well as providing regular lunches for pensioners and organizing a mothers' project and nursery for local women.[32]

In the atmosphere of hostility to the estate which followed the death of a police officer during the riot, Dolly Kiffin was singled out for vicious treatment by the popular press. Her personal finances were investigated as part of serious allegations of fraud involving local government grants and investigators were dispatched to the Caribbean to look into her background. In an article entitled 'The rise and rise of estate Godmother' which was also reproduced in the *Daily Mail*, the *Sun* presented her in the following terms:

They call Dolly Kiffin the Godmother. Her word is law – the only law – on London's riot-backed Broadwater Farm estate where P.C. Keith Blakelock was hacked to death. . . . To scores of jobless black youths on Broadwater who use Dolly's self-help training and social centre, she is a hero and a left-wing political guru. But worried community leaders fear plump Dolly's 'unhealthy' influence on the sprawling complex of council blocks.[33]

According to this article Dolly was known to her deviant followers as 'Mama Queen'. Under this alias, she 'has become the ruler of a mini-empire where fear and race-hate are the dreadful main exports'. The inversion of national symbols in this description and the defacement which results from Dolly's blackening them provides a striking illustration of the proximity of 'race' to nation which has been described in more detail in Chapter 2. It is also memorable for the link it presents between family and 'race'. Dolly is known not as the 'Queen' but as 'Mama Queen'; her regal status is inseparable from her role as a mother; she is a matriarch and her disorderly subjects are simultaneously her children.

These connotations of female strength and power, however desirable they might be in a real monarch, become, in Dolly's case, evidence of black family pathology which departs from the acceptable norm. The same theme was continued in another, later report about Dolly which also cemented the connection between the disorders and drug use in the black community. This variation on the black crime theme had emerged most strongly in police reports from the West Midlands (West Midlands Police, 1985).

Carol Francis, a young black woman caught smuggling £3900 worth of cannabis was discovered to have worked as an aide to Dolly, handled her dubious accounts and even been the girlfriend of her son Tony. Ms Francis, jailed for three months for her crime, told the *Daily Mail:* 'To young unemployed blacks she [Dolly] is both a matriarchal figure and a political heroine.' It seems that in the form of this 'plump, 49-year-old mother of six' Powell's wide-grinning piccanninies had finally found a maternal figure.[34]

Dolly's lawless empire extends no further than the concrete parameters of the riot-racked complex of sprawling concrete blocks. The difference between it and the real thing, which is by implication being subverted and destroyed by the unpatriotic activities of Dolly and her riotous brood, is expressed in its local scope. The racial culture which provides its inhabitants with their alternative identity exists within strict territorial boundaries.

This local dimension was conveyed in reports of the Handsworth, Tottenham and Brixton riots by accounts of rioters simply retreating into their homes once contained in their immediate local area by the police. Reicher, who notes that rioters in Bristol did not pursue police beyond the symbolic boundaries of St Paul's, observed the same phenomenon in his account.

Once the police had been chased out of St Pauls, they were not followed. The only area involved consisted of City and Grosvenor Roads and the streets backing off them . . . even later during the looting the participants did not stray beyond the boundaries of St Pauls. Not only that, but once police were drawn out no one else was stopped from entering the area, indeed crowd members even helped to organize the traffic flow.[35]

The strong association of identity and territory which is revealed by these reports is also expressed in the language of community employed by riot participants. This language suggests that area-based notions of group solidarity provided an important unifying factor for crowd behaviour. Community is a strong theme in subsequent local political organizing around the issues which had generated the riots.

The initial organization arising out of the Brixton disorders called itself 'The Groce Family Support and Community Defence Campaign' thus setting support for the immediate victims of police violence alongside the longer-term objective of community defence: 'The Campaign has been set up to seek justice for Mrs Cherry Groce, support her family in this time of stress, and also to ensure the defence of the community. . . .' Analysts should not take the congruence of these different aims for granted. A press release/leaflet issued by the organization stating its demands and aims made much of the campaign's origins in 'a meeting of the black community'. The community was presented as the source of the campaign's moral authority. In Handsworth, members of the 'African/Caribbean community' issued a leaflet simply headed 'Community statement' which presented the demands and aims of post-riot organizing in a similar fashion. Both leaflets stressed the role of the media in creating the situation in which the riots had developed and in distorting the experiences of black residents in the riot areas. They are included as an appendix to this chapter.

Regardless of the difficulty of speaking of a single community in the areas concerned, the riotous protests can themselves symbolize such a possibility. Bearing multiple meanings for their various active and passive participants, they can appear to represent the whole community in ridding it of the illegitimate encroachments of police. The use of curfew orders and geographical restrictions in the control of those who were arrested in the riots, like the Handsworth tale of Rastas on patrol, suggests that police may also have recognized the symbolic dimensions of space in the problem of re-imposing and symbolizing order once the riots were over. The well-publicized confinement of Cherry Groce's son Michael to his grandmother's house under bail-conditions, which were described by the magistrate in the case as a form of 'house arrest',[36] was another example of this awareness (Holdaway, 1983).

The issue of 'outside agitators' supposedly responsible for fomenting hatred and stirring up riot in the various communities was an obvious means to deny the local responsibility and rationality which lay behind the disorders. Brixton's senior police officer, Commander Alex Marnoch, informed the press that his force

had been aware of the presence of militants from the West Midlands in Brixton after the riot in Handsworth. . . . They had tried to 'stir up trouble' with [sic] local people, but had been rebuffed and left before the South London disturbances began![37]

Contradicting Marnoch's implicit analysis of the riots' origins, a Home Office study of the Handsworth disorders of 1981 put forward a view of their roots in spontaneous local factors. Nearly half of the (all male) respondents to the Home Office survey of participants

said they knew in advance that there was going to be trouble; particularly among the youngest in the sample this information had been spread by word of mouth (Field and Southgate, 1982 p. 68).

Father Lamont Phillips, a black preacher who spoke to the funeral of Cynthia Jarrett in Tottenham, told mourners to 'beware of certain groups who will try and use you as fodder to further their own aims'.[38] Here too it would appear that a self-conscious community, constituting solidarity out of the symbolism surrounding a local

244

tragedy – Mrs Jarrett's death – jealously guarded its political autonomy and ideological integrity.

An ending

This brief discussion of riotous protest has been necessary not merely because it illustrates the theoretical points made towards the beginning of this chapter, nor because it ties an overtly political argument to the cultural analyses of Chapters 4 and 5. In the representation of recent riots, it is possible to glimpse a struggle, a sequence of antagonisms which has moved beyond the grasp of orthodox class analysis. Unable to control the social relations in which they find themselves, people have shrunk the world to the size of their communities and begun to act politically on that basis. The politics of the urban social movements supply an answer to the question of historical agency posed in the first chapter.

We saw in Chapter 1 that forms of political calculation ordered by the priorities and experiences of the dwindling industrial proletariat find it difficult to make sense of these new social struggles. They are written off as mere deviancy or marginality. This dismissal is the penalty for disappointing the teleology of economistic socialism (Lea and Young, 1984; Taylor, 1982).

One of this book's conclusions is that if these struggles (some of which are conducted in and through 'race') are to be called class struggles, then class analysis must itself be thoroughly overhauled. I am not sure whether the labour involved in doing this makes it either a possible or a desirable task. The liberatory rationality which informs these struggles has found new modes of expression which stress what can be called neo-populist themes. They appeal directly to 'the people'. By contrast, the political languages of class and socialism have been so thoroughly discredited by Labourism at home and 'actually existing socialism' abroad that they may be completely beyond resuscitation. The dynamism and cultural vitality of the neo-populist social movements of which struggles around 'race' are only one example, contrasts sharply with the decadent corporate organizations and political styles from which the new movements tell us we must disengage if authentic politics is to be re-born. Whether such disengagement leads to an enhancement of radical, democratic politics is likely to depend to a considerable degree on local factors. In examining the demand for tactical withdrawal, I hope to have shown that the organizational possibilities provided by 'race' and the forms of consciousness which have emerged with the rejection of racism by urban communities, are now at least as likely to provide strong foundations for radical collective action as the equivalent appeal derived from narrowly-based class politics – Labourist or Leninist, 'Eurocommunist' or Fundamentalist (Fine *et al.*, 1983).

I believe that this argument can also be sustained at a more general level. As Craig Calhoun has shown in *The Question of Class Struggle*, rootedness in tradition and immediate social relations is the essential basis of a radical response to social change (Calhoun, 1982). This sense of rootedness is powerfully expressed today in the politics of the inner-city communities, particularly where locality, ethnicity or 'race' grounds them in potent historical memories. The significance of this general point has evaded Marxism whether it has made 'class consciousness the pre-requisite of class struggle' (Lenin) or 'class consciousness largely the outcome of that struggle' (Gramsci).

If, as Gorz has argued, class membership is increasingly being lived out as a 'contingent and meaningless fact' (1982), the ground on which the whole productivist, Marxian edifice has been erected is in jeopardy. The proletariat of yesterday, classically conceived or otherwise, now has rather more to lose than its chains. The real gains which it has made have been achieved as the cost of a deep-seated accommodation with capital and the political institutions of corporatism. Its will, as Calhoun has also pointed out 'is apt to be a reformist will' and this prompts a further question: Where is radical collective action to come from in the miserable years of crisis and crisis management which await Britain?

The answer suggested by this book is that it is likely to arise from those groups who find the premises of their collective existence threatened. In earlier phases of capitalist development and in peripheral states these may have been workers tied to pre-capitalist modes of production locked into the capitalist system in a subordinate position or those whose traditional social relations were displaced by its consolidation.

These groups, who were not and are not still classes in the Marxian sense, responded to their situation, not as isolated individuals but as social actors. Their histories (Adas, 1979) point to fundamental problems in Marxist theory which has rested for far too long on an idealized view of the modern proletariat. The Marxist view has been criticized above for being based on Hegel's notion of a universal class and on a loose analogy with 'the emergence of the bourgeoisie out of feudalism' as a class for itself (Bookchin, 1982).

In the present, studying the potency of racism and nationalism and observing the capability of movements formed around 'racial' subjectivities involves an examination of the social relations within which people act and their junctions with forms of politics which articulate themselves through historical memory's 'traditional' roots. 'Race' and its attendant imaginary politics of community, affect and kinship provides a contemporary example of how 'traditional' ties are created and re-created out of present rather than past conditions.

Taking on board C. L. R. James's important observation that 'there is nothing more to organize' because 'organization as we have known it is at an end' (1980) it is possible to comprehend how people can act socially and cohesively without the structures provided by formal organizations. Collective identities spoken through 'race', community and locality are, for all their spontaneity, powerful means to co-ordinate action and create solidarity. The constructed 'traditional' culture becomes a means, as we saw in Chapter 5, to articulate personal autonomy with collective empowerment focused by a multi-accented symbolic repertoire and its corona of meanings.

The word 'radical' carries with it connotations of rootedness which, if the thrust of this book is accepted, are once again becoming highly significant for British political culture. 'Race' must be retained as an analytic category not because it corresponds to any biological or epistemological absolutes, but because it refers investigation to the power that collective identities acquire by means of their roots in tradition. These identities, in the forms of white racism and black resistance, are the most volatile political forces in Britain today.

Notes

1 Freddie McGregor's song 'Jogging' exemplifies this theme.
2 Stafford Scott, leader of Broadwater Farm Youth Association, addressing a public meeting in Haringey Town Hall, 10.11.85.
3 *Daily Express*, 7.10.85. See also Charles Moore's *The Old People of Lambeth* Salisbury Papers, no. 9, 1982.
4 *Sun*, 7.9.85
5 *Standard*, 17.6.83.
6 *Sun*, 24.10.85.
7 See, for example, John Rex's 'The sociology of a zone of transition' and Ruth Glass 'Conflict in cities' both in Raynor and Harden (eds.), *Cities, Communities and the Young* (RKP/Open University Press, 1973).
8 A good account of community struggles around education is included in the CARF study of Southall, *Southall The Birth of A Black Community* (IRR, London 1981) pp. 33–4. A useful overview of Afro-Caribbean community activism emerges from David Pearson's *Race, Class and Political Activism. A Study of West Indians in Britain* (Gower, Farnborough 1981).
9 'It seems to me that the entire concept of the proletariat was never completely free from the Hegelian antithesis between (rational, essential) reality and (merely empirical accidental) existence, and this for reason of their own subjective needs. The actual empirical proletariat, even though summoned by them to represent the whole of humanity in its progress, is a class that, left to its own devices, only attains trade-union expression of its interests. As the result of an overwhelming structure

of historical reality, the same as formerly affected church organisations concerned with the saving of souls, consciousness of its "true", world-historical goals had to be brought into the workers' movement from outside' (Bahro, 1978, p. 195).

10 See Richard Hyman's 'Andre Gorz and the Disappearing Proleteriat' in Miliband and Saville (eds), *The Socialist Register 1983* (Merlin, London).
11 Jeff Rooker MP, *Sun*, 11.9.85.
12 Lea and Young (1982).
13 The Right Hon. Douglas Hurd, quoted in the *Observer*, 15.9.85.
14 *Guardian*, 22.11.85.
15 15.9.85.
16 *Sun*, 11.9.85.
17 *Mail on Sunday*, 29.9.85.
18 *Sunday Times*, 29.9.85.
19 Stafford Scott quoted in the *Guardian*, 17.1.86.
20 *Guardian*, 30.9.85.
21 *Mirror*, 30.9.85.
22 See the *Sun* reports of the demolition of houses in Brixton's front line – Railton Road – 2.11.82.
23 *People, Sunday Telegraph*, 29.9.85.
24 *Sun*, 11.9.85.
25 *Sunday Times*, 29.9.85.
26 3.10.85.
27 *Daily Telegraph*, 12.9.85.
28 12.9.85.
29 CCCS, 1982, p. 163; HMSO, 1981, p. 106.
30 29.9.85.
31 30.9.85.
32 *Haringey Star*, January 1986.
33 16.12.65.
34 19.12.86.
35 ibid, p. 12; see also *Sunday Times*, 6.4.80.
36 *Sun*, 1.10.85.
37 *Guardian*, 1.10.85
38 *Guardian*, 19.10.85.

Appendices to Chapter 6

1 Press Release

At a meeting of the black community in Brixton at Lambeth Town Hall on 3rd October 1985 the GROCE FAMILY SUPPORT AND COMMUNITY DEFENCE CAMPAIGN was established. The Campaign has been set up to seek justice for Mrs Cherry Groce, support her family in their time of stress and also to ensure the defence of the community and those arrested in the aftermath of the events of the weekend.

The meeting decided upon the following:-

That Inspector Lovelock should be arrested and charged with attempted murder.

That there should be a totally independent public enquiry to look into the details of the shooting and police tactics generally and that the community itself should determine the nature and form of such an enquiry.

There was much concern about the media coverage of the shooting itself and the events of the weekend. Reports on Saturday evening that Mrs Groce had died and totally false reports of the deaths of three young white women inevitably inflamed an already volatile situation. We believe that the media should be forced to act more responsibly; efforts are being made to raise the issues with the appropriate authorities.

The Campaign will be organising a petition demanding the arrest and charge of the officer and also the establishment of an independent public enquiry. It was resolved that the community be mobilised by way of a demonstration and March in November, the date of which will be announced.

In the meantime the Groce family which includes six young children need material support. Fund raising efforts are being organised but we take this opportunity to make a public appeal for donations to assist them at this most difficult time. Much help is also required to organise effective defence for those arrested and charged on Saturday 28th and Sunday 29th September. Donations and contact can be made to

> THE GROCE FAMILY SUPPORT & COMMUNITY DEFENCE CAMPAIGN
> c/o 506 Brixton Road
> London SW9
> Tel 326 1397

2 Community Statement

At a meeting of members of the African/Caribbean Community of Handsworth on 10th September, 1985 at 7.00pm at Gerrard Street Church Centre, the following statement was agreed by the Community members present:

1) To counter the misinformation projected by the media coverage of the events of Monday afternoon and evening we would like to bring to the attention of the general public that the causes triggering off the disturbances were as follows:

a) A white vigilante group at a recent resident association meeting declared its intention to burn down the old Villa Cross bingo hall to stop it becoming a 'drugs den' in response to moves that it be turned into an amusement arcade.

b) Around 5.00pm on Monday 9th September, 1985, the police, in pursuing a minor traffic offence proceeded to manhandle a motorist in such a way that a black woman felt compelled to intervene. She was punched in the face by one or more of the officers. At this point black youths intervened on her behalf.

c) The police presence was increased by a series of hoax calls claiming that there was a fire in the disused bingo hall.

d) The fire was mysteriously started after these calls.

2) The rebellion itself was not racially motivated in any way, as suggested by the police. White, Asian and Afro-Caribbean were involved.

3) We extend our condolences and sympathy to the relatives of those who have died.

4) We condemn the white establishment who through the BBC have prejudged the issue by labelling the deaths as murder before any enquiry has taken place, whilst at the same time failing to disclose the fact that several youths have been beaten by the police, and some of whom are reported to have been seriously injured [*sic*].

5) We condemn the police on their clear lack of sensitivity.

6) It is our belief that the fire was started by the vigilante group and the hoax calls were made to draw the police and fire brigade into the area to create confrontation between our community and the police in order to cover their tracks.

7) We call upon the Prime Minister and the Home Secretary to call a public judicial enquiry into the causes of the rebellions.

Bibliography

Abdul-Malik, M. (1968), *From Michael DeFreitas to Michael X*, Sphere, London

ABSWAP (1983), *Black Children in Care: Evidence to the House of Commons Social Services Committee*

Adas, M. (1979), *Prophets of Rebellion: Millenarian Protest Movements against the European Colonial Order*, University of North Carolina Press, Chapel Hill

Adorno, T. (1977), 'Commitment' in Jameson (ed.), *Aesthetics and Politics*, New Left Books, London

Allen, R. (1969), *Black Awakening in Capitalist America: an Analytic History*, Anchor, Garden City

Anderson, B. (1983), *Imagined Communities: Reflections on the Origin and Spread of Nationalism*, Verso, London

Anderson, P. (1983), *In the Tracks of Historical Materialism*, Verso, London

Appignanesi, L. (ed.) (1986), *Postmodernism*, ICA Documents 4 and 5, ICA, London

Attali, J. (1985), *Noise: The Political Economy of Music*, Manchester University Press

Bahro, R. (1984), *From Red to Green*, New Left Books, London

Bahro, R. (1982), *Socialism and Survival*, Heretic Books, London

Bahro, R. (1978), *The Alternative in Eastern Europe*, New Left Books, London

Baker, H. A. (1984), *Blues, Ideology, and Afro-American Literature: A vernacular theory*, University of Chicago Press

Bakhtin, M. (1984), *Rabelais and His World*, Indiana University Press, Bloomington

Bakhtin, M. (1981), *The Dialogic Imagination*, University of Texas Press, Austin

Baldwin, J. (1986), *Evidence of Things Not Seen*, Michael Joseph, London

Balibar, E., *et al.* (1980), 'Is the Crisis "Above All National,"?: A View of the Policy of the French Communist Party', *Contemporary Marxism*, no. 2, Winter

Banton, M. and Harwood, J. (1975), *The Race Concept*, David and Charles, Newton Abbott

Barker, M. (1981), *The New Racism*, Junction Books, London

Baraka, A. (1984), *Daggers and Javelins Essays*, Quill, New York

Barnett, A. (1984), 'Fortress Thatcher' in Ayrton, Englehart and Ware (eds.), *World View 1985*, Pluto Press, London

Barnett, A. (1983a), 'Getting it wrong and making it right', *New Socialist*, Sept./Oct.

Barnett, A. (1983b), 'The dangerous dream', *New Statesman*, **105**, no. 2726, 17 June

Barnett, A. (1982), 'Iron Britannia', *New Left Review*, no. 134, July/August

Barthes, R. (1973), *Mythologies*, Paladin, London

Bastide, R. (1978), *The African Religions of Brazil*, Johns Hopkins University Press, Baltimore and London

Bauman, Z. (1982), *Memories of Class: The Pre-history and After-life of Class*, Routledge & Kegan Paul, London

Bebey, F. (1975), *African Music a People's Art*, Lawrence Hill and Co., Westport

Beetham, D. (1970), *Transport and Turbans*, IRR/Oxford UP

Benedict, R. (1943), *Race and Racism*, The Book Club

Ben-Habib, S. (1981), 'Modernity and the Aporias of Critical Theory', *Telos*, no. 49

Benjamin, P. (1984), 'The Afro-American Musician: Messengers of a Unique Sensibility in Western Culture', *Views on Black American Music Proceedings of the 12th and 13th Annual Black Musician's Conferences, University of Massachusetts at Amherst*, no. 2, 1984–5

Benn, Tony (1981), 'Britain as a colony', *New Socialist*, no. 1., Sept./Oct.

Bennett, G. (1962), *The Concept of Empire from Burke to Attlee* (2nd edn), Adam and Charles Black, London

Ben-Tovim, G. *et al.* (1981), 'Race, Left Strategies and The State', *Politics and Power*, **3**

Berghahn, M. (1977), *Images of Africa in Black American Literature*, Macmillan, London

Bertram, G. C. L. (1958), *West Indian Immigration*, The Eugenics Society, London

Bhaskar, R. (1980), 'Scientific Explanation and Human Emancipation', *Radical Philosophy*, **26**, autumn

Bhaskar, R. (1979), *The Possibility of Naturalism*, Harvester, Hassocks

Birley, D. and Bright, J. (1985), *Crime in the Community: Towards a Labour Party Policy on Crime Prevention and Public Safety*, Labour Campaign for Criminal Justice, London

Black and In Care Steering Group (1984), Conference Report, October

Boddy, M. and Fudge, C. (eds.) (1984), *Local Socialism*, Macmillan, London

Bolt, C. and Drescher, S. (eds.) (1980), *Anti-slavery, Religion and Reform*, William Dawson and Sons, Folkestone

Bookchin, M. (1982), 'Finding The Subject: Notes of Whitebook and Habermas Ltd', *Telos*, no. 52, summer

Bookchin, M. (1978), 'Beyond Neo-Marxism', *Telos*, no. 36, summer

Bradshaw, P. (1981), 'A Big Sound System Splashdown', *New Musical Express*, 21 February

Brathwaite, E. K. (1984), *History of the Voice: The development of nation language in anglophone Caribbean poetry*, New Beacon Press, London

British Medical Association (1965), *Report of the Working Party on the Medical Examination of Immigrants*, BMA, Tavistock Square, London

Buci-Glucksmann, C. (1980), *Gramsci and The State*, Lawrence and Wishart, London

Bull, D. and Wilding, P. (1983), *Thatcherism and The Poor*, Child Poverty Action Group Poverty Pamphlet, no. 59

Butt, R. (1985), 'Multi Cultural Consequences', *Times Educational Supplement*, 24.5.85

Calhoun, C. (1982), *The Question of Class Struggle*, Basil Blackwell, Oxford

Calhoun, C. (1980), 'Community: Toward a variable conceptualisation for comparative research', *Social History*, **5**, no. 1, January

Campbell, B. (1983), 'Taking The Sexism Out of Class', *New Statesman*, **106**, no. 2739, 16 September

Campbell, H. (1985), *Rasta and Resistance: From Marcus Garvey to Walter Rodney*, Hansib Publications, London

Carby, H. (1982), 'Schooling in Babylon' in CCCS (eds.), *The Empire Strikes Back*, Hutchinson, London

CARF (1981), *Southall: Birth of a Black Community*, IRR, London

Carmichael, S. and Hamilton, C. (1967), *Black Power: The Politics of Liberation in America*, Vintage, New York

Carter, A. (1983), 'Masochism for the Masses', *New Statesman*, 3.6.83

Carter, B. (1985), *Capitalism, Class conflict and the New Middle Class*, Routledge & Kegan Paul, London

Casey, J. (1982), 'One Nation: The Politics of Race,' *Salisbury Review*, no. 1

Casey, J. (1978), 'Tradition and Authority', in Cowling (ed.), *Conservative Essays*

Cashmore, E. (1979), *Rastaman: The Rastafarian Movement in England*, Allen and Unwin, London

Castells, M. (1983), *The City and the Grassroots*, Edward Arnold, London

Castleman, C. (1982), *Getting Up – Subway Graffiti in New York*, MIT Press, London

CCCS (1982), *The Empire Strikes Back*, Hutchinson, London

Chambers, I. (1985), *Urban Rhythms: Pop Music and Popular Culture*, Macmillan, London

Chater, A. (1966), *Race Relations in Britain*, Lawrence and Wishart, London

Chernoff, J. M. (1979), *African Rhythm and African Sensibility*, University of Chicago Press

Clark, K. B. (1966), 'The Civil Rights Movement – Momentum and Organisation', *Daedalus*, **95**, winter

Clarke, S. (1980), *Jah Music*, Heinemann, London

Clutterbuck, R. (1978), *Britain in Agony: The Growth of Political Violence*, Penguin, Harmondsworth

Cohen, A. P. (1985), *The Symbolic Construction of Community*, Tavistock, London

Cone, J. H. (1984), *For My People: Black Theology and the Black Church*, Skotaville Publishers, Braamfontein

Cone, J. H. (1972), *The Spirituals and the Blues: An Interpretation*, Greenwood Press, Westport, Connecticut

Cooke, M. G. (1984), *Afro-American Literature in the Twentieth Century: The Achievement of Intimacy*, Yale University Press

Coon, C. (1977), *1988: The New Wave Punk Rock Explosion*, Orbach and Chambers, London

Cosgrove, S. (1985), 'Up Jumped a Monkey from the Coconut Grove', *Echoes*, 9 February

Cowley, J. (1985), *West Indian Gramophone Records in Britain: 1927–1950*, ESRC Occasional Papers in Ethnic Relations, no. 1

Cowling, M. (ed.) (1978), *Conservative Essays*, Cassell, London

Craib, I. (1984), *Modern Social Theory From Parsons To Habermas*, Wheatsheaf, Brighton

Critchley, T. A. (1978), *A History of Police in England and Wales* (2nd edn), Constable, London

Daly, M. (1979), *Gyn/Ecology: The Meta-ethics of Radical Feminism*, The Women's Press, London

Davis, J. (1980), 'The London Garotting Panic of 1862: A Moral Panic and the Creation of a Criminal Class in mid-Victorian England', in Gatrell, Lenman and Parker (eds.), *Crime and the Law: The Social History of Crime in Western Europe since 1500*, Europa Publications, London

Demuth, C. (1978), *'Sus': A report on the Vagrancy Act 1824*, Runnymede Trust, London

Dhondy, M. (1974), 'Immigrant Workers on Strike', *Radical America*, **8**, no. 5., Sept./Oct.

Dick, O. (1984), 'Mixers', *The Face*, May

Douglass, F. (1974), *Narrative of the Life of Frederick Douglass: An American Slave Written by Himself*, (ed.) Benjamin Quarles, Belknap/Harvard

DuBois, W. E. B. (1969), *The Souls of Black Folk*, Signet, New York

Duffield, M. (1984), 'New Racism . . . New Realism: Two Sides of The Same Coin', *Radical Philosophy*, **37**, summer

Ellison, R. (1964), *Shadow and Act*, Random House, New York

Elton, The Lord (1965), *The Unarmed Invasion: A survey of Afro-Asian Immigration*, Geoffrey Bles Ltd, London

Essien-Udom, E. U. (1966), *Black Nationalism: The Rise of the Black Muslims in the USA*, Pelican, Harmondsworth

Evans, S. (1980), *Personal Politics: The Roots of Women's Liberation in the Civil Rights Movement and the New Left*, Vintage, New York

Fanon, F. (1967), *Toward the African Revolution*, Pelican, Harmondsworth

Farmer, J. (1985), *Lay Bare the Heart: An Autobiography of the Civil Rights Movement*, Arbor House, New York

Field, S. and Southgate, P. (1982), *Public Disorder: a review of research and a study in one inner city area*, Home Office Research Unit, London

Fielding, N. (1981), *The National Front*, Routledge and Kegan Paul, London

Fine, B. *et al.* (1984), *Class Politics: An Answer To Its Critics*, Leftover Pamphlets, London

Fitzgerald, M. (1984), *Political Parties and Black People: participation, representation and exploitation*, Runneymede/GLC

Fladeland, B. (1984), *Abolitionists and Working-Class Problems in the Age of Industrialisation*, Macmillan, London

Foot, M. (1986), *Loyalists and Loners*, Collins, London. See also 'The Lives of Enoch', an extract from this book, *Guardian*, 12.3.86

Foot, P. (1969), *The Rise of Enoch Powell*, Penguin, Harmondsworth

Foot, P. (1965), *Immigration and Race in British Politics*, Penguin, Harmondsworth

Foucault, M. (1970), *The Order Of Things*, Tavistock, London

Fox-Piven, F. and Cloward, R. (1977), *Poor People's Movements: why they succeed and how they fail*, Pantheon, New York

Freeman, J. (ed.) (1983), *Social Movements of the Sixties and Seventies*, Longman, New York

Futrell, J. (1980), 'The Lovers Beat', *Black Echoes*, 13.12.80

Fyvel, T. R. (1961), *The Insecure Offenders: Rebellious Youth in the Welfare State* (3rd edn 1964), Penguin, Harmondsworth

Gabriel, J. and Ben-Tovim, G. (1979), 'The conceptualisation of race relations in sociological theory', *Ethnic and Racial Studies*, **2**, no. 2

Gamble, A. (1974), *The Conservative Nation*, RKP, London

Garland, D. (1985a), *Punishment and Welfare: A History of Penal Strategies*, Gower Press, Aldershot

Garland, D. (1985b), 'Politics and Policy in Criminological Discourse', *International Journal of Law and Society*, February

Garon, P. (1975), *Blues and The Poetic Spirit*, Eddison Bluesbooks, London

Garratt, S. (1985), 'Lovers Rock', *The Face*, March

Gartner, L. P. (1973), *The Jewish Immigrant in England 1870–1914*, Simon, London

Gates, H. L. (ed.) (1984a), *Black Literature and Literary Theory*, Methuen, London

Gates, H. L. (1984b), 'The blackness of blackness: a critique of the sign and The Signifying Monkey', in Gates (ed.), 1984a

Geiss, I. (1974), *The Pan-African Movement*, Methuen, London

Gellner, E. (1983), *Nations and Nationalism*, Basil Blackwell, Oxford

Genovese, E. (1979), *From Rebellion to Revolution*, University of Louisiana, Baton Rouge

George, N. *et al.* (1985), *Fresh Hip Hop Don't Stop*, Random House, New York

Gillett, C. (1972), 'The Black Market Roots of Rock', in Denisoff and Peterson (eds.), *The Sounds of Social Change studies in popular culture*, Rand McNally, Chicago

Gilroy, P. (1984a), 'Hip Hop Technology', in Ayrton, Englehart and Ware (eds.), *World View 1985*, Pluto Press, London

Gilroy, P. (1984b), 'African Influences in Popular Music', in P. Ayrton (ed.), *World View 1984*, Pluto Press, London

Gilroy, P. (1983), 'Channel 4, Bridgehead or Bantustan?', *Screen*, **24**, no. 4–5, July–October

Gilroy, P. (1981), 'You Can't Fool The Youth Race and Class formation in the 1980s', *Race and Class*, **XXIII**, no. 2/3

Gilroy, P. and Lawrence, E. (1982), 'Two-tone Britain, Black Youth White Youth and the politics of anti-racism', in Bains and Cohen (eds.), *Youth in Multi-racist Britain*, Macmillan (forthcoming)

Gilroy, P. and Sim. J. (1985), 'Law Order and the State of the left', *Capital and Class*, no. 25, spring

Glazer, N. and Moynihan, P. (eds.) (1975), *Ethnicity, Theory and Experience*, Harvard University Press

GLC (1986), *Policing London: Collected Reports of the GLC Police Committee Support Unit*

GLC (1985), *Anti Racist Programme 1984: Review and Assessment*, unpublished paper

GLC (1984a), *Rastafarianism in Greater London*, Ethnic Minorities Unit

GLC (1984b), *Ethnic Minorities and the Abolition of the GLC*, Ethnic Minorities Unit

Glean, M. (1973), 'Whatever Happened to CARD?', *Race Today*, January

Gorz, A. (1985), *Pathways To Paradise on the liberation from work*, Pluto Press, London

Gorz, A. (1982), *Farewell To The Working Class*, Pluto Press, London

Gorz, A. (1980), *Ecology as Politics*, South End Press, Boston

Gramsci, A. (1971), *Selections from the prison notebooks*, Lawrence and Wishart

Griffiths, P. (1966), *A Question Of Colour?*, Leslie Frewin and Co., London

Hackney CRE (1983), *Policing in Hackney: A record of HCRE's Experience 1978–82*, HCRE

Hager, S. (1985), *Hip Hop*, St Martin's Press, New York

Hager, S. (1982), 'Afrika Bambaataa's Hip Hop,' *Village Voice*, 21.9.82

Hall, S. (1985), 'Authoritarian Populism: a reply', *New Left Review*, **151**, May/June

Hall, S. (1980), 'Race Articulation and Societies Structured in Dominance', in UNESCO 1980

Hall, S. (1978), 'Race and Moral Panics in Post-War Britain', in CRE (ed.), *Five Views of Multi-racial Britain*, CRE, London

Hamilton, C. (1984), 'A Way of Seeing: The Use of Culture in the works of C. L. R. James', *Solid Ground*, winter/spring 1984, no. 2–3, **2**

Haralambos, M. (1974), *Right On: From Blues To Soul in Black America*, Eddison Bluesbooks

Harding, V. (1980), *The Other American Revolution*, Afro-American culture and society monograph series, volume 4, Center for Afro-American Studies, University of California, Los Angeles and Institute of the Black World, Atlanta, Georgia

Harding, V. (1969), 'Religion and Resistance Among Antebellum Negroes', in Meier and Rudwick (eds.), *The Making of Black America*, vol. 1, Atheneum, New York

Hebdige, D. (1985), 'The Bottom Line on Planet One', *Ten 8*, no. 19

Hebdige, D. (1983), 'Ska Tissue: The Rise and Fall of Two Tone', in Simon and Davis (eds.), *Reggae International*, Thames and Hudson, London

Hebdige, D. (1979), *Subculture: The Meaning of Style*, Methuen, London

Heilbut, A. (1985), *The Gospel Sound: Good News and Bad Times* (revised edn), Limelight Editions, New York

Higginbotham, A. L. jnr (1978), *In The Matter of Colour: Race and the American Legal Process: the Colonial Period*, Oxford University Press, New York

Hind, J. and Mosco, S. (1985), *Rebel Radio: The Full Story of British Pirate Radio*, Pluto Press, London

Hiro, D. (1971), *Black British White British*, Eyre and Spottiswoode, London

HMSO (1981), *The Brixton Disorders 10–12 April 1981: Report of An Inquiry by the Rt. Hon. Lord Scarman OBE*, Cmnd. 8427

HMSO (1977), *Report of the Commissioner of Police of the Metropolis for the year 1976*, Cmnd. 6821

HMSO (1976), Select Committee on Race Relations and Immigration Session 1975–6, *The West Indian Community*, Metropolitan Police Evidence Thursday 25 March (47–vii)

HMSO (1973), *Police Immigrant Relations in England and Wales:*

Observations on the Report of the Select Committee on Race Relations and Immigration, Cmnd. 5438

HMSO (1972), Select Committee on Race Relations and Immigration Session 1971–2, *Police/Immigrant Relations*, 1, 471–I

Hoare, I. *et al.* (1975), *The Soul Book*, Methuen, London

Hoare, I. (1975), 'Mighty, mighty spade and whitey: soul lyrics and black-white crosscurrents', in Hoare *et al.* (eds.), *The Soul Book*

Hobsbawm, E. (1985), 'Retreating into extremism,' *Marxism Today*, April

Hobsbawm, E. (1984), 'Labour: Rump or Rebirth', *Marxism Today*, March

Hobsbawm, E. (1983), 'Falklands Fallout', *Marxism Today*, January

Hobsbawm, E. (1978), 'The Historians' Group of the Communist Party', in Cornforth (ed.), *Rebels and Their Causes: Essays in Honour of A. L. Morton*, Lawrence and Wishart, London

Holdaway, S. (1983), *Inside The British Police – A Force At Work*, Basil Blackwell, Oxford

Holmes, C. (1979), *Anti-semitism in British Society 1876–1939*, Edward Arnold, London

Honeyford, R. (1984), 'Education and race – an alternative view', *Salisbury Review*, winter

Honeyford, R. (1983), 'Multi-Ethnic Intolerance', *Salisbury Review*, summer

Howe, D. (1985), *Black Sections in The Labour Party*, Race Today Publications, London

Huddle, R. (1978), 'Hard Rain', *Socialist Review* (GB), July/August

Humphries, S. (1981), *Hooligans or Rebels? An Oral History of Working Class Childhood and Youth 1889–1939*, Basil Blackwell, Oxford

Humphry, D and John, G. (1972), *Police Power and Black People*, Panther, London

Hunte, J. (1965), *Nigger Hunting in England?*, West Indian Standing Conference, London

Institute of Race Relations (1979) *Police Against Black People*, evidence submitted to the Royal Commission on Criminal Procedure, IRR, London

Jagan, C. (1984), *The Caribbean – Whose Backyard?* (No publisher's mark)

Jah Bones (1982), 'Rastafari: An Attempt at a Definition', *Caribbean Times*, 23.7.82

James, C. L. R. (1985), *A History of Negro Revolt*, Race Today, London

James, C. L. R. (1980), *Notes On Dialectics*, Alison and Busby, London

James, C. L. R. (1938), *The Black Jacobins*, Alison and Busby, London

Jameson, F. (1984), 'Postmodernism or The Cultural Logic of Capital', *New Left Review*, no. 146, July/August

Jenkins, B. and Minnerup, G. (1984), *Citizens and Comrades: Socialism in a world of nation states*, Pluto Press, London

Jones, A. (1985), 'Local Body Foreign Mind', *New Musical Express*, 7.12.85

Jones, L. (1967), *Black Music*, Quill, New York

Jones, L. (1963), *Blues People*, Morrow Quill, New York

Jones, S. (1986), *White Youth and Jamaican Culture*, unpublished Ph.D. thesis, University of Birmingham, Centre for Contemporary Cultural Studies

Jordan, J. (1985), *On Call*, South End Press

Jordan, J. (1981), *Civil Wars*, Beacon Press, Boston

Karenga, M. R. (1968), extract from *The Quotable Karenga* in Barbour (ed.), *The Black Power Revolt*, Collier Books, Boston

Keil, C. (1972), 'Motion and Feeling Through Music', in Kochman (ed.), *Rappin' and Stylin' Out*

Keil, C. (1970), *Urban Blues*, Chicago University Press

Kerridge, R. (1985), 'Fostering Apartheid', *The Spectator*, 6.7.85

Kimberley, N. (1982), 'Ska How Jamaica found a sound of its own', *The Encyclopaedia of Rock*, 5, issue 49

Kiple, K. F. and King, V. H. (1981), *Another Dimension to the Black Diaspora: diet, disease and racism*, Oxford University Press

Kitching, G. (1985), 'Nationalism: the instrumental passion', *Capital and Class*, no. 25, spring

Kitzinger, S. (1969), 'Protest and Mysticism: The Rastafari Cult of Jamaica', *Journal for The Scientific Study of Religion*, 8, no. 2, autumn

Knox, D. (1967), 'Britain's Black Powerhouse: Michael X. A soft-voiced fighter's gospel for the ghettos', *Life*, 43, no. 8, 16 October

Kochman, T. (1972), *Rappin' and Stylin' Out: Communication in Urban Black America*, University of Illinois Press, Chicago and London

Kofsky, F. (1970), *Black Nationalism and the Revolution in Music*, Pathfinder Press, New York

Kohl, H. and Hinton, J. (1972), 'Names, Graffiti and Culture', in Kochman (ed.), *Rappin' and Stylin' Out*

Laclau, E. and Mouffe, C. (1985), *Hegemony and Socialist Strategy*, Verso, London

Laing, D. (1985), *One Chord Wonders: Power and Meaning in Punk Rock*, Open University Press, Milton Keynes

Lambert, J. (1970), *Crime, Police and Race relations*, IRR/Oxford University Press

Lambeth, London Borough of (1981), *Final Report Of The Working Party Into Community/Police Relations in Lambeth*, LBL

Langer, P. (1984), 'Sociology – Four Images of Organised Diversity: Bazaar, Jungle, Organism and Machine', in Rodwin and Hollister (eds.), *Cities of the Mind: Images and Themes of the City in Social Science*, Plenum Press, London

Larsen, N. (1929), *Passing*, Negro Universities Press, New York (reissue 1969)

Latimer, D. (1984), 'Jameson and Post-Modernism', *New Left Review*, **148**, November/December

Lawrence, E. (1982), 'In the Abundance of Water the Fool is Thirsty: Sociology and Black Pathology', in CCCS (eds.), *The Empire Strikes Back*, Hutchinson, London

Lea, J. and Young, J. (1984), *What Is To Be Done About Law and Order?*, Penguin/Socialist Society, London

Lea, J. and Young, J. (1982), 'The Riots in Britain 1981: Urban Violence and Political Marginalisation', in Cowell, D. *et al.* (eds.), *Policing The Riots*, Junction Books, London

Lee, B. M. (1982), *Rastafari: The New Creation*, Jamaica Media Productions Ltd

Levitas, R. (1986), *The Ideology of the New Right*, Polity Press, Oxford

Linebaugh, P. (1984), 'Reply To Sweeny', *Labour/Le Travail*, no. 14, autumn

Linebaugh, P. (1982), 'All The Atlantic Mountains Shook', *Labour/Le Travail*, no. 10, autumn

Little, K. (1948), *Negroes In Britain*, Routledge & Kegan Paul, London

Loach, L. (1985), 'We'll Be Here Right To The End . . . And After: Women in The Miners' Strike', in Beynon, H. (ed.), *Digging Deeper: Issues in The Miners' Strike*, Verso, London

Lomax, A. (1968), *Folk Song Style and Culture*, Transaction, New Brunswick

McAdam, D. (1982), *Political Process and the Development of Black Insurgency, 1930–1970*, University of Chicago Press

Mackenzie, J. M. (1984), *Propaganda and Empire*, Manchester University Press

Mackenzie, J. M. (1986), *Imperialism and Popular Culture*, Manchester University Press

Maclennan, G. (1984), 'Class Conundrum', *Marxism Today*, May

MacMillan, H. (1973), *At The End of the Day*, Macmillan, London

Makonnen, R. (1973) [George Griffith], *Pan Africanism from Within*, Oxford University Press, Nairobi

Manley, M. (1983), 'Reggae: A Revolutionary Impulse', in Davis and Simon (eds.), *Reggae International*, Thames and Hudson

Marable, M. (1985), *Black American Politics from The Washington Marches to Jesse Jackson*, Verso, London

Marable, M. (1984), *Race, Reform and Rebellion: The Second Reconstruction in Black America, 1945–1982*, Macmillan, London

Marable, M. (1981), *Blackwater Historical Studies in Race, Class Consciousness and Revolution*, Black Praxis Press, Dayton

Marcus, G. (1977), *Mystery Train: Images of America in Rock n' Roll Music*, Omnibus Press, London

Marcuse, H. (1972), *Eros and Civilisation*, Abacus, London

Mark, R. (1978), *In The Office of Constable*, Fontana, London

Marx, K. and Engels, F. (1973), D. Fernbach (ed.), *The Revolutions of 1848*, Penguin, Harmondsworth

Massey, D. (1984), *Spatial Divisions of Labour*, Macmillan, London

Massey, D. and Miles, N. (1984), 'Mapping out the unions', *Marxism Today*, May

Mbiti, J. (1969), *African religions and philosophy*, Heinemann, London

Melucci, A. (1981a), 'Ten Hypotheses for the Analysis of New Movements', in Pinto (ed.), *Contemporary Italian Sociology*, Cambridge University Press

Melucci, A. (1981b), 'New Movements, Terrorism and the Political System: Reflections on The Italian Case', *Socialist Review* (US), no. 56, March–April

Melucci, A. (1980), 'The new social movements: A Theoretical Approach', *Social Science Information*, **19**, no. 2

Mepham, J. and Hillel-Ruben, D. (eds.) (1979), *Issues in Marxist Philosophy, Volume 2: Materialism*, Harvester Press, Brighton

Miles, R. (1984), 'Marxism versus the sociology of "race relations" ', *Ethnic and Racial studies*, 7, no. 2

Miles, R. (1982), *Racism and Migrant Labour*, Routledge & Kegan Paul, London

Miles, R. (1978), *Between Two Cultures? The Case of Rastafarianism*, SSRC Working Papers in Ethnic Relations, no. 10

Mingone, E. (1981), *Social Conflict and the City*, Blackwell, Oxford

Mitchell-Kernan, C. (1972), 'Signifying Loud Talking and Marking', in Kochman (ed.), *Rappin' and Stylin' Out*

Moore, C. (1982), *The Old People of Lambeth*, Salisbury Papers, no. 9

Morse, D. (1976), 'Blues, Soul Music and Black Consciousness', *Afras Review*, no. 2, summer

Morse, D. (1971), *Motown and the Arrival of Black Music*, Studio Vista

Mulhern, F. (1984), 'Towards 2000: News From You Know Where', *New Left Review*, no. 148, November/December

Murji, K. (1985), 'Observing The Brixton Riot', *New Society*, 4.10.85

Nairn, T. (1977), *The Break Up of Britain*, New Left Books, London

Newman, K. (1983a), *Policing and Social Policy in Multi-ethnic Areas in Europe*, Keynote speech to Cambridge Colloquium on 'Policing and Social Policy in Multi-Ethnic Areas in Europe' 30.8.83; see also article in *The Times*, 31.8.83

Newman, K. (1983b), *Policing London: Post Scarman*, Sir George Bean Memorial Lecture 1983, 30.10.83

Newman, K. (1983c), *Public Order in Free Societies*, Talk to the European Atlantic Group, 24.10.83

Newton, H. (1974), *Revolutionary Suicide*, Wildwood House, London

Nicholas, A. X. (1971), *The Poetry of Soul*, Bantam, New York

Nicholson, B. (1974), *Racialism, Fascism and The Trade Unions*, Transport and General Workers Union, London

Nimni, E. (1985), 'The great historical failure: Marxist theories of Nationalism', *Capital and Class*, no. 25, spring

Nketia, J. K. (1982), *The Music of Africa*, Victor Gollancz, London

Omi, M. and Winant, H. (1983), 'By The Rivers of Babylon: Race in the United States', pts 1 and 2. pt 1 *Socialist Review*, **13**, no. 5; pt 2, **13**, no. 6

Ousley, H. *et al.* (1986), *A Different Reality: An Account of Black people's experiences and their grievances before and after the Handsworth rebellions of September 1985*, West Midlands County Council

Padmore, G. (1956), *Pan-Africanism or Communism*, Dennis Dobson, London

Palmer, C. (1975), 'Religion and Magic in Mexican Slave Society', in Engerman and Genovese (eds.), *Race and Slavery in The Western Hemisphere: Quantitative Studies*, Princeton University Press, New Jersey

Palmer, R. (1974), 'Avant Garde Funk', *Black Music*, October

Panitch, L. (1981), 'Trades unions and the state', *New Left Reivew*, no. 125

Pannell, N. and Brockway, F. (1966), *Immigration What Is The Answer? Two Opposing Views*, Routledge & Kegan Paul, London

Parmar, P. (1984), 'Hateful Contraries', *Ten 8*, no. 16

Patterson, O. (1980), *Slavery and Social Death*, Harvard University Press

Patterson, O. (1977), *Ethnic Chauvinism: The Reactionary Impulse*, Stein and Day, New York

Patterson, O. (1966), 'The Dance Invasion,' *New Society*, reprinted in *Pressure Drop*, no. 2, undated

Pearson, D. G. (1981), *Race, Class and Political Activism: A Study of West Indians in Britain*, Gower Press, Farnborough

Perry, M. (1976), *Silence To The Drums: A Survey of the Literature of The Harlem Renaissance*, Greenwood Press, London

Phizaclea, A and Miles, R. (1980), *Labour and Racism*, Routledge & Kegan Paul, London

Platt, S. (1985), 'The Innocents of Broadwater Farm', *New Society*, 11.10.85

Powell, E. (1978), *A Nation or No Nation?*, Batsford, London

Powell, E. (1969), *Freedom and Reality*, Paperfront, Kingswood

Preston, M. B. *et al.* (eds.) (1982), *The New Black Politics The Search for Political Power*, Longman, Brentwood

Prezworski, A. (1977), 'Proletariat into a class: the process of class formation from Kautsky's "The Class Struggle" to recent controversies', *Politics and Society*, **7**, no. 4

Proffitt, R. (undated), *Labour Party Black Sections: Answers to questions frequently asked about Black Sections*, East Lewisham Labour Party

Rabstein, M. (1981), 'The Empire Strikes Back: Why Britain Needs

National Liberation', in Bridges, G. and Brunt, R. (eds.), *Silver Linings*, Lawrence and Wishart, London

Raynor, J. and Harden, J. (1973), *Cities, Communities and the Young*, Open University Press/RKP, London

RCG (1978), *The Anti-Nazi League and the Struggle against Racism*, Revolutionary Communist Group, London

Reed, I. (1973), *Mumbo Jumbo*, Doubleday, Garden City, New York

Reed, I. (1972), *Conjure: Selected Poems, 1963–1970*, University of Massachusetts Press, Amherst

Reicher, S. D. (1984), 'The St Pauls' Riot: an explanation of the limits, of crowd action in terms of a social identity model', *European Journal of Social Psychology*, **14**, pp. 1–21

Reiner, R. (1985), *The Politics of The Police*, Harvester Press, Brighton

Rex, J. and Tomlinson, S. (1979), *Colonial Immigrants in a British City*, Routledge & Kegan Paul, London

Rex, J. (1970), *Race Relations in Sociological Theory*, Weidenfeld and Nicolson, London

Rex, J. (1968), 'The Race Relations Catastrophe', in Burgess, T. (ed.), *Matters of Principle Labour's last chance*, Penguin, Harmondsworth

Roberts, K., Duggan, J. and Noble, M. (1981), *Unregistered youth unemployment and outreach careers work*, Final report, pt 1, Non-registration, University of Liverpool Department of Sociology Research paper, no. 31

Robinson, C. (1982), *Black Marxism*, Zed, London

Rockwell, J. (1985), *All American Music*, Kahn and Averill, London

Rooney, B. (1980), 'Active Mistakes – A Grass Roots Report', *Multiracial Social Work*, no. 1

Rose, S. and Lewontin, R. (1983), *Not in Our Genes*, Penguin, Harmondsworth

Rubin, G. (1975), 'The Traffic In Women', in R. Reiter (ed.), *Toward an Anthropology of Women*, Monthly Review, New York

Said, E. (1985), 'Opponents, Audiences, Constituencies and Community', in Foster (ed.), *Postmodern Culture*, Pluto Press, London

Sayers, J. (1982), *Biological Politics*, Tavistock, London

Scarman, Lord Justice (1975), *The Red Lion Square Disorders of 15 June 1974*, Cmnd. 5919, HMSO, London

Scott, H. (1954), *Scotland Yard*, Andre Deutsch, London

Scraton, P. (1985), *The State of The Police*, Pluto Press, London

Seabrook, J. (1986), 'The war against jingoism', *Guardian*, 31.3.86. See also the reply by Dafydd Elis Thomas, 'In a loveless state', *Guardian*, 14.4.86.

Seidel, G. (1985), 'The White discursive order: The British New Right's discourse on cultural racism with particular reference to the Salisbury Review', unpublished paper presented to the University of Utrecht summer school of Critical Theory, June

Sheppard, E. *et al.* (1875), *The Story of the Jubilee Singers with Their Songs*, Hodder and Stoughton, London

Sherman, A. (1979), 'Britain Is Not Asia's Fiancée', *Daily Telegraph*, 9.11.79

Shyllon, F. (1977), *Black People in Britain*, Oxford University Press

Shyllon, F. (1974), *Black Slaves in Britain*, IRR/Oxford University Press

Sidran, B. (1971), *Black Talk*, Holt, Rinehart, Winston, New York

Siggerson, D. (1977), 'Love and Money – Crossover Jazz in The Seventies', pts 1 and 2, *Black Music*, March and ApriL

Sim, J. (1982), 'Scarman The Police Counter Attack', in Eve and Musson (eds.), *The Socialist Register 1982*, Merlin, London

Sithole, E. (1972), 'Black Folk Music', in Kochman (ed.), *Rappin' and Stylin' Out*

Sivanandan, A. (1982), *A Different Hunger*, Pluto Press, London

Slater, D. (1982), 'David King', *Camerawork*, no. 24

Small, J. W. (1984), 'The Crisis In Adoption', *International Journal of Social Psychiatry*, **30**, nos. 1/2, spring

Smith, D. J. and Gray, J. (1983), *Police and People in London – volume iv, The police in action*, Policy Studies Institute, London

Soper, K. (1986), *Humanism and Anti-Humanism*, Hutchinson, London

Soper, K. (1979), 'Marxism, Materialism and Biology', in Mepham and Hillel-Rubin (eds.), *Issues in Marxist Philosophy*, Harvester, Brighton

Southern, E. (1983), *The Music of Black Americans* (2nd edn), W. W. Norton and Co., New York

Stedman-Jones, G. (1983), *Languages of Class*, Cambridge University/Press

Stedman-Jones, G. (1971), *Outcast London: A Study of The Relationship Between Classes in Victorian Society*, Oxford University Press

Storm-Roberts, J. (1972), *Black Music of Two Worlds*, Morrow and Co., New York

Stubbs, P. (1985), 'The employment of black social workers: from "ethnic sensitivity" to anti-racism?', *Critical Social Policy*, no. 12

Studlar, D. (1985), ' "Waiting for the catastrophe": Race and the Political Agenda in Britain', *Patterns of Prejudice*, **19**, no. 1

Studlar, D. (1984), 'Nonwhite Policy Preferences, Political Participation, and the Political Agenda in Britain', unpublished paper prepared for Conference on Race and Politics, St Hughs College, Oxford, 28–30 September

Studlar, D. (1983), 'The Ethnic Vote problems of analysis and interpretation', *New Community*, **11**

Taylor, I. (1982), 'Against Crime and for Socialism', *Crime and Social Justice*, no. 18

Thompson, E. P. (1983), *The Defence of Britain*, END/CND, London

Thompson, E. P. (1982), *Zero Option*, Merlin, London

Thompson, E. P. (1980), *The Making of the English Working Class*, Penguin, Harmondsworth

Thompson, E. P. (1978), *The Poverty of Theory and Other Essays*, Merlin, London

Thompson, L. (1985), *An Autobiography*, Rabbit Press, Crawley

Timpanaro, S. (1972), *On Materialism*, New Left Books, London

Touraine, A. (1983a), *Anti-nuclear protest the Opposition to nuclear energy in France*, Cambridge University Press

Touraine, A. (1983b), *Solidarity Poland 1980–81*, Cambridge University Press

Touraine, A. (1981), *The Voice and The Eye An analysis of social movements*, Cambridge University Press

Touraine, A. (1977), *The Self-production of Society*, University of Chicago Press, London

UNESCO (1980), *Sociological Theories: race and colonialism*, Paris

Vansina, J. (1985), *Oral Tradition as History*, James Currey Ltd, London

Wallerstein, I. (1980), 'Eurocommunism: Its Roots in European Working Class History', *Contemporary Marxism*, no. 2, winter

Wallerstein, I. (1979), 'Class formation in the capitalist world-economy', *The Capitalist World Economy*, Cambridge University Press

Wallis, R. and Malm, K. (1984), *Big sounds from small peoples*, Constable, London

Walvin, J. (1985), 'Abolishing the slave trade: anti-slavery and popular radicalism, 1776–1807', in Emsley and Walvin (eds.), *Artisans, Peasants and Proleterians*, Croom Helm, London

Weightman, G. (1978), 'Flogging anti-racism', *New Society*, 11.5.78

Weiner, M. J. (1981), *English Culture and the Decline of Industrial Spirit 1850–1980*, Cambridge University Press

Weldon Johnson, J. (1965), *The Autobiography of an ex-Coloured Man*, Avon Books, New York

Wells, I.B. (1970), *Crusade For Justice: The Autobiography of Ida B. Wells*, (ed.) Alfreda M. Duster, University of Chicago Press

West, C. (1982), *Prophecy Deliverance! an afro-american revolutionary christianity*, Westminster Press, Philadelphia

West Midlands Police (1985), *Report of The Chief Constable West Midlands Police: Handsworth/Lozells – September 1985* (unpublished Report into the Handsworth Riots of 1985), Birmingham

Williams, G. (1982), 'Land of our fathers', *Marxism Today*, August

Williams, R. (1983), *Towards 2000*, Pelican, Harmondsworth

WING (1985), *Worlds Apart Women Under Immigration and Nationality Law*, Pluto Press, London

WMACAS (Western Massachusetts Association of Concerned African Scholars) (1978), *U.S. Military Involvement in Southern Africa*, South End Press, Boston

Wolf, E. (1982), *Europe and The People Without History*, University of California Press, London

Wolpe, H. (1980), 'Capitalism and cheap labour-power in South Africa: from segregation to apartheid', in Wolpe (ed.), *The Articulation of Modes of Production*, Routledge & Kegan Paul, London

Wright, P. (1985), *On Living in an Old Country*, Verso, London

Wright, R. (1956), Foreword to Padmore, G., *Pan Africanism or Communism*, Dennis Dobson, London

Yawney, C. (1985a), 'Strictly Ital: Rastafari Livity and Holistic Health', unpublished paper to Society for Caribbean Studies conference, 2–4 July

Yawney, C. (1985b), 'Don't Vex Then Pray The Methodology of Initiation Fifteen Years Later', unpublished paper to Qualitative Research conference, University of Waterloo, May

Yawney, C. (1979), *Lions In Babylon The Rastafarians of Jamaica as a visionary movement*, unpublished Ph.D. dissertation, Dept of Anthropology, McGill University

Young, C. M. (1977), 'Rock is Sick and Living in London', *Rolling Stone*, 20.10.77

Index